Bl

COLT

Firearms & Values

By S.P. Fjestad

Publisher's Suggested List Price
$14.95

Content Disclaimer:

Due to space considerations, this book does not contain information or values on machine guns, select fire, NFA classified firearms, firearms accessories (scopes, bayonets, etc.), airguns, modern black powder reproductions and replicas. For current information on airguns and modern black powder replicas, please refer to the *Blue Book of Airguns* and the *Blue Book of Modern Black Powder Arms*. Visit BlueBookOfGunValues.com for more info on how to order either online or in print.

Blue Book Publications, Inc.
8009 34th Avenue South, Suite 250
Minneapolis, MN 55425 U.S.A.
Customer Service: 800-877-4867, ext. 3 (domestic only)
Phone No.: 952-854-5229 (International)
Fax No.: 952-853-1486
General Email: support@bluebookinc.com
Website: BlueBookOfGunValues.com
Published and printed in the United States of America

ISBN-13: 978-1-947314-11-5
ISBN-10: 1-947314-11-4

Distributed in part to the book trade by Ingram Book Company and Baker & Taylor.

Table of Contents

The author/publisher would like to thank the following individuals for their contributions to this Seventh Edition *Blue Book Pocket Guide for Colt Firearms & Values*:

Beverly Haynes (Colt Historian) and Joseph Canali from Colt Archives, LLC

Kevin Cherry and Gurney Brown from Cherry's

Richard Burdick

Richard Churchill

Rick Crosier

Tom Covault

Kurt House

Willmer Kellogg

John Kopec

Charles Layson

Jesse Lewallen

Josh Loewensteiner

Greg Martin

Tom Mintner

Orvin Olson

Joe Pittenger

Dave Trauth

Carol Wilkerson

the late R.L. Wilson (honorary)

CCA (Colt Collector's Association) and members

CREDITS:

Cover artwork: Clint H. Schmidt

Printing: POD by BR Printers located in East Windsor, NJ.

How to Use This Book

The values listed in this 7th Edition *Blue Book Pocket Guide for Colt Firearms & Values* are based on national average retail prices for both modern and antique firearms, and some accessories/accoutrements. This is not a firearms wholesale pricing guide. More importantly, do not expect to walk into a gun/pawn shop or gun show and think that the proprietor/dealer/collector should pay you the retail values listed within this text for your gun(s). Resale offers on many models could be anywhere from near retail to 20%-50% less than the values listed, depending upon locality, desirability, dealer inventory, and profitability. In other words, if you want to receive 100% of the retail value, then you have to do 100% of the work (become the retailer, which also includes assuming 100% of the risk).

Percentages of original condition (with corresponding values) are listed between 10%-100% for most antiques (unless configuration, rarity, and age preclude upper conditions). 60%-100% condition factors are listed on most modern firearms since condition below 60% is seldom encountered (or purchased). Please consult our revised Photo Percentage Grading System™ (PPGS) available on our website: bluebookofgunvalues.com to learn more about the condition of your firearm(s). Since condition is the overriding factor in price evaluation, study these photos and captions carefully to learn more about the condition of your specimen(s).

A copy of NRA Condition Standards and Grading Criteria have been included to help make the conversion to percentages easier. To find a Colt model in this text, first look under the correct category name, then find the model, sub-model, or variation you are looking for. Colt Commemoratives will appear last in this text. When applicable, antiques will appear before modern guns, and are typically listed in chronological sequence.

Trademarks are listed alphabetically in uppercase bold typeface, like this:

COLT'S MANUFACTURING COMPANY, LLC

Manufacturer/trademark information is listed directly beneath the trademark heading:

Current manufacturer with headquarters located in West Hartford, CT.

Manufacturer notes may appear next under individual heading descriptions and can be differentiated by the following typeface:

Manufactured from 1836-1842 in Paterson, NJ; 1847-1848 in Whitneyville, CT; 1854-1864 in London, England; and from 1848-date in Hartford, CT. Colt Firearms became a division of Colt Industries in 1964. In March 1990, the Colt Firearms Division was sold to C.F. Holding Corp. located in Hartford, CT, and the new company was called Colt's Manufacturing Company, Inc.

The next classification is the category name (normally, in alphabetical sequence) in uppercase lettering (inside a screened gray box) which primarily refers to a firearm's configuration. Category names can be differentiated by the following typeface:

REVOLVERS: PERCUSSION

A further sub-classification may appear under a category name, as depicted below. These sub-categories of a major category name appear in both upper and lower case type, and typically appear in alphabetical order. Sub-category names can be differentiated by the following typeface:

Revolvers: Percussion, Paterson Variations

A category note may follow a category or sub-category name to help explain the category, and/or provide limited information on the models and values listed within the category. This appears as follows:

All pistols in this section are .45 ACP cal., unless otherwise noted.

Model names appear flush left, are bold faced, and are in uppercase lettering either in chronological order (normally) or alphabetical order (sometimes, the previous model name and/or close sub-variation will appear at the end in parentheses) and are listed under the individual category and sub-category names. Examples include:

GOVERNMENT MODEL 1911A1

Model descriptions are denoted by the following typeface and usually include the following information:

- calibers, gauges/bore, action type, barrel length(s), finish(es), weight, and other descriptive data are provided adjacent to model names in this typeface. This is where most of the information is listed for each specific model, including identifiable features and possibly some production data, including quantity, date of manufacture, and discontinuance date, if known.

Variations (and possible production periods) within a model appear as sub-models - they are differentiated from model names by an asterisk (*), are italicized and indented, and appear in upper and lowercase type, as follows:

* ***Anaconda 1st Edition***

This is usually followed by a short description of that sub-model. These sub-model descriptions have the same typeface as the model descriptions, such as:

- .40 S&W (new 1992) or .45 ACP cal., 4 ¼ in. barrel, 8 shot mag., white dot sights, 36 oz. Mfg. 1991-1996.

Also included is yet another layer of model/information nomenclature differentiating sub-models from variations of sub-models or a lower hierarchy of sub-model information. These items are indented from the sub-models, and have the icon graphic », for example:

» ***New Service Model Shooting Master .38 Spl.***

A description for this level of sub-model information may appear next to the sub-entry, and uses the same typeface as model and sub-model descriptions shown above.

Model notes and information appear in smaller type, generally after the price line, and should be read since they contain important, critical, and interesting facts/information. In some cases, factory recalls (some include serialization) are also provided. Examples include:

This model has the full grip length of the .380 Government Model.

Extra features/special orders which can add or subtract value are placed either under category names, model/sub-model descriptions, or pricing lines. On current models that don't have a price line, the MSR will also appear in this typeface, in addition to other pricing information regarding that model. These individual lines appear bolder than other descriptive typeface, such as the following:

Add 10% for original box.
Subtract 15% if without extra cylinder.
Current MSR on this model is $6,528.

On many discontinued models/variations after 1985, the following line may appear under the price line, indicating the last manufacturer's suggested retail price flush right on the page, like this:

Last MSR was $1,195.

Last MSR in 2002 was $3,500.

Grading lines normally appear at the top of each page, and in the middle if price lines change. If you are uncertain as to how to properly grade a particular firearm, please refer to the digital color Photo Percentage Grading System (PPGS) at BlueBookOfGunValues.com for more assistance. The most commonly encountered grading line (shown with a typical price line underneath) in this text is for 100%-60% condition factors:

MSR	100%	98%	95%	90%	80%	70%	60%

Price line formats are as follows - when the price line shown below (with proper grading line) is encountered, it automatically indicates the gun is currently manufactured, and the MSR is shown left of the 100% column. Following this are the 100%-60% values. This 100% value is the national average price a consumer will typically expect to pay for that model in NIB unfired condition. 100% specimens without boxes, warranties, etc., which are currently manufactured may be discounted (5%-20%, depending on the desirability of make and model). This 100% price on currently manufactured guns also assumes not previously sold at retail.

.45 LC cal.	$2,800	$2,450	$2,100	$1,905	$1,540	$1,260	$980
.44 Spl. cal.	$2,600	$2,275	$1,950	$1,770	$1,430	$1,170	$910
	$2,050	$1,795	$1,550	N/A	N/A	N/A	N/A

When "N/A" (Not Applicable) is listed instead of a value, this indicates that this particular model is not encountered enough in those condition factors to warrant a value - especially true on antiques in upper condition factors and with commemoratives and special/limited editions under 95%.

Values for conditions under 60% will typically be no less than 50% (1/2) of the 60% price, unless the gun has been shot to a point where the action may be loose or questionable. Obviously, no "MSR" will appear in the left margin, but a last manufacturer's suggested retail price may appear flush right below the price line, automatically indicating a discontinued gun, like this:

Last MSR was $670.

On older Colt models grading and values are provided from 100%-10%, and an example of this grading line is as follows:

100%	98%	95%	90%	80%	70%	60%	50%	40%	30%	20%	10%

Typically, 100%-10% values are listed for these older firearms and a few examples of the price lines are as follows:

N/A	N/A	$175,000	$140,000	$100,000	$80,000	$65,000	$55,000	$45,000	$35,000	$25,000	$20,000
N/A	N/A	$140,000	$115,000	$90,000	$75,000	$60,000	$45,000	$35,000	$28,000	$24,000	$16,000

Again, N/A's are abbreviations for not applicable, which indicates this model is not encountered enough in those upper condition factors to warrant a value.

Most commemorative/limited edition grading and price lines will appear as follows:

100%	Issue Price	Qty. Made
$2,500	$275	100

Included for your convenience at the end of this pocket guide is an Index of all category names, Abbreviations listings and company contact information.

Most dealers and collectors are now utilizing what is essentially an objective method for deciding the condition of a gun: THE PERCENTAGE OF ORIGINAL FACTORY FINISH(ES) REMAINING ON THE GUN. After looking critically at a variety of firearms and carefully studying the Photo Percentage Grading System™ (available online at BlueBookOfGunValues.com), it will soon become evident if a specific gun has 98%, 90%, 70% or less finish remaining. Remember, sometimes an older unfired gun described as NIB can actually be 98% or less condition, simply because of the wear accumulated by taking it in and out of the box and excessive handling. Commemoratives are especially prone to this problem. Of course, factors such as quality of finish(es), engraving (and other embellishments), special orders/features, historical significance and/or provenance, etc. can and do affect prices immensely. Also, it seems that every year bore condition (especially on antiques) becomes more important in the overall grading factor (and price) of both collectible and desirable Colt models. Because of this, bore condition must be listed separately for those guns where it makes a difference in value.

Every gun's unique condition factor - and therefore the price - is best determined by the percentage of original finish(es) remaining, with the key consideration being the overall frame/receiver finish. The key word here is "original", for if anyone other than the factory has refinished the gun, its value as a collector's item has been diminished. The exceptions would be rare and historical guns that have been properly restored. Every year, top quality restorations have become more accepted, and prices have gone up proportionately with the quality of the workmanship. Also popular now are antique finishes, and a new question has come up, "What is 100% antique finish on new reproductions?" Answer - a gun that started out as new, and then has been aged to a lower condition factor to duplicate natural wear and tear.

When examining a gun's condition, note where the finishes of a firearm typically wear off first. These are usually places where the gun accumulates wear from holster/case rubbing, and contact with the hands or body over an extended period of time.

It should be noted that the older a collectible firearm is, the smaller the percentage of original finish one can expect to find. Some very old and/or very rare firearms are sought by collectors in almost any condition!

PHOTO PERCENTAGE GRADING SYSTEM CONVERSION GUIDELINES

New/Perfect - 100% condition with or without box. 100% on currently manufactured firearms assumes NIB (New In Box) condition and not sold previously at retail.

Mint - typically 98%-99% condition with almost no observable wear. Probably sold previously at retail, and may have been shot occasionally.

Excellent - 95%+ - 98% condition.

Very Good - 80% - 95% condition (all parts/finish should be original).

Good - 60% – 80% condition (all parts/finish should be original).

Fair - 20% - 60% condition (all parts/finish may or may not be original, but must function properly and shoot).

Poor - under 20% condition (shooting not a factor).

NRA CONDITION STANDARDS

The NRA conditions listed below have been provided as guidelines to assist the reader in converting and comparing condition factors. Once the gun's condition has been accurately assessed, only then can values be accurately ascertained. Please refer to the Photo Percentage Grading System (PPGS) available online at BlueBookOfGunValues.com to learn more about condition factors. Why guess when you can be sure?

NRA MODERN CONDITION DESCRIPTIONS

New – not previously sold at retail, in same condition as current factory production.

Perfect – in new condition in every respect, may have previously been sold at retail.

Excellent – near new condition, used but little to no noticeable marring of wood or metal, bluing near perfect (except at muzzle or sharp edges).

Very Good – in perfect working condition, no appreciable wear on working surfaces, no corrosion or pitting, only minor surface dents or scratches.

Good – in safe working condition, minor wear on working surfaces, no broken parts, no corrosion or pitting that will interfere with proper functioning.

Fair – in safe working condition, but well worn, perhaps requiring replacement of minor parts or adjustments which should be indicated in advertisement, no rust, but may have corrosion pits which do not render article unsafe or inoperable.

NRA ANTIQUE CONDITION DESCRIPTIONS

Factory New – all original parts; 100% original finish; in perfect condition in every respect, inside and out.

Excellent – all original parts; over 80% original finish; sharp lettering, numerals and design on metal and wood; unmarred wood; fine bore.

Fine – all original parts; over 30% original finish; sharp lettering, numerals and design on metal and wood; minor marks in wood; good bore.

Very Good – all original parts; none to 30% original finish; original metal surfaces smooth with all edges sharp; clear lettering, numerals and design on metal; wood slightly scratched or bruised; bore disregarded for collectors firearms.

Good – less than 20% original finish, some minor replacement parts; metal smoothly rusted or lightly pitted in places, cleaned or reblued; principal lettering, numerals and design on metal legible; wood refinished, scratched, bruised or minor cracks repaired; in good working order.

Fair – less than 10% original finish, some major parts replaced; minor replacement parts may be required; metal rusted, may be lightly pitted all over, vigorously cleaned or reblued; rounded edges of metal and wood; principal lettering, numerals and design on metal partly obliterated; wood scratched, bruised, cracked or repaired where broken; in fair working order or can be easily repaired and placed in working order.

Poor – little or no original finish remaining, major and minor parts replaced; major replacement parts required and extensive restoration needed; metal deeply pitted; principal lettering, numerals and design obliterated, wood badly scratched, bruised, cracked or broken; mechanically inoperative, generally undesirable as a collector's firearm.

COLT'S MANUFACTURING COMPANY, LLC

Current manufacturer with headquarters located in West Hartford, CT.

Manufactured from 1836-1842 in Paterson, NJ; 1847-1848 in Whitneyville, CT; 1854-1864 in London, England; and from 1848-date in Hartford, CT. Colt Firearms became a division of Colt Industries in 1964. In March 1990, the Colt Firearms Division was sold to C.F. Holding Corp. located in Hartford, CT, and the new company was called Colt's Manufacturing Company, Inc. The original Hartford plant was closed during 1994, the same year the company was sold again to a new investor group headed by Zilkha Co., located in New York, NY. During 1999, Colt Archive Properties LLC, the historical research division, became its own entity.

In late 1999, Colt discontinued many of their consumer revolvers, but reintroduced both the Anaconda and Python Elite through the Custom Shop. Production on both models is now suspended. The semi-auto pistols remaining in production are now referred to as Model "O" Series.

In November 2003, Colt was divided into two separate companies, Colt Defense LLC (military/law enforcement) and Colt's Manufacturing Company LLC (handguns and match target rifles). The largest portion of Colt Defense's business is now in sporting rifles, a line of business the company got back into during 2011. Military orders have been on the decline since 2009.

During 2013, Colt Defense LLC acquired Colt's Manufacturing LLC for $60.5 million and reunited Colt's military and civilian handgun businesses. By combining the two companies after a decade long split, Colt Defense has eliminated the risk that its contract with Colt's Manufacturing to sell commercial firearms to civilian sportsmen and hunters under its namesake brand wouldn't be extended beyond March 2014. The company plans to remain in West Hartford.

For more information and current pricing on both new and used Colt airguns, please refer to the *Blue Book of Airguns* by Dr. Robert Beeman & John Allen (also available online). For more information and current pricing on both new and used Colt black powder reproductions and replicas, please refer to the *Blue Book of Modern Black Powder Arms* by John Allen (also available online).

REVOLVERS: PERCUSSION

Prices shown for percussion Colts are for guns only. Original cased guns with accessories will bring a healthy premium over non-cased models (200%-350% over a gun only is common). Be very careful when buying an "original" cased gun, as many fake cases have shown up in recent years.

If possible, it is advisable to procure a factory letter (available only within the following ser. no. ranges) before buying, selling, or trading Models 1851 Navy (ser. range 98,000-132,000), 1860 Army (ser. range 1,000-140,000), or 1861 Navy (ser. range 1-12,000). These watermarked letters are available by writing Colt Archive Properties LLC in Bloomfield, CT, with a charge of $300 or more per serial number (if they can research it). Some 1849 Pockets can also be researched for $200. Include your name and address, Colt model name, serial number, and check or credit card information to: COLT ARCHIVE PROPERTIES LLC, 1295 Blue Hills Avenue, Bloomfield, CT 06002. Please allow 90-120 days for a response.

Prices shown for extremely rare Colt's firearms might not include values in the 90%, 95%, 98%, and 100% condition columns. Prices are very hard to establish since these excellent to mint specimens are seldom seen or sold.

The author wishes to express his thanks to Greg Martin from Greg Martin Auctions for his pricing updates on Colt percussion revolvers, Conversions, Open Tops, Pocket models, and the New Line Series.

Revolvers: Percussion, Paterson Variations

PATERSON NO. 1 POCKET MODEL - also known as "Baby Paterson," .28 cal., single action with folding trigger, 5 shot, 2 1/2-4 3/4 in. octagon barrels, blue metal, varnished walnut grips. Serial range 1 to approx. 500. Standard barrel marking "Patent Arms M'g Co. Paterson N.J.-Colt's Pt." Centaur scene with four horse head trademark and "COLT" on 1 1/16 in. cylinder of round or square type. Mfg. 1837-1838.

This and all other Paterson models have 5 shot cylinders and serial numbers are not commonly in evidence externally. Disassembly of the arm is usually necessary to determine the serial number.

The Pocket Model Paterson No. 1 (Baby Paterson) is the first production-made handgun in Colt's Paterson, N.J. facility. It is very small in size, almost appearing as a toy or miniature.

* ***Paterson No. 1 Pocket Model Standard Production Model*** - without attached loading lever.

100%	98%	95%	90%	80%	70%	60%	50%	40%	30%	20%	10%
N/A	N/A	$125,000	$100,000	$85,000	$72,500	$60,000	$55,000	$50,000	$45,000	$40,000	$35,000

* ***Paterson No. 1 Pocket Model Late Production Ehlers Model*** - with attached loading lever, 31/32 round back cylinder and recoil shield milled for ease of capping. Barrel marked "Patent Arms Paterson N.J.-Colt's Pt." Approx. 500 mfg. including the Ehlers Model under Belt Model No. 2 Mfg. 1840-1843.

100%	98%	95%	90%	80%	70%	60%	50%	40%	30%	20%	10%
N/A	N/A	$90,000	$75,000	$67,500	$60,000	$55,000	$50,000	$47,500	$45,000	$40,000	$35,000

PATERSON NO. 2 BELT MODEL - .31 or .34 cal., single action with folding trigger, 5 shot, 2 1/2-5 1/2 in. octagon barrels, blue metal, varnished walnut grips, serial range 1-approx. 850 which includes the Belt Model No. 3. All standard production Belt Models No. 2 have straight bottom style grips. Standard barrel markings "Patent Arms M'g Co. Paterson N-J. Colt's Pt." Centaur scene with four horse head trademark and "COLT" on cylinder of round or square backed type. Mfg. 1837-40. Somewhat heavier than the Pocket No. 1 revolver.

100%	98%	95%	90%	80%	70%	60%	50%	40%	30%	20%	10%

* ***Paterson No. 2 Belt Model Standard Production Model*** – without attached loading lever.

N/A N/A $80,000 $70,000 $65,000 $60,000 $55,000 $50,000 $47,500 $45,000 $40,000 $35,000

* ***Paterson No. 2 Belt Model Ehlers*** – with attached loading lever, 1 1/16 in. round back cylinder, recoil shield milled for ease of capping. Barrel marked "Patent Arms Paterson N-J. Colt's Pt." Approx. 500 mfg. including the Ehlers Model under Pocket Model No. 1. Mfg. 1840-43.

N/A N/A $125,000 $100,000 $85,000 $75,000 $70,000 $65,000 $57,500 $50,000 $45,000 $40,000

PATERSON NO. 3 BELT MODEL – .31 or .34 cal., single action with folding trigger, 5 shot, 3 1/2-5 1/2 in. octagon barrels, blue metal, a few having case hardened hammers, varnished walnut grips. Serial range 1-approx. 850 which includes the Belt Model No. 2. All standard production Belt Models No. 3 have the flared bottom style grips. Standard barrel markings "Patent Arms M'g Co. Paterson N-J. Colt's Pt." The square backed cylinder is seen less often than the more common round back, both bearing the Centaur scene with four horse head trademark and "COLT," with both Belt Models, revolvers exhibiting attached loading levers are less common than those without a lever. Mfg. 1837-1840.

* ***Paterson No. 3 Belt Model Standard w/o Lever*** – without attached loading lever.

N/A N/A $95,000 $85,000 $80,000 $75,000 $67,500 $60,000 $57,500 $55,000 $50,000 $45,000

* ***Paterson No. 3 Belt Model Standard With Lever*** – with attached loading lever and recoil shield milled for ease of capping (scarce).

N/A N/A $140,000 $110,000 $90,000 $75,000 $67,500 $60,000 $57,500 $55,000 $50,000 $45,000

PATERSON NO. 5 HOLSTER MODEL – also known as "Texas Paterson" - .36 cal., single action with folding trigger, 5 shot, 4 to 12 in. octagon barrels, blue metal with case hardened frame and hammer. All cylinders bear the stage coach hold-up scene. Varnished walnut grips of flared bottom style. Serial range 1 to approx. 1,000. As with all models of Patersons, the serial number usually cannot be seen without disassembly of the revolver. Very large and heavy compared to the other Paterson models. Enjoys more popularity with collectors because of its military and frontier use. Mfg. 1838-1840.

Many specimens encountered in this variation show extreme use. Consequently, fine to mint specimens are quite rare and highly prized by collectors. Values are given for non-military marked specimens. Any specimen bearing an authenticated martial marking is truly a rarity and should be appraised individually. NOTE: Watch for fakes here. There are now many times more faked martial markings, often times on non-original Patersons, than there are originals.

* ***Paterson No. 5 Holster Model Standard Production Model w/o Lever*** – without attached loading lever, round or square backed cylinder.

N/A N/A $160,000 $140,000 $125,0000 $110,000 $90,000 $85,000 $80,000 $75,000 $65,000 $60,000

100%	98%	95%	90%	80%	70%	60%	50%	40%	30%	20%	10%

* ***Paterson No. 5 Holster Model Standard Production Model With Lever*** - with attached loading lever, round backed cylinder and recoil shield milled for ease of capping.

N/A N/A $200,000 $175,000 $150,000 $125,000 $100,000 $95,000 $82,500 $75,000 $70,000 $65,000

Revolvers: Percussion, Walker Model

WALKER MODEL - .44 cal., single action, 9 in. part round/part octagon barrel, 6 shot cylinder, brass trigger guard, one-piece walnut grips, blue metal with case hardened frame, lever, and hammer, cylinder left in the white without finish, barrels marked "Address SamL Colt New-York City," found on right side of barrel lug is "US" over "1847," cylinder bears Texas Ranger/Indian fight scene, various metal parts and walnut grips stamped with Govt. Inspectors' marks, Ser. numbers beginning with no. 1 were applied for each of five different military companies (A,B,C,D, & E). The total for the military issue Walkers was approx. 1,000 revolvers; the remaining approx. 100 revolvers were produced for civilian distribution. Total production approx. 1,100 mfg. 1847.

Because of these arms being subjected to great extremes of use, they will exhibit high degrees of wear, often to the extent that most or all markings will be worn off. Replaced parts are common and many badly worn and damaged specimens have been extensively rebuilt and restored. NOTE: Use great caution when contemplating the purchase of a Walker. A multitude of out-and-out fakes and "antiqued" reproduction Walkers have been fed into the market over the past few decades. Some of these are old enough (and have aged enough naturally) to almost resemble an authentic specimen. Enlist the services of a qualified expert before your dollars are spent. Only 10%-12% of the original production of approx. 1,100 specimens have been accounted for. The acquisition of an authenticated Walker revolver is the ultimate goal of serious Colt handgun collectors.

* ***Walker Standard Military Issue Model***

N/A N/A N/A N/A N/A N/A $500,000 $400,000 $250,000 $150,00 $125,000 $100,000

* ***Walker Limited Civilian Issue Model*** - .44 cal., serial range 1001 to approx. 1100. Similar to military model except Govt. inspectors' marks were not applied.

N/A N/A N/A N/A N/A N/A $500,000 $400,000 $250,000 $150,00 $125,000 $100,000

Pricing is difficult on the civilian issue arms. They tend to be in considerably better condition than the much more common military specimens. The factors of scarcity and condition will often bring higher prices from the advanced collector of means, especially in the finer grades of condition. On the other hand, the collector appreciating military usage will pay more for military marked examples. This publication tries to reflect the latest trends on purchase of civilian models.

100%	98%	95%	90%	80%	70%	60%	50%	40%	30%	20%	10%

Revolvers: Percussion, Dragoon Series

WHITNEYVILLE HARTFORD DRAGOON - .44 cal., 6 shot, 7 1/2 in. part octagon/part round barrel, some of the left-over Walker parts were used in Dragoons, blue metal with case hardened frame, lever, hammer, brass trigger guard, and steel cylinder bears Texas Ranger and Indian battle scene. Total production approx. 240. Serial range approx. 1,100 to 1,340 in sequence following civilian Walkers. Mfg. 1847.

* ***Whitneyville Hartford Dragoon w/Rear frame cut out for grips***

N/A N/A $350,000 $175,000 $150,000 $100,000 $85,000 $75,000 $65,000 $50,000 $45,000 $40,000

* ***Whitneyville Hartford Dragoon w/Straight rear frame***

N/A N/A $250,000 $150,000 $125,000 $90,000 $75,000 $65,000 $55,000 $40,000 $30,000 $25,000

FIRST MODEL DRAGOON - .44 cal., 6 shot, 7 1/2 in. round and octagon barrel, blue metal with case hardened frame, lever, hammer, brass grip straps, silvered straps for civilian market, serial range numbered after Hartford Dragoon, 1341 to around 8000. Oval cyl. slots, square back trigger guard, Texas Ranger and Indian fight scene on cylinder. Total production approx. 7,000. Mfg. 1848-1850.

* ***First Model Dragoon Military Model***

N/A N/A $125,000 $80,000 $60,000 $45,000 $27,500 $25,000 $20,000 $15,000 $12,500 $10,000

* ***First Model Dragoon Civilian Model***

N/A N/A $80,000 $60,000 $50,000 $25,000 $22,500 $20,000 $17,500 $15,000 $12,500 $10,000

FLUCK MODEL DRAGOON - basically a First Model Dragoon, with 7 1/2 in. altered Walker barrels and fully martially marked, should be extensively checked over, used to replace defective Walkers. Mfg. 1848. Total production 300. Serial range approx. 2,216 to 2,515.

N/A N/A $85,000 $75,000 $65,000 $30,000 $25,000 $20,000 $17,500 $15,000 $13,500 $12,000

SECOND MODEL DRAGOON - .44 cal., 6 shot, 7 1/2 in. round and octagon barrel, serial range following the First Model Dragoon 8,000-10,700. Texas Ranger and Indian fight scene on cylinder. Mfg. 1850-1851.

* ***Second Model Dragoon Military Model***

N/A N/A $85,000 $70,000 $50,000 $30,000 $25,000 $20,000 $16,000 $12,000 $10,000 $7,500

* ***Second Model Dragoon Civilian Model***

N/A N/A $75,000 $60,000 $40,000 $35,000 $22,500 $20,000 $17,500 $15,000 $11,000 $6,000

* ***Second Model Dragoon New Hampshire or Massachusetts*** - notice state markings on front portion of trigger guard.

N/A N/A $80,000 $65,000 $52,500 $40,000 $37,500 $25,000 $20,000 $15,000 $12,500 $10,000

THIRD MODEL DRAGOON - .44 cal., 6 shot, 7 1/2 in. round and octagon barrel, same basic features as earlier models, but with round trigger guard and rectangular cylinder slots, Texas Ranger and Indian fight scene on cylinder, serial range approx. 10,200-19,600, some overlapping of numbers, with approx. 10,500 mfg. from 1851-1861.

* ***Third Model Dragoon Civilian***

N/A N/A $60,000 $45,000 $35,000 $30,000 $25,000 $17,500 $15,000 $12,000 $10,000 $7,500

100% 98% 95% 90% 80% 70% 60% 50% 40% 30% 20% 10%

* ***Third Model Dragoon Martially Marked U.S.***

N/A N/A $55,000 $40,000 $35,000 $25,000 $22,500 $20,000 $17,500 $15,000 $12,000 $8,500

* ***Third Model Dragoon Third Model*** - 8 in. barrel.

N/A N/A $65,000 $55,000 $40,000 $30,000 $25,000 $22,000 $21,000 $19,500 $14,000 $9,500

* ***Third Model Dragoon First and Second Variation*** - shoulder stock model.

N/A N/A $60,000 $45,000 $35,000 $25,000 $22,500 $20,000 $17,500 $15,000 $12,500 $9,500

* ***Third Model Dragoon Third Variation***

N/A N/A $60,000 $45,000 $35,000 $25,000 $20,000 $17,500 $15,000 $12,000 $10,000 $7,500

* ***Third Model Dragoon C.L. Dragoon***

N/A N/A $75,000 $65,000 $50,000 $35,000 $26,000 $22,500 $19,000 $15,000 $12,500 $10,000

ENGLISH HARTFORD DRAGOON - basically a Third Model Dragoon, assembled at Colt's London factory, with unique serial range 1-700, some were assembled from earlier parts inventories, easy to spot with British proofs of crown over V and crown over GP, the blue was of the English type, many were engraved.

N/A N/A $55,000 $40,000 $32,000 $22,500 $19,000 $15,000 $12,500 $10,000 $8,750 $7,500

1848 BABY DRAGOONS - .31 cal., 5 shot, 3, 4, 5, or 6 in. octagon barrels, most without loading lever, serial range 1-15,500, a scaled down version of the .44 caliber Dragoons, early ones with Texas Ranger scene and later ones with the holdup scene.

* ***1848 Baby Dragoon Type I*** - left-hand barrel stamping, Texas Ranger and Indian scene, approx. serial range 1-150.

N/A N/A $25,000 $15,000 $11,000 $7,500 $7,000 $6,5000 $6,000 $5,500 $5,000 $4,500

* ***1848 Baby Dragoon Type II*** - with Texas Ranger and Indian scene, 11,600 serial range, without loading lever.

N/A N/A $17,500 $12,000 $9,500 $6,500 $6,250 $6,000 $5,200 $4,500 $4,000 $3,500

* ***1848 Baby Dragoon Type III*** - with Stagecoach scene and oval cylinder slots, serial range 10,400-12,000.

N/A N/A $17,500 $12,000 $9,500 $6,500 $6,250 $6,000 $5,200 $4,500 $4,000 $3,500

* ***1848 Baby Dragoon Type IV*** - with Stagecoach holdup scene, rectangle cylinder slots, serial range 11,000-12,500.

N/A N/A $17,500 $12,000 $9,500 $6,500 $6,250 $6,000 $5,200 $4,500 $4,000 $3,500

* ***1848 Baby Dragoon Type V*** - with Stagecoach holdup scene, rectangle cylinder slots and loading lever, serial range 11,600-15,500.

N/A N/A $17,500 $12,000 $9,500 $6,500 $6,250 $6,000 $5,200 $4,500 $4,000 $3,500

Revolvers: Percussion, Models 1849, 1851, 1855, 1860, 1861, 1862, & 1865

1849 POCKET MODEL - .31 cal., 5 or 6 shot, 3, 4, 5, and 6 in. octagon barrels, most with loading levers, blue metal with case hardened frame, lever and hammer, grip straps of brass (silver plated), or steel (silver plated or blue), stagecoach hold-up scene on cylinder, serial range 12,000 to 340,000. Mfg. 1850-73.

100%	98%	95%	90%	80%	70%	60%	50%	40%	30%	20%	10%

* ***1849 Pocket Model First Type*** – 4, 5, or 6 in. barrel, loading lever and small or large brass trigger guard.

N/A N/A $5,000 $4,000 $3,000 $2,250 $1,750 $1,500 $1,200 $800 $625 $500

* ***1849 Pocket Model Second Type*** – 4, 5, or 6 in. barrel, loading lever and steel grip straps.

N/A N/A $4,500 $3,000 $2,500 $1,500 $1,200 $950 $850 $750 $625 $500

* ***1849 Pocket Model Wells Fargo Model*** – 3 in. barrel, without loading lever and with small round trigger guard.

N/A N/A $18,500 $15,000 $10,000 $8,500 $5,000 $4,000 $3,000 $2,500 $2,250 $2,000

1849 LONDON POCKET MODEL – London pistols were of the same general configuration, but of better finish, serial range 1-11,000. Mfg. 1853-57.

* ***1849 London Pocket Model Early Type*** – serial numbered under 1500, with small trigger guard and brass grip straps.

N/A N/A $7,500 $4,500 $4,000 $3,500 $2,900 $2,250 $1,750 $1,200 $1,075 $950

* ***1849 London Pocket Model Late Type*** – oval trigger guard and steel grip straps.

N/A N/A $4,750 $3,750 $3,000 $2,250 $1,500 $1,200 $1,075 $950 $850 $750

1851 NAVY – .36 cal., 6 shot, 7 1/2 in. octagon barrel and loading lever, blue metal with case hardened frame, lever, and hammer, one-piece walnut finished grips, cylinder scene of Texas Navy battle with Mexico, serial range 1-highest recorded number was 215,348, three barrel addresses 1-74,000 (ADDRESS SAML COLT, NEW YORK CITY), 74,000-101,000 (ADDRESS SAML COLT, HARTFORD, CT.) 101,000-215,348 (ADDRESS COL. SAML COLT, NEW YORK, U.S. AMERICA). Mfg. 1850-1873.

* ***1851 Navy First Model*** – square back trigger guard, bottom wedge screw, serial range 1-1,250.

N/A N/A $28,000 $24,000 $20,000 $17,500 $12,500 $10,000 $8,250 $6,500 $5,500 $4,500

* ***1851 Navy Second Model*** – square back trigger guard, top wedge screw, serial range 1,250-4,000.

N/A N/A $25,000 $20,000 $17,500 $12,000 $10,000 $7,500 $6,250 $5,000 $4,250 $3,500

* ***1851 Navy Third Model*** – small round brass trigger guard, serial range 4,200-85,000.

N/A N/A $7,500 $6,500 $5,000 $4,000 $3,000 $2,000 $1,600 $1,200 $1,100 $1,000

* ***1851 Navy Fourth Model*** – large round brass trigger guard, serial range 85,000-215,348.

N/A N/A $7,500 $6,500 $5,000 $4,000 $3,000 $2,000 $1,600 $1,200 $1,100 $1,000

* ***1851 Navy Iron Gripstrap Model*** – most often seen in fourth model.

N/A N/A $7,500 $6,500 $5,000 $4,000 $3,000 $2,200 $1,850 $1,500 $1,350 $1,200

* ***1851 Navy Martially Marked U.S. Navys*** – brass or iron gripstrap.

N/A N/A $22,500 $18,500 $15,000 $11,000 $8,500 $6,000 $4,750 $3,500 $3,000 $2,500

100%	98%	95%	90%	80%	70%	60%	50%	40%	30%	20%	10%

* ***1851 Navy Cut for shoulder stock*** - first and second type (like third model Dragoon).

N/A	N/A	$15,000	$10,000	$9,250	$8,500	$6,750	$5,000	$3,500	$2,000	$1,750	$1,500

* ***1851 Navy Third Type*** - four screw frame.

N/A	N/A	$7,500	$6,500	$5,000	$4,000	$3,000	$2,500	$2,250	$2,000	$1,750	$1,500

51 NAVY LONDON MODEL - basically the same gun as the Hartford piece with London barrel address, with British proof marks in serial range 1-42,000. Mfg. 1853-1857.

* ***51 Navy London Early First Model*** - serial range below 2000, brass grip straps and small trigger guard.

N/A	N/A	$7,500	$6,500	$5,000	$4,000	$3,000	$2,500	$2,250	$2,000	$1,750	$1,500

* ***51 Navy London Late Second Model*** - balance of production, large round trigger guard, steel grip straps, all London parts.

N/A	N/A	$8,000	$4,500	$4,000	$3,500	$3,000	$2,500	$2,000	$1,500	$1,350	$1,200

1855 SIDEHAMMER POCKET MODEL (ROOT MODEL) - .28 cal., had 3 1/2 in. octagon barrel, .31 cal. usually had 3 1/2 in. or 4 1/2 in. round barrel. Blue with case hardened lever and hammer, one-piece wraparound style walnut grips.

Commonly called the "Root" Model by collectors, manufactured 1855 through 1870. The .28 cal. model serial numbered 1 through approx. 30,000. The .31 cal. round barrel model serial numbered 1 through approx. 14,000. Total production approx. 44,000.

Easily recognizable by its side mounted hammer and cylinder rotation ratchet at rear of frame.

* ***1855 Sidehammer Pocket Model 1 and 1A*** - .28 cal., 3 7/16 in. octagonal bbl., oct. load lever, Indian/cabin cyl. scene, Hartford barrel address. Serial range 1 to 384.

N/A	N/A	$12,500	$8,000	$6,500	$5,000	$4,250	$3,500	$3,000	$2,500	$2,250	$2,000

* ***1855 Sidehammer Pocket Model 2*** - .28 cal., 3 1/2 in. oct. bbl., Indian/cabin cyl. scene, Hartford barrel address with pointed hand. Serial range 476 to 25,000.

N/A	N/A	$3,500	$2,000	$1,600	$1,200	$1,000	$950	$850	$750	$625	$500

* ***1855 Sidehammer Pocket Model 3*** - .28 cal., 3 1/2 in. oct. bbl., full fluted cylinder, Hartford barrel address with pointed hand. Serial range 25,001 to 30,000.

N/A	N/A	$4,250	$2,500	$2,000	$1,200	$1,075	$950	$850	$750	$625	$500

* ***1855 Sidehammer Pocket Model 3A*** - .31 cal., 3 1/2 in. oct. bbl., full fluted cylinder, Hartford barrel address. Serial range 1 to 1,350.

N/A	N/A	$3,500	$2,000	$1,600	$1,200	$1,000	$950	$850	$750	$625	$500

* ***1855 Sidehammer Pocket Model 4*** - .31 cal., 3 1/2 in. oct. bbl., full fluted cylinder, Hartford barrel address. Serial range 1,351 to 2,400.

N/A	N/A	$4,500	$3,500	$3,000	$2,250	$1,500	$1,200	$1,075	$950	$850	$750

100%	98%	95%	90%	80%	70%	60%	50%	40%	30%	20%	10%

* ***1855 Sidehammer Pocket Model 5*** - .31 cal., 3 1/2 in. round bbl., full fluted cylinder, "COL. COLT NEW-YORK" barrel address. Serial range 2,401 to 8,000.

N/A N/A $4,500 $3,500 $3,000 $2,250 $1,500 $1,200 $1,075 $950 $850 $750

* ***1855 Sidehammer Pocket Model 5A*** - .31 cal., 4 1/2 in. round bbl., included in same serial range as Model 5.

N/A N/A $4,500 $3,500 $3,000 $2,250 $1,875 $1,500 $1,350 $1,200 $1,075 $950

* ***1855 Sidehammer Pocket Model 6*** - .31 cal., 3 1/2 in. round bbl., stage coach hold-up cylinder scene, "COL. COLT NEW-YORK" barrel address. Serial range 8,001 through 11,074.

N/A N/A $4,500 $3,500 $3,000 $2,250 $1,800 $1,500 $1,350 $1,200 $1,075 $950

* ***1855 Sidehammer Pocket Model 6A*** - .31 cal., 4 1/2 in. round bbl., included in same serial range as Model 6.

N/A N/A $4,500 $3,500 $3,000 $2,250 $1,800 $1,500 $1,350 $1,200 $1,075 $950

* ***1855 Sidehammer Pocket Model 7*** - .31 cal., 3 1/2 in. round bbl., stage coach hold-up cylinder scene, "COL. COLT NEW-YORK" barrel address. Cylinder pin retained by screw-in cylinder. Serial range 11,075 through 14,000.

N/A N/A $5,500 $4,000 $3,500 $3,000 $2,750 $2,500 $2,000 $1,500 $1,350 $1,200

* ***1855 Sidehammer Pocket Model 7A*** – .31 cal., 4 1/2 in. round bbl., including same cylinder scene, barrel address and serial range as Model 7.

N/A N/A $5,000 $4,000 $3,500 $3,000 $2,750 $2,250 $1,750 $1,200 $1,100 $1,000

1860 MODEL ARMY - .44 cal., 6 shot, 7 1/2 and 8 in. round barrels with loading lever, blue metal with case hardened frame, lever and hammer, one piece walnut grips, normally blue steel back strap and brass trigger guard, barrel markings were "ADDRESS SAM COLT, HARTFORD, CT." on early productions and "ADDRESS COL. SAM COLT, NEW YORK, U.S. AMERICA" on balance, serial range 1-about 200,500, Texas Navy scene on round cylinder model. Mfg. 1860-73.

* ***1860 Model Army Fluted Cylinder*** - full length cylinder flutes and no cylinder scene, 7 1/2 or 8 in. barrel, grips of Navy (very rare) or Army size, usually 4 screw frames.

N/A N/A $22,500 $15,000 $12,000 $7,500 $6,000 $5,000 $4,250 $3,500 $3,000 $2,500

* ***1860 Model Army Round Cylinder*** - roll engraved Texas Navy scene, some with early Hartford address, Army grips, four screw frame to about 50,000 range, most were sold to the U.S. Government and will be martially marked.

N/A N/A $13,500 $9,250 $8,000 $5,000 $4,250 $3,500 $3,000 $2,500 $2,000 $1,500

* ***1860 Model Army Civilian*** - same general configurations as Round Cylinder Model, but with 3 screw frame, no shoulder stock cuts and better blue finish than military pieces, late New York barrel address.

N/A N/A $7,500 $6,500 $5,000 $4,000 $3,000 $2,500 $2,000 $1,500 $1,350 $1,200

100%	98%	95%	90%	80%	70%	60%	50%	40%	30%	20%	10%

1861 MODEL NAVY – .36 cal., 6 shot, 7 1/2 in. round barrel with loading lever, blue metal with case hardened frame, lever and hammer, silver plated brass grip straps, the barrel address was "ADDRESS COL. SAM COLT, NEW YORK, U.S. AMERICA", serial range 1-38,843, cylinder scene of Texas Navy and Mexico Battle. Mfg. 1861-1873.

* ***1861 Model Fluted Cylinder Navy*** – in serial range 1-100, with fluted cylinder and without rolled cylinder scene.

N/A N/A $40,000 $35,000 $30,000 $25,000 $21,500 $17,500 $15,000 $12,000 $10,000 $7,500

* ***1861 Model Navy Regular Production model***

N/A N/A $20,000 $12,000 $10,000 $7,500 $6,000 $5,000 $4,250 $3,500 $2,750 $2,000

* ***1861 Model Martially Marked Navys*** – will bear the U.S. stamp and inspector's marks, those marked U.S.N. on butt were of a 650 piece order for the Navy.

N/A N/A $35,000 $22,500 $15,000 $8,500 $7,500 $6,000 $5,000 $4,000 $3,250 $2,500

* ***1861 Model London Marked Navy*** – with "ADDRESS COL. COLT, LONDON", for barrel address.

N/A N/A $22,500 $12,000 $10,000 $7,500 $6,000 $5,000 $4,750 $4,500 $3,250 $2,000

* ***1861 Model Shoulder Stock Cut Navy*** – 4 screw frames in serial range 11,000-14,000, made for third style stock (see Dragoon stocks).

N/A N/A $25,000 $15,000 $12,000 $9,000 $7,500 $6,500 $5,500 $4,500 $4,000 $3,500

1862 POLICE MODEL – .36 cal., 5 shot half fluted and rebated cylinder, 4 1/2, 5 1/2, and 6 1/2 in. round barrels (also 3 1/2 in. barrel but quite rare) and loading lever. Mfg. 1861-1873. Serial numbered with Model 1862 Pocket Navy, approx. 28,000 1862 Police Models were produced. Blue with case hardened frame, lever, and hammer, grip straps silver plated, one-piece walnut grips. Serial range 1 through approx. 47,000. Standard barrel marking "ADDRESS COL. SAML COLT NEW-YORK U.S. AMERICA" "COLTS/PATENT" on left side of frame, "PAT SEPT. 10TH 1850" stamped in cyl. flute.

Many Model 1862 Police and 1862 Pocket Navy revolvers were converted to cartridge with the advent of the metallic cartridge. Consequently these models in their original cap and ball chambering are quite desirable to collectors.

* ***1862 Police Early Model*** – "ADDRESS SAM COLT/HARTFORD CT" barrel address, silvered iron or brass grip straps.

N/A N/A $6,000 $5,000 $4,000 $3,000 $2,500 $2,250 $2,000 $1,750 $1,500 $1,200

* ***1862 Police Standard Production Model*** – with New York barrel address.

N/A N/A $4,750 $3,500 $3,000 $2,500 $2,000 $1,750 $1,500 $1,250 $1,100 $950

* ***1862 Police Export Production Model*** – with "L" below serial numbers (for export to England), steel grip straps. Most often but not always bearing British proofs.

N/A N/A $4,000 $3,000 $2,500 $2,250 $2,000 $1,750 $1,500 $1,250 $1,100 $950

100%	98%	95%	90%	80%	70%	60%	50%	40%	30%	20%	10%

* *1862 Police London Marked Model* - similar to above, except with "ADDRESS, COL. COLT/LONDON" address on barrel.

N/A	N/A	$17,500	$12,000	$9,000	$6,000	$5,000	$5,000	$4,000	$3,000	$2,500	$2,000

POCKET MODEL OF NAVY CALIBER (MODEL 1865) - .36 or .38 cal., 5 shot rebated cylinder, 4 1/2, 5 1/2, and 6 1/2 in. octagonal barrels with loading lever. Mfg. 1865-1882. Blue with case hardened frame, lever and hammer, grip straps silver plated brass, one-piece walnut grips. Standard barrel markings "ADDRESS COL. SAML COLT NEW-YORK U.S. AMERICA" "COLTS/PATENT" on left side of frame, stage coach hold-up scene on cylinder. Serial numbered with Model 1862 Police Model, approx. 19,000 produced. Serial range 1 through approx. 47,000. Mfg. began 1865.

This model has been identified for decades to collectors as the Model 1853 or the Model 1862 Pocket Model Navy. Recent research indicates that a more correct model name for this revolver is the Pocket Model of Navy Caliber.

Because of being produced during the advent of the metallic cartridge, the number remaining in the original cap and ball configuration is rather few; scarce with any serial number, but particularly so in numbers over approx. 19,800.

* *Pocket Model of Navy Caliber Standard Model* - 4 1/2, 5 1/2 or 6 1/2 in. barrel lengths.

N/A	N/A	$12,000	$9,000	$7,500	$5,000	$3,500	$3,000	$2,750	$2,500	$2,000	$1,500

* *Pocket Model of Navy Caliber Export Production Model* - with "L" below serial numbers (for export to England), steel grip straps. Often found with British proofs.

N/A	N/A	$10,000	$7,500	$6,000	$4,500	$3,500	$3,000	$2,750	$2,500	$2,000	$1,500

* *Pocket Model of Navy Caliber London Marked Model* - similar to above but "ADDRESS COL. COLT/LONDON" address on barrel.

N/A	N/A	$17,500	$12,500	$10,000	$7,500	$6,000	$5,000	$4,250	$3,500	$3,250	$3,000

REVOLVERS: PERCUSSION CONVERSIONS

Colt Thuer Conversions

Subtract approx. 50% for factory nickel plating on models listed below.

COLT THUER CONVERSIONS (c. 1868-1872) - .31, .36, or .44 centerfire cal., less than 5,000 produced in all models. This was Colt's first commercial attempt at converting percussion revolvers to fire fixed ammo. Standard features: usually threaded inside rammer for a Thuer loading tool, a hardened flat face on hammer, deepened loading cutout on right side of lug, Thuer ring and back of cylinder have matching assembly numbers. Beware of fakes! Only non-experimental Colt models are listed. Rarity by barrel length will not be considered here. Serial numbers are often missing on cylinder.

Prices for Colt Conversions reflect values for blue and case hardened examples. Nickel plated specimens are rarely seen, but typically sell

100%	98%	95%	90%	80%	70%	60%	50%	40%	30%	20%	10%

for 20%-40% less than blue finish.

Any defects, excessive wear, or dulled blue will affect value. Nickeled conversions that have lost their translucence (become cloudy) should be discounted more than usual 20%-40% from blue and case hardened examples, especially on near-mint to mint specimens.

* ***Colt Thuer Conversion 1849 Pocket***

N/A N/A $70,000 $40,000 $32,500 $25,000 $21,500 $18,000 $15,000 $12,000 $10,000 $7,500

* ***Colt Thuer Conversion 1851 Navy***

N/A N/A $30,000 $27,500 $25,000 $22,000 $18,500 $15,000 $11,500 $8,500 $7,250 $6,000

* ***Colt Thuer Conversion 1860 Army*** – the most common Thuer, but popular because it's a large frame model.

N/A N/A $35,000 $27,500 $23,750 $20,000 $18,750 $17,500 $15,500 $12,500 $10,750 $9,000

* ***Colt Thuer Conversion 1861 Navy***

N/A N/A $35,000 $25,000 $21,000 $17,500 $16,250 $15,000 $12,500 $10,000 $8,750 $7,500

* ***Colt Thuer Conversion 1862 Police***

N/A N/A $22,500 $18,500 $16,750 $15,000 $13,500 $12,000 $10,250 $8,500 $7,500 $6,500

* ***Colt Thuer Conversion 1862 Pocket Navy***

N/A N/A $30,000 $27,000 $22,500 $17,500 $16,250 $15,000 $12,500 $10,000 $8,750 $7,500

Richards Conversions: All Variations

Subtract approx. 50% for factory nickel plating on models listed below.

RICHARDS CONVERSION, COLT 1860 ARMY REVOLVER - .44 CF cal., produced circa 1870s, special machining to barrel and breech of cylinder for conversion to a cartridge weapon. Produced in three serial ranges: one numbered under 10,000, a separate group generally in the 190,000 to 200,000 range, and approx. 9,000 produced 1873-1878 in the 24,000-144,000 serial range.

* ***1860 Army First Model Richards*** – integral rear sight and floating firing pin on breech plate, front edge of barrel lug is same as 1860 Percussion Army. Breech plate extends over rear edge of cylinder.

N/A N/A $25,000 $15,000 $11,750 $8,500 $7,000 $5,500 $5,000 $4,500 $4,000 $3,500

* ***1860 Army Second Model Richards*** – standard Richards type barrel. A space between face of conversion ring and rear of cylinder when viewed from the side. No integral sight on breechplate, cut away at top allowing hammer to directly strike the cartridge.

N/A N/A $25,000 $20,000 $14,500 $8,500 $7,750 $7,000 $5,750 $4,500 $4,250 $4,000

* ***1860 Army Twelve Stop Cylinder Variation Richards*** – generally the same as the Second Model Richards except cylinder has extra "safety" notches between the locking notches. This variation was usually produced in the 100-300, 1,000-1,700 and 200,000 serial ranges. Cylinder locking notches over chambers often broken through. Watch for alterations.

N/A N/A $35,000 $25,000 $18,500 $12,000 $10,500 $9,000 $8,250 $7,500 $7,000 $6,500

100%	98%	95%	90%	80%	70%	60%	50%	40%	30%	20%	10%

* *1860 Army U.S. Marked Richards* - generally the same as 1st Model Richards (many minor differences). Has "U.S." stamped on left barrel lug and "A" (Ainsworth) inspector marks in several places. They are converted 1860 percussion Armys, so original numbers are typically in 23,000-144,000 range plus a second set of assembly numbers. Oiled grips, military soft blue finish.

N/A	N/A	$35,000	$25,000	$18,500	$12,000	$10,500	$9,000	$8,250	$7,500	$7,000	$6,500

Richards-Mason Conversions: All Variations

Subtract approx. 50% for factory nickel plating on models listed below.

1860 ARMY RICHARDS-MASON - .44 CF cal., overall, much rarer than Richards Army Conversions, circa 1870s, approximately 2100 produced. A rare variation has an 1860 Army rebated cylinder and a barrel with a lug shaped similar to 1861 Navy Conversion. breechplate without integral rear sight, cutout at top so hammer can strike primer directly. A space can be seen between breechplate and rear of cylinder. Rear of lug is a vertical line instead of the bullet shape cutout seen on Richards models.

N/A	N/A	$30,000	$20,000	$17,500	$15,500	$12,500	$9,500	$8,000	$6,500	$5,750	$5,000

1851 NAVY RICHARDS-MASON - .38 CF and RF cal., circa 1870s. Produced in two different serial ranges. Has improved Richards-Mason breechplate that is flush with diameter of recoil shield. Difficult to locate in prime condition.

* *1851 Navy Civilian Model Richards-Mason* - Richards-Mason breechplate which is same diameter as recoil shield, octagon barrel, mirrored civilian blue. Nickel finish commonly seen.

N/A	N/A	$17,500	$12,000	$9,500	$6,500	$5,500	$4,500	$4,000	$3,500	$2,500	$2,000

* *1851 U.S. Navy Richards-Mason* - Richards-Mason breechplate, oiled grips, soft blue military finish, produced in US. percussion range of 40,000-90,000. Inconsistent "U.S.N." and other inspector markings. Iron straps, "U.S." on frame.

N/A	N/A	$20,000	$15,000	$12,000	$8,500	$7,500	$6,500	$5,500	$4,500	$4,000	$3,500

1861 NAVY RICHARDS-MASON - produced in civilian and military versions, circa 1870s, made in RF and CF cal. in two serial ranges. Round 7 1/2 in. barrel.

* *1861 Navy Civilian Model Richards-Mason* - Richards-Mason breechplate, round 7 1/2 in. barrel with attached ejector housing, unrebated cylinder. When blue, has a commercial high gloss finish.

N/A	N/A	$25,000	$17,000	$13,750	$10,000	$8,750	$7,000	$6,250	$5,000	$4,000	$3,000

* *1861 Navy U.S. Navy Richards-Mason* - soft military blue finish, oiled grips, converted from percussion U.S. Navy revolvers, inconsistent military markings, centerfire, set of extra serial numbers often seen on cylinder.

N/A	N/A	$25,000	$20,000	$16,000	$12,000	$10,500	$8,000	$7,250	$6,000	$4,750	$3,500

100%	98%	95%	90%	80%	70%	60%	50%	40%	30%	20%	10%

COLT 1862 POLICE & POCKET NAVY RICHARDS-MASON CONVERSIONS (circa 1870s) - .38 RF and CF cal., parts for 1862 Police, Pocket Navy, as well as 1849 Pockets are often intermixed. As parts bins were depleted, Colt used whatever components that would fit, resulting in a tremendous amount of minor variations. Some barrels were converted from percussion models while others were newly made as cartridge barrels without rammer plugs and loading slots in the lug. There are five different serial ranges (1849, 1862 Police, Pocket Navy, Conversion). 3 1/2 to 6 1/2 in. barrels, again not all features available on all models.

Nickel plated conversions will bring 20%-40% less than blue and case hardened specimens.

* ***1862 Police & Pocket Navy Richards-Mason Conversion 4 1/2 in. Octagon Barrel Model*** - 4 1/2 in. octagon barrel without ejector. Rebated Pocket Navy Cylinder.

100%	98%	95%	90%	80%	70%	60%	50%	40%	30%	20%	10%
N/A	N/A	$9,500	$6,500	$5,000	$3,500	$2,600	$1,750	$1,350	$950	$850	$750

* ***1862 Richards-Mason Conversion Round (Percussion) Barrel Pocket Navy with Ejector*** - plug in rammer slot; ejector housing, loading cutout in right side of lug, barrel remachined from Pocket Navy percussion barrel, Pocket Navy rebated cylinder. Similar appearance to cartridge barrel variation.

100%	98%	95%	90%	80%	70%	60%	50%	40%	30%	20%	10%
N/A	N/A	$10,000	$8,000	$6,750	$5,000	$4,000	$3,000	$2,250	$1,500	$1,200	$850

1862 POLICE AND POCKET (1865 POCKET MODEL) NAVY CONVERSION - 4 1/2, 5 1/2, or 6 1/2 in. barrels with 1862 Police percussion profile and added ejector housing. Has rebated Pocket Navy cylinder or rarer half fluted 1862 Police cylinder. 6 1/2 in. barrel will bring a premium.

* ***1862 Police/Pocket Navy with Rebated Pocket Navy Cylinder*** - 1862 Police profile barrel with ejector housing and rebated 1862 Pocket Navy cylinder.

100%	98%	95%	90%	80%	70%	60%	50%	40%	30%	20%	10%
N/A	N/A	$9,500	$6,000	$5,250	$4,000	$3,100	$2,250	$1,550	$850	$750	$650

* ***1862 Police/Pocket Navy with Half Fluted Cylinder*** - 1862 Police profile barrel with ejector housing and 1/2 fluted Police cylinder.

100%	98%	95%	90%	80%	70%	60%	50%	40%	30%	20%	10%
N/A	N/A	$12,000	$8,500	$6,750	$5,000	$4,000	$3,000	$2,250	$1,500	$1,175	$850

Conversions with Round Cartridge Barrel

Subtract approx. 50% for factory nickel plating on models listed below.

ROUND CARTRIDGE BARREL WITH EJECTOR

See Baby Open Top listing under Revolvers:"Open Top" models.

3 1/2 IN. ROUND CARTRIDGE BARREL CONVERSION - .38 RF or CF cal., sometimes seen with serial numbers that are from 1849 Pocket Model (300,000 range). Barrel newly made for cartridges, not converted from a percussion barrel, only type conversion with 3 1/2 in. barrel. No ejector, no loading lever slot or loading cutout in lug area. Pocket Navy rebated cylinder.

N/A N/A $6,000 $4,000 $3,250 $2,500 $2,000 $1,500 $1,250 $1,000 $875 $750

REVOLVERS: "OPEN TOP" MODELS

If possible, it is advisable to procure a factory letter before buying/selling this Open Top Revolver. These watermarked letters are available by writing Colt Archive Properties LLC in Bloomfield, CT, with a charge of $200 or more per serial number (if they can research it). Send your name and address, Colt model name, serial number, and check or credit card information to: COLT ARCHIVE PROPERTIES LLC, 1295 Blue Hills Avenue, Bloomfield, CT 06002. Please allow 90-120 days for a response.

1871-72 OPEN TOP MODEL RIMFIRE - .44 RF cal., 6 shot, 7 1/2 in. barrel, without frame top strap, blue metal with case hardened hammer, serial range 1-approx. 7,000, barrel address "ADDRESS COL. SAM COLT, NEW YORK, U.S. AMERICA", forerunner of the single action Army, quite desirable. Mfg. 1871-72.

Add 20% for blue finish on models listed below.

* ***Baby Open Top Prototype*** - .38 RF and CF cal., 4 1/2, 5 1/2, or 6 1/2 in. barrels produced as a cartridge component without rammer slots and lug cutouts inherent to a percussion barrel, much shorter lug area than similar model converted from percussion barrel, no slots or loading cutouts on barrel, with ejector housing and Pocket Navy rebated cylinder, only unnumbered and single digit serial numbers have been observed, very scarce.

N/A N/A $10,000 $6,000 $4,750 $3,500 $3,000 $2,500 $2,000 $1,500 $1,350 $1,200

* ***1871-72 Open Top Model Rimfire Regular Production Model*** - 7 1/2 in. barrel, New York address, Navy grips.

N/A N/A $45,000 $27,000 $24,000 $20,000 $16,500 $12,000 $10,000 $7,500 $6,250 $5,000

* ***1871-72 Open Top Model Rimfire Regular Production*** - with Army grips.

N/A N/A $45,000 $27,000 $24,000 $20,000 $16,500 $12,000 $10,000 $7,500 $6,250 $5,000

* ***1871-72 Open Top Model Rimfire Late Production*** - with address "COLT PT. F. A. MANUFACTURING CO., HARTFORD, CT., U.S.A."

N/A N/A $45,000 $25,000 $21,500 $17,500 $13,750 $10,000 $8,250 $6,500 $5,500 $4,000

Add 40% for models with 8 in. barrel or COLTS/PATENT frame markings.

REVOLVERS: PERCUSSION, 2ND & 3RD GENERATION BLACK POWDER SERIES

To learn more about the 2nd & 3rd Generation Percussion Black Powder Series, it is recommended to purchase the *Blue Book of Modern Black Powder Arms* by John Allen. The latest edition contains more information on the Colt 2nd Generation Black Powder Series than anything else previously published. These definitive books are available from Blue Book Publications, Inc. To order, please call, fax, email, or visit bluebookofgunvalues.com.

DERRINGERS

FIRST MODEL DERRINGER - .41 RF cal., single shot, 2 1/2 in. barrel,

100%	98%	95%	90%	80%	70%	60%	50%	40%	30%	20%	10%

all steel construction, scroll engraving standard, blue, nickel, or silver plated barrel, downward pivoting barrel, no grips, serial numbered 1-6,500. Mfg. approx. 1870-1890.

100%	98%	95%	90%	80%	70%	60%	50%	40%	30%	20%	10%
$3,750	$2,850	$2,450	$2,200	$2,000	$1,600	$1,200	$1,075	$875	$750	$675	$650

SECOND MODEL DERRINGER - .41 RF or CF cal., single shot, 2 1/2 in. barrel, scroll engraving standard, blue, nickel, or silver plated barrel, downward pivoting barrel, checkered and varnished walnut grips, "No 2" marked on top of barrel, serial numbered 1-9,000. Mfg. approx. 1870-1890.

100%	98%	95%	90%	80%	70%	60%	50%	40%	30%	20%	10%
$1,775	$1,475	$1,275	$1,100	$950	$850	$750	$650	$585	$550	$500	$475

* ***Second Model Derringer .41 Centerfire cal.***

100%	98%	95%	90%	80%	70%	60%	50%	40%	30%	20%	10%
$3,850	$2,950	$2,550	$2,200	$2,000	$1,750	$1,500	$1,300	$1,175	$1,000	$975	$950

THIRD MODEL DERRINGER (THUER MODEL) - .41 RF or CF (rare) cal., single shot, side pivoting 2 1/2 in. barrel, varnished walnut grips, blue barrels, bronze frames, engraving optional, Colt barrel address, spur trigger, serial numbered approx. 1-45,000. Mfg. approx. 1875-1912.

100%	98%	95%	90%	80%	70%	60%	50%	40%	30%	20%	10%
$1,750	$1,500	$1,250	$1,100	$1,000	$800	$650	$575	$500	$450	$400	$350

Add 30%-50% for .41 centerfire cal. Early models are worth considerably more.

MSR	100%	98%	95%	90%	80%	70%	60%

FOURTH MODEL DERRINGER (FIRING) - .22 Short cal., single shot similar in appearance to the 3rd Model, 2 1/2 in. barrel, approx. 112,000 mfg. 1959-1963 with either D or N suffix. A few were put in books (sometimes as pairs), picture frames, penholders, bookends, etc. (these will command premiums).

	100%	98%	95%	90%	80%	70%	60%
Gun only	$100	$90	$75	$70	$55	$45	$35
Gun w/accessories	$375	$330	$280	$255	$205	$170	$130

* ***Fourth Model Derringer (non-firing)*** - this variation was normally used for decoration and is normally encountered in books, picture frames, penholders, bookends, etc. Values below assume all factory materials intact - if not, prices are reduced to $50-$75 for gun only.

MSR	100%	98%	95%	90%	80%	70%	60%
	$375	$330	$280	$255	$205	$170	$130

Non-firing guns usually do not have the barrel notch, thus preventing the hammer from striking the cartridge.

LORD DERRINGER - .22 Short cal. only, side pivoting Thuer action, gold plated with black chrome barrel and walnut grips. Mfg. 1970-76 by Colt, cased.

MSR	100%	98%	95%	90%	80%	70%	60%
	$175	$155	$130	$120	$95	$80	$60

LADY DERRINGER - .22 Short cal. only, side pivoting Thuer action, full gold plated finish with pearlite grips. Mfg. 1970-76 by Colt, cased.

MSR	100%	98%	95%	90%	80%	70%	60%
	$175	$155	$130	$120	$95	$80	$60

MSR	100%	98%	95%	90%	80%	70%	60%

LORD & LADY CASED SET - one each of the Lord & Lady Derringers or combinations, consecutive serial numbers, numbered 1,001-up, with DER suffix.

	$495	$435	$370	$335	$270	$225	$175

LADY CASED SET - cased pair of Lady Derringers. Approx. 12,000 pairs shipped first year.

	$495	$435	$370	$335	$270	$225	$175

LORD CASED SET - cased pair of Lord Derringers. Approx. 3,000 pairs shipped first year.

	$495	$435	$370	$335	$270	$225	$175

BOOKCASE DERRINGER PAIR - .22 Short cal., consecutively numbered Derringers with synthetic ivory grips and nickel finish, cased inside unique hardcover "Colt Derringers" labeled book with red velvet lining, limited mfg. in early 1960s.

	$350	$300	$265	$240	$195	$160	$125

100%	98%	95%	90%	80%	70%	60%	50%	40%	30%	20%	10%

REVOLVERS: POCKET MODELS

If possible, it is advisable to procure a factory letter before buying/selling this variation (open top only). These watermarked letters are available by writing Colt Archive Properties LLC in Bloomfield, CT, with a charge of $200 or more per serial number (if they can research it). Send your name and address, Colt model name, serial number, and check or credit card information to: COLT ARCHIVE PROPERTIES LLC, 1295 Blue Hills Avenue, Bloomfield, CT 06002. Please allow 90-120 days for a response.

CLOVERLEAF HOUSE PISTOL - .41 Short or long RF cal., cloverleaf configured 4 shot cylinder, spur trigger, 1 1/2 or 3 in. barrel, blue or nickel plated, approx. 7,500 mfg. in ser. no. range 1-8,300 during 1871-76.

$2,550	$2,300	$1,850	$1,600	$1,400	$1,200	$1,100	$925	$825	$725	$650	$600

Add 30% for blue finish.

Add 80% for 1 1/2 in. barrel.

This model is sometimes referred to as the Jim Fisk model, as he was murdered by Edward Stokes with a Cloverleaf.

* ***5-shot Cloverleaf*** - similar to 4 shot model, except has round 5 shot cylinder and 2 5/8 in. barrel only, approx. 2,500 mfg. in ser. no. range 6,160-9,950 during 1871-76.

$2,175	$1,900	$1,600	$1,325	$1,150	$975	$850	$750	$650	$600	$550	$500

OPEN TOP REVOLVER (OLD LINE) - .22 Short or long RF cal., 2 3/8 or 2 7/8 in. barrel, 5 variations with a variety of finishes, engraving, and grips, first model has cone shaped firing pin that drops through frame (up to approx. ser. no. 125), without topstrap on frame, with or without integral ejector, varnished walnut grips were standard. Approx. 114,200 mfg. 1871-1877.

$1,450	$1,250	$1,150	$950	$850	$750	$700	$600	$550	$450	$375	$325

Add 30% for blue finish.

100%	98%	95%	90%	80%	70%	60%	50%	40%	30%	20%	10%

This model is also known as the Open Top .22 seven shot revolver, the Old Line .22, and the Open Top .22 Pocket. After 1873, Colt referred to this model as the O.M., or Old Model.

* ***Open Top Revolver (Old Line, Early Model)*** – has ejector and high hammer spur.

$3,195	$2,750	$2,525	$2,100	$1,875	$1,650	$1,550	$1,325	$1,200	$995	$825	$725

REVOLVERS: NEW LINE SERIES & VARIATIONS

If possible, it is advisable to procure a factory letter before buying/selling New Line Revolvers. These watermarked letters are available by writing Colt Archive Properties LLC in Bloomfield, CT, with a charge of $100 or more per serial number (if they can research it). Send your name and address, Colt model name, serial number, and check or credit card information to: COLT ARCHIVE PROPERTIES LLC, 1295 Blue Hills Avenue, Bloomfield, CT 06002. Please allow 90-120 days for a response.

Add 30% for blue finish on models listed below.

1ST MODEL – .22, .30, .32, .38, or .41 RF and CF cal., mfg. 1873-1876, 7 (.22 cal. only) or 5 shot, short cylinder flutes, cylinder stop slots cut on exterior of cylinder, 1 3/4, 2 1/4, or 4 in. barrel, full nickel or blue/case hardened finish, spur trigger. Many thousands mfg. 1873-1884.

$1,250	$1,050	$925	$825	$750	$675	$600	$550	$450	$350	$300	$250

2ND MODEL – similar to 1st Model, except has longer cylinder flutes and cylinder stop slots are on the back of cylinder, may or may not have loading gate. Mfg. 1876-1884.

$1,125	$995	$875	$800	$725	$650	$575	$500	$400	$325	$275	$225

Caliber rarity on both models from highest mfg. to lowest is: .22, .32, .30, .41, and .38.

NEW HOUSE MODEL – .38 or .41 CF cal., 5 shot, 2 1/4 in. barrel, spur trigger, checkered hard rubber grips. Approx. 4,000 mfg. 1880-1886 starting at ser. no. 10,300.

$1,475	$1,150	$1,000	$875	$800	$675	$600	$500	$425	$375	$350	$325

NEW POLICE MODEL – .32, .38, or .41 CF cal., 5 shot, 2 1/4, 4 1/2, 5, or 6 in. barrel, spur trigger, with or without ejector, stamped or etched "NEW POLICE" on barrel. Approx. 4,000 mfg. 1882-1886.

N/A	N/A	$1,950	$1,750	$1,500	$1,100	$725	$650	$600	$550	$525	$475

REVOLVERS: SAA, 1873-1940 MFG. (SER. NOS. 1-357,000)

The author wishes to express thanks to Charles Layson for making the following information available and reformatting the Colt 1st Generation SAA section.

The Colt SAA was produced in 36 calibers with many special order features or combinations available directly from the Colt factory. These factory special order features can greatly enhance the value of the revolver. The Single Action Colt, or "Peacemaker," as it is often called, is undoubtedly the most collectible handgun in the world, and as such, can command very high prices.

Standard barrel markings include the "short" two-line address on 4 3/4 in. or shorter barrels, or "long" one-line address on all other barrel lengths.

It is prudent to secure several professional opinions as to originality when contemplating an expensive purchase, since many SAAs have been altered or "improved" over the decades. Before he died, Keith Cochran, author of the

Colt Peacemaker Encyclopedia, Vol. II, guesstimated that over 1/2 of all pre-WWII revolvers were no longer factory original. Because of this, it is advisable to procure a factory letter when buying or selling older or recently manufactured Colt Single Actions (hence guaranteeing original configuration and value credibility). These watermarked letters are based on the original factory handwritten shipping ledgers and are available by contacting Colt Archive Properties LLC in Bloomfield, CT. While not totally infallible, these letters are normally very accurate. The cost to document a 1st Generation SAA is $100. This research can be expedited by phone service for either $100 (2nd and 3rd Generation SAA), or $150 (First Generation SAA through ser. number 343,000). The expedite service provides a verbal report over the phone within 24 hours and a documentation letter follows in 2-3 weeks. Single actions shipped during the time period of 1933-1945 cannot be documented due to lost records. The serial number range typically affected is 354,000-357,859. Documentation letters for .44 rimfire SAA require a $200 research fee.

Additionally, historical research premium charges apply for factory engraving ($100-150, depending on if standard, expert, or master engraving with no gold inlays), and unique shipping destinations such as company executives, famous Western personalities or Colt family members ($50-$200). To contact the Archive Department for assistance call 1-800-962-2658, Ext. 1343. Once contacted, they can advise you what the exact historical research charge will be for the service you are requesting. The address to write to is COLT ARCHIVE PROPERTIES LLC, 1295 Blue Hills Avenue, Bloomfield, CT 06002. For a complete Archive Services price list, please refer to the Colt website at coltsmfg.com.

Values shown are for guns without special order features. Factory engraving, ivory grips, very rare special order barrel lengths, and special finishes would add considerably to the values shown below. One final word on single action Colts: Black Powder Colts (pre 165,000 serial range) should be scrutinized carefully for potential problems, including refinishing (including aging), replacement parts, restamped serial numbers, and added, non-factory special order features. This makes a major difference in pricing the SAA, since a genuine, original SAA's price tag will vary immensely from a non-original, made-up "parts gun."

SAA 1st Generation Civilian/Commercial (Mfg. 1873-1940)

One of the most well known handguns, and certainly the most collected revolver in the world, the Colt Single Action Army has been produced almost continuously since 1873, with only a minor interruption between 1940 and 1955. It is without a doubt, the most copied revolver with over fifteen clones currently in production.

Better known as the "Peacemaker", this firearm has appreciated in value at an accelerated rate over the last fifty years. Spurred by the popularity of television westerns in the 1950s and 60s, a standard pre-war, 1st generation single action in excellent condition has gone from $250 in 1960 to approximately $10,000 today, and in some cases much higher.

Not every Colt Peacemaker, however, is worth thousands of dollars. While many factors determine the actual value, the single most important has to be the overall condition of the gun now, compared to the day it left the factory. Because of the demand for Peacemakers in excellent condition many have been reworked and/or reblued, both by private gunsmiths and by the Colt factory itself. Unfortunately only the factory marked its refinished guns, while private individuals normally did not.

100%	98%	95%	90%	80%	70%	60%	50%	40%	30%	20%	10%

The Colt company has used at least three different methods of marking handguns that are to be reworked and/or refinished, and while there is some disagreement among collectors as to exactly what these marks indicate, e.g., refinishing, major parts replacement, or both, it is the opinion of this writer that the first to be used was a six pointed star stamped on the rear right bow of the trigger guard, from approximately 1890 to 1920. The second was a small ampersand placed in the same location, from approximately 1920 to 1945. The third was completely different, and is occasionally found in addition to the ampersand. It was a series of three numbers stamped on most major parts. Called "bin" numbers, they correspond to the numbers on small boxes or "bins" in the custom shop, into which are placed all the parts of a disassembled handgun destined to be reworked and /or refinished. On the Single Action Army, these numbers were placed on the rear flat of the loading gate, visible when it is open (not to be confused with the assembly number stamped on the rear curve of the loading gate), on the front of the cylinder, on the left side of the grip straps, and on the bottom of the barrel, near the frame.

Any reworking or refinishing has a negative effect on the value of a gun to the collector, and the amount varies depending upon the age of the gun, what was actually done and the quality of the workmanship. For example, an early black powder single action that has been expertly refinished by the factory or a qualified restorer is worth only 10 to 20% of what the same gun would be worth in original, mint condition. A late smokeless powder Single Action similarly redone, however, is still worth 30%-40% of one in near new condition. In many cases, the factory had an irritating habit of adding then current markings to an earlier gun, e.g., a caliber designation added to the barrel of a pre-1890 Single Action, or a rampant Colt to the frame.

Values quoted relate only to original, unaltered examples.

SINGLE ACTION ARMY (SAA) - STANDARD MFG. – over 30 cals., six shot single action revolver, three standard barrel lengths. The 4 3/4 in. barrel had a two line address, while the 5 1/2 in. and 7 1/2 in. had a one line address. Blue with color case hardened frame or full nickel finish were both available. Of the many (36) calibers offered, .45 Colt was by far the most popular, accounting for 42% of total production, followed by .44/.40 (18%), .38-40 (11%), .32-20 (8%) and .41 (4.5%). One piece, varnished walnut grips were standard for the first ten years, then gradually replaced with two piece hard rubber. When grips are "not listed" on Colt historical letters, you should assume that they were the standard for their time period, either wood or rubber; not the pearl or ivory that someone added at a later date.

* ***Pinch Frame SAA (ser. no. range 1-160)*** – very rare and seldom found with any original finish, .44 S&W American and .45 Colt calibers, 7 1/2 in. barrel, blue and case hardened finish, one piece varnished wood grips, distinctive rear sight situated one-half inch in front of hammer notch, which gives the impression that the top strap has been "pinched." Mfg. 1873.

N/A	N/A	N/A	N/A	N/A	N/A	$150,000	$130,000	$100,000	$75,000	$50,000	$25,000

Add 50% for original .44 S&W American caliber (it is estimated that only 20-25 were produced in this caliber, and most were later converted).

Be aware! There are many counterfeits in this variation.

100%	98%	95%	90%	80%	70%	60%	50%	40%	30%	20%	10%

* ***Early Black Powder SAA (Mfg. 1873-1876, ser. no. range 160-22,000)*** – .45 LC cal., 7 1/2 in. barrel standard, blue or nickel finish, rear sight changed to standard "V" notch, first few hundred have German silver front sight, distinctive italic script style lettering used in barrel address, two line, two date patent marking on frame, one piece varnished wood grips has more distinctive flair at bottom rear on early guns, serial numbers shared with early martial production, 5 1/2 in. barrels introduced in 1875 in guns for export. Mfg. 1873-76.

» ***Ser. Nos. 160-999 (Mfg. 1873)***

100%	98%	95%	90%	80%	70%	60%	50%	40%	30%	20%	10%
N/A	N/A	$80,000	$74,000	$55,000	$52,000	$44,000	$38,000	$30,000	$24,000	$18,000	$13,000

» ***Ser. Nos. 1,000 - 9,999 (Mfg. 1873-1874)***

100%	98%	95%	90%	80%	70%	60%	50%	40%	30%	20%	10%
N/A	N/A	$67,000	$60,000	$50,000	$44,000	$35,000	$31,000	$24,000	$19,000	$14,000	$11,000

» ***Ser. Nos. 10,000 - 22,000 (Mfg. 1874 - 1876)***

100%	98%	95%	90%	80%	70%	60%	50%	40%	30%	20%	10%
N/A	$55,000	$51,000	$45,000	$35,000	$30,000	$24,000	$21,000	$16,000	$13,000	$11,000	$8,000

Subtract 20%-40% for nickel finish, depending on original condition.

* ***Intermediate Black Powder SAA (Mfg. 1876-1890, ser. no. range 22,000-130,000)*** – the italic style of lettering in the barrel address is changed to a block letter style in the 22,000 range, the first two piece hard rubber grips with eagle motif appear in 1882 and became the standard by 1888, the .44-40 (.44WCF) caliber is introduced in 1878, the round head ejector is changed to oval shape in the 52,000 serial range, 4 3/4 in. to 5 1/2 in. barrels are becoming more popular, and Colt gradually abandons the practice of placing serial numbers on the cylinders and barrels of civilian revolvers. Nickel plated single actions seldom have numbered barrels and cylinders after the 60,000 serial range. Blue guns normally have numbers on both up to the 110,000 range, and occasionally thereafter up to 125,000. Two line, two date patent markings change to three line, three dates by 1878.

Subtract 25% for nickel finish.

Add 30% for original box.

Add 10% for 4 3/4 in. barrel.

One-piece wood grips are more desirable than two-piece rubber grips.

» ***Ser. Nos. 22,000 - 54,000 (Mfg. 1876 - 1880)***

100%	98%	95%	90%	80%	70%	60%	50%	40%	30%	20%	10%
N/A	$40,000	$35,000	$30,000	$23,000	$20,000	$15,000	$12,000	$9,000	$7,000	$5,500	$4,500

» ***Ser. Nos. 54,000 - 130,000 (Mfg. 1880 - 1890)***

100%	98%	95%	90%	80%	70%	60%	50%	40%	30%	20%	10%
N/A	$38,000	$33,000	$27,000	$21,000	$16,000	$13,000	$9,500	$8,000	$6,500	$5,500	$4,500

* ***Late Black Powder SAA (Mfg. 1890 - 1896, ser. no. range 130,000-165,000)*** – three line patent date format changes to two lines with three dates, circled rampant Colt trademark is added to left side of frame, grips transition from wood and rubber w/eagle to plain two piece rubber by 1892, and caliber designation is added to the barrel and eliminated from trigger guard.

100%	98%	95%	90%	80%	70%	60%	50%	40%	30%	20%	10%
N/A	$30,000	$25,000	$20,000	$15,000	$12,000	$9,500	$8000	$6,000	$5,600	$4,800	$4,000

100%	98%	95%	90%	80%	70%	60%	50%	40%	30%	20%	10%

Subtract 40% for nickel finish.

Add 25% for original box.

Add 10% for 4 3/4 in. barrel.

Add 20% for wood or rubber w/eagle grips.

* ***Early Smokeless Powder SAA (Mfg. 1896 - 1908)*** – several important physical characteristics were changed during this transition period. Most notably, in 1896 the vertical screw retaining the cylinder pin was eliminated in favor of the horizontal latch. This was identical to what had already been used on the double action models since 1877. This change coincided with the introduction of ammunition loaded with white or smokeless powder, which was more powerful and less corrosive than black powder. It was necessary for firearms manufacturers, therefore, to modify and strengthen their products to safely use the new ammunition. By adopting the more modern and tool-free horizontal latch for the Single Action at this time, Colt gave its customers an easy way to tell the new from the old, the stronger from the weaker, and a good excuse to purchase a new Peacemaker! As a result, sales boomed and more Single Actions were sold in the next ten years, than any other ten year period in Colt's history.

* ***The knurling pattern on the hammer spur began a two step revision in 1906. Up until this time, the knurling was enclosed in a border with a line underneath. Beginning in 1906, for approximately two years, the border remained, but the line underneath was eliminated. By late 1908, the border was also eliminated, and thereafter, the knurling ran to the very edges of the hammer spur. Although Colt advertised their improved smokeless powder Single Actions as early as 1897, they did not add the "VP" proof mark (verified proof, Colt's guarantee for smokeless powder use) to the trigger guard until 1904. While the highest production and sales figures were reached during this period, quality did not suffer. Many collectors feel that the fitting, polishing and finishing work performed during this period was superior to any other.***

» ***Ser. Nos. 165,000 - 182,000 (Mfg. 1896 - 1899)*** – the first three years of this period, 1896 to 1899, have recently become known as the "blackpowder transition" period, to distinguish Single Actions made with the modern, stronger frame and yet still considered "antique" by federal law that uses January 1st, 1899 as the beginning of the modern gun era.

N/A	$25,000	$21,000	$13,000	$11,000	$8,000	$6,500	$5,300	$4,000	$3,100	$2,800	$2,400

» ***Ser. Nos. 182,000 - 300,000 (Mfg. 1899 - 1908)***

N/A	$20,000	$17,000	$11,000	$7,500	$6,200	$4,800	$4,400	$4,000	$3,200	$2,500	$2,000

Add 25% for original box.

Subtract 10% for nickel finish.

* ***Intermediate Smokeless Powder SAA (Mfg. 1908 - 1920, ser. no. range 300,000-339,000)*** – physical changes continued to occur during this

100%	98%	95%	90%	80%	70%	60%	50%	40%	30%	20%	10%

period. Rampant Colt medallions were inserted into pearl, ivory, and checkered walnut grips in 1909, the .44 Special caliber was introduced circa 1912, the blueing process was gradually changed, and the circled rampant Colt on the frame began to lose its circle as the die stamps wore. The company, however, did not quickly give up the use of black powder rifling (wide grooves and narrow lands) completely until 1914, although an experimentation and transition period with narrower grooves and wider lands had begun about 1910. Similarly, the small and low black powder front sight did not change to the larger and higher smokeless profile until 1914. WWI came and went, and SAA sales began to decline. The year 1920 is very significant to Single Action collectors since this was the year that the serial number relocation was completed. Those numbers on the trigger guard and backstrap were moved under the grips beginning in the late 338,000 serial range (1919), leaving only the number on the frame visible from exterior. This brought to a close a practice which had begun in the 1840s with the percussion revolvers. Many collectors regard this as the end of the "cowboy" period.

» *Ser. Nos. 300,000 - 328,000 (Mfg. 1908 - 1914)*

100%	98%	95%	90%	80%	70%	60%	50%	40%	30%	20%	10%
N/A	$18,000	$13,000	$9,000	$7,500	$5,700	$5,000	$3,800	$3,200	$2,800	$2,400	$2,100

Add 20% for original box.

Add 10% for smooth, two-piece walnut grips.

Add 25% for checkered, varnished walnut grips with deep set medallions.

Subtract 25% for nickel finish.

» *Ser. Nos. 328,000 - 339,000 (Mfg. 1914 - 1920)*

100%	98%	95%	90%	80%	70%	60%	50%	40%	30%	20%	10%
N/A	$15,000	$12,000	$9,000	$6,500	$5,000	$4,300	$3,600	$3,100	$2,700	$2,300	$2,000

Add 20% for original box.

Add 15% for smooth, two-piece walnut grips.

Add 25% for checkered, varnished walnut grips with deep set medallions.

Subtract 30% for nickel finish.

* ***Late Smokeless Powder SAA** (ser. no. range 339,000-357,000)* – single action sales continued to diminish after 1920, as sales of semi-automatics increased. Only 19,000 SAAs were sold in the twenty year period, with only 100 being produced in 1936. The complete serial number is visible only on the frame, but many cylinders are stamped on the rear with the last two or three digits. In 1928, the caliber marking on the left side of the barrel was changed to read "Colt Single Action Army," followed by the caliber. In 1930, the "V" notch rear sight was replaced with a square groove to match the wider front sight, and in 1935, the finish on the hammer was changed from color case hardened to blue with polished sides. Colt special order grip medallions also made a three step, transitional change by 1923. Since 1909, deep set bronze medallions on pearl, ivory or checkered walnut grips had been recessed into the grips and both horses faced forward. They were first changed to a less expensive, flush mount design, still facing forward and then

100%	98%	95%	90%	80%	70%	60%	50%	40%	30%	20%	10%

within the same year to a flush mount, with one facing forward and one backward, a cost cutting measure which required only one die. The finish on the checkered wood grips was also changed from a varnish to an oil finish in 1924.

It is important to remember that while special order grips such as pearl, ivory, or checkered wood may add as much as 25% to an SAA's value, they must be factory original to that particular gun, and be recorded as such in the factory records.

» *Ser. Nos. 339,000 - 350,000 (Mfg. 1920 - 1928)*

100%	98%	95%	90%	80%	70%	60%	50%	40%	30%	20%	10%
$13,000	$11,000	$9,000	$7,000	$5,000	$4,000	$3,500	$3,000	$2,800	$2,600	$2,400	$2,000

Add 20% for original box in good condition.

Add 25% for original checkered wood, pearl, or ivory grips.

Add 10% for original stag horn grips (very rare!).

» *Ser. Nos. 350,000 - 355,000 (Mfg. 1928 - 1935)*

100%	98%	95%	90%	80%	70%	60%	50%	40%	30%	20%	10%
$12,000	$10,000	$8,000	$6,000	$4,500	$4,000	$3,200	$2,800	$2,600	$2,500	$2,200	$2,000

Add 20% for original box in good condition.

Add 25% for original checkered wood, pearl, or ivory grips.

» *Ser. Nos. 355,000 - 357,000 (Mfg. 1935 - 1940)*

100%	98%	95%	90%	80%	70%	60%	50%	40%	30%	20%	10%
$11,000	$8,500	$6,500	$5,500	$4,000	$3,200	$2,700	$2,400	$2,200	$2,000	$1,900	$1,800

Add 20% for original box in good condition.

Add 25% for original checkered wood, pearl, or ivory grips.

SAA 1st Generation Commercial, Non-Standard Mfg.

SINGLE ACTION ARMY (SAA) - NON-STANDARD MFG. - between 1873-1940, Colt mfg. approx. 327,000 Commercial SAA revolvers. There were several distinct types or configurations of SAAs that varied from the standard and therefore, have special significance to the collector.

* ***.44 Rimfire SAA*** - .44 Henry rimfire cal., 7 1/2 in. barrel, blue and nickel finishes, most were shipped to the southwest and saw hard use, rare with any original finish remaining, many barrels shortened during their period of use, serial numbered in their own range, 1 - 1,863, mfg. from 1875 to 1880.

100%	98%	95%	90%	80%	70%	60%	50%	40%	30%	20%	10%
N/A	N/A	N/A	N/A	$75,000	$60,000	$47,000	$35,000	$27,000	$22,000	$18,000	$15,000

Beware! Many have been found with cut and/or stretched barrels.

A factory letter on this model is available for $200.

* ***.22 Rimfire SAA*** - blue or nickel finish, 5 1/2 in. and 7 1/2 in. barrels, manufactured in two distinct runs, slightly less than 100 converted from unsold .44 RF still in inventory in the late 1880s, and approximately 20 mfg. new in 1891.

100%	98%	95%	90%	80%	70%	60%	50%	40%	30%	20%	10%
N/A	$40,000	$35,000	$32,000	$28,000	$25,000	$22,000	$20,000	$18,000	$15,000	$12,000	$9,000

Add 10% for rare 5 1/2 in. barrel.

Subtract 50% for factory refinished models.

Subtract 10% for those converted from .44 rimfire.

100%	98%	95%	90%	80%	70%	60%	50%	40%	30%	20%	10%

* ***Buntline Special Model SAA*** – .45 LC cal., long barrel model named after Ned Buntline, author of dime novels in the late 19th century. Only 28 believed to be mfg. with folding adjustable rear sight and extended hammer screw for attachment of nickel plated metal skeleton shoulder stock, all in the 28,800 serial range, most with 10, 12, or 16 in. barrel. Very rare.

Values for most original Colt Buntlines can vary a lot depending on condition and barrel length (12 or 16 in. is the most desirable). Values for most original condition Buntlines with the shoulder stock are in the $75,000-$275,000 range.

Individual appraisals are highly recommended for this model.

* ***Etched Panel .44-40 SAA*** – the most desirable of all Commercial black powder era SAAs, this variant has the words "Colt Frontier Six Shooter" acid etched in a panel on the left side of the barrel. This marking was the result of a request in January 1878 by J. P. Moore's and Sons, one of Colt's largest distributors in New York. to help them market the new .44-40 Winchester chambered SAA. Colt agreed, and shipped the first "etched panels" to Moore's and Sons in February 1878. The lowest serial numbered known etched panel .44-40 is in the 41,000 serial range (1878) and the highest in the 129,000 range circa 1890.

100%	98%	95%	90%	80%	70%	60%	50%	40%	30%	20%	10%
N/A	$50,000	$40,000	$30,000	$20,000	$16,000	$14,000	$12,000	$9,000	$8,000	$7,000	$6,000

Subtract 50% for nickel finish.

Add 20% for one-piece wood grips.

Add 20% for 4 3/4 in. barrel.

Add 30% for 5 1/2 in. barrel.

* ***Ejectorless (Sheriff's Model) Model SAA*** – this term denotes Single Actions without ejectors and ejector housings. Most were produced in .45 LC and .44-40 WCF cal., with 3 1/2 in. or 4 in. barrels, but 2 1/2 in., 3 in., 4 3/4 in., and 7 1/2 in. were made. According to collector and researcher Wynn Paul, the first ejectorless Sheriff's or Storekeeper's models were shipped from the factory on February 22, 1882 to Hibbard, Spencer, Bartlett & Co., Chicago, IL, in two shipments of ten each, one group with 3 1/2 in. barrels, one group with 4 in. barrels. At least 1,500 were produced, most in the latter part of the 19th century.

Factory nomenclature never referred to the Ejectorless Model SAA's as Sheriff's or Storekeepers Models.

» ***Ejectorless (Sheriff's Model) Smokeless Powder Frame SAA***

100%	98%	95%	90%	80%	70%	60%	50%	40%	30%	20%	10%
N/A	$67,000	$52,000	$44,000	$30,000	$27,000	$21,000	$18,000	$16,000	$13,000	$11,000	$8,000

Add 20% for .44-40 cal. w/etched panel.

Add 30% for original special order grips.

Add 50% for 2 1/2 in. or 7 1/2 in. barrel.

Subtract 15% for nickel finish.

Factory nomenclature never referred to the Ejectorless Model SAA's as Sheriff's or Storekeepers Models.

100%	98%	95%	90%	80%	70%	60%	50%	40%	30%	20%	10%

» ***Ejectorless (Sheriff's Model) Black Powder Frame SAA*** – pre-1896 mfg. with old style black powder frame.

N/A	$85,000	$75,000	$60,000	$47,000	$33,000	$27,000	$22,000	$19,000	$15,000	$11,500	$9,000

Add 20% for .44-40 cal. w/etched panel.

Add 30% for original special order grips.

Add 50% for 2 1/2 in. or 7 1/2 in. barrel.

Subtract 15% for nickel finish.

Beware of fakes! The *Blue Book of Gun Values* strongly recommends getting a historical letter from Colt, then checking the authenticity of the serial numbers. Many guns have had numbers altered to match records.

* ***Flat-top Target Model SAA*** – many calibers from .22 RF to .476 Eley were available, target version of the SAA with flat-top frame and adj. sights, approximately 925 were manufactured from 1888-1896, both in 5 1/2 and 7 1/2 in. barrel and full blue finish, two-piece smooth walnut, two-piece rubber, or two-piece checkered walnut grips are known.

N/A	$20,000	$18,000	$15,000	$13,000	$11,000	$9,000	$8,000	$7,000	$6,000	$5,000	$4,500

Add 10% for 5 1/2 in. barrel.

Beware! Many target models were returned to the factory for refinishing.

* ***Long Flute Series SAA*** – in 1913, Colt decided to make use of approximately 1500 cylinders left over from the model 1878 double action production. Since it was necessary to add a bolt lock notch and a lead-in groove on these long flute cylinders, a block of serial numbers, 330,000 to 331,480, was set aside to be used for this special production. Manufactured in 1913 and 1914, specimens are known in .32 WCF, .38 WCF, .41 LC, .44 S&W Spl., .44 WCF, and .45 LC cals.

According to researchers Hull and Rowcliffe, whose survey includes 114 long flute Single Actions, no .44 WCF have been noted. The actual total mfg. may possibly exceed 1,500, and while quite rare, these long flute variations sell for only 5% to 10% more than other Single Actions of this period.

* ***Pre-war/Post-war Mfg. SAAs*** – made from pre WWII parts remaining in inventory after production of the Single Action Army had ended in 1940, many of these post-war guns were given as gifts to dignitaries and retiring Colt employees, known calibers include .30 Carbine, .357 Mag., .38 Spl., .44 Spl., .44-40 WCF and .45 Colt. Most are found with 5 1/2 in. barrels and blue and case hardened finish; nickel is rare. Shipping cartons vary from pre-war dark maroon and brown, hinged top, circa 1950, to black 2nd generation style. Approximately 338 were assembled and shipped between 1947-1961.

Add 10% for nickel finish.

Add 20% plus for important or well known recipient.

Most of these guns are found in 95% or better condition, and are valued like the last of the pre-war 1st generation Single Actions.

* ***Factory Engraved SAAs*** - slightly less than 1% (approximately 3,400) Single Actions are thought to have been engraved at the factory or elsewhere by authority from Colt between 1873 and 1940. Between 1873-circa 1929 Colt offered three basic grades of engraving with alphabetical designations - A (least coverage), B, and C (most coverage). Circa 1929-1936 Colt changed these alphabetical engraving designations to numerical, and became No. 1 (least coverage), 2, and 3 (most coverage). Many of these early SAA's also carried special inscriptions, initials, grips, etc., and because of this, the value ranges are very wide. Condition also plays a huge role here. Factory engraved black powder SAAs typically sell in the $10,000 to $100,000 range, while factory engraved smokeless powder SAAs usually peak in the $50,000 range. Very special or one of a kind pieces, such as the six known "panel" engraved guns, or one carried by a famous outlaw or lawman may bring upward of $300,000, depending on condition and particulars. Most factory work is documented in the records.
* ***Special Order SAAs*** - Included in the approximate 3,400 factory engraved SAAs, there are a small number of one of a kind, custom special ordered guns. These are, of course, well documented in the Colt held factory archives by serial number and can be accessed through the office of Beverly Haynes, Colt Firearms Historian. While most of these special order guns were factory engraved, some were not, and their orders include request such as initials, monograms, inscriptions, trigger pulls, alternate sights, stocks and special targeting requirements. On handguns made between 1889 and 1914, it is possible to access some of these special order details. The original Colt Special Order and Repair Ledgers and now the property of the Colt Collectors Association Historian, Don Jones, and he is available to all members of the CCA. To quote Mrs. Haynes and Mr. Jones, "As a supplement to the Colt Factory letter, the Colt Special Order Ledger entries dovetail nicely in corroborating the original configuration detailed in the Factory letter. In effect the special order entry is the build order for the Colt firearm, tracing the order from receipt through production. As such they will document configuration details and changes that are sometimes left silent in the Colt shipping based production record. In addition, the Colt Repair Ledgers that are available are very limited in scope, but they do stand alone in their serial number based, period documentation or repairs, factory refinishing, and ownership of certain Colt handguns and rifles." Obviously the information contained in these Colt Special Order and Repair ledgers is very important to Colt collectors, as it may seriously affect the value of certain guns.
* ***Non-Factory Engraved SAAs*** - value depends on when and where the engraving was done. Early "New York" or "dealer" engraved Single Actions done outside the factory were usually shipped from Colt in the "soft" and w/o finish. The majority of these were done in the 1870s or 1880s, and condition being equal, are generally priced at 25% to 50% of factory original specimens. Later guns, well done by a known

100%	98%	95%	90%	80%	70%	60%	50%	40%	30%	20%	10%

contemporary artist, are usually priced by adding the value of the gun to the cost of the engraving. Poor execution may actually lower the value of a plain, but original gun, much as refinishing would. The notation of "soft" in the factory records is desirable, since the large wholesalers in the northeast used many of the same engravers as Colt. There are and have been some 20th century engravers who stand out, however, and their work commands higher prices, e.g. Lynton McKenzie, Ben Lane, Cole Agee and Weldon Bledsoe - the two latter being famous for their "cattle brand" style, and Ben Lane for his meticulous duplication of the patterns of Cuno Helfricht, the most famous of all Colt factory engravers.

* ***Bisley Model SAA*** – numbered in the same serial range as the standard Single Action Army, the Bisley model featured a more curved forward and longer grip strap and a smaller, raked back hammer. It was designed with the target shooter in mind and named after Bisley, England, the location of the international shooting matches during the late 19th and early 20th century. It was offered in the same barrel lengths, the same finishes and most all of the more popular Single Action calibers, .32 WCF (.32-20) being the most popular. It was advertised from 1896 (approx. ser. no. 165,900) to 1912 (approx. ser. no. 323,000). The highest number known (331,916) was assembled in 1915, but not shipped until November, 1919. Slightly over 45,000 were produced.

N/A	$10,000	$8,500	$7,500	$6,200	$5,000	$4,200	$3,500	$2,800	$2,200	$1,800	$1,500

Add 30% for nickel finish.

Add 25-40% for original box.

Add 15% for pre-1899 serial number.

Only approx. one dozen black powder Bisley boxes known.

* ***Flat-top Target Bisley SAA*** - a target version similar to the flat-top target Single Action with adj. sights. Available in all standard calibers with a 7 1/2 in. barrel, blue finish and either walnut or rubber grips. Offered from 1894 to 1912, the most popular caliber was .455 Eley followed closely by .32 WCF. Only 976 were manufactured.

N/A	$18,000	$16,000	$13,500	$11,500	$10,000	$8,000	$7,200	$6,700	$6,000	$5,000	$4,000

Add 30% for any barrel length other than 7 1/2 in.

* ***Battle of Britain SAA*** - late 1st generation Single Action Armys purchased by the British government in anticipation of invasion from Germany in 1940. A total of 163, mostly .38 and .45 cal. in both blue and nickel finish were sent to England by Colt. These guns were fully inspected and proofed by the British, in many cases showing the exact specifications of the cartridge on the bottom of the barrel. Most, if not all, were unissued, and remain today in 90% plus condition.

$12,000	$10,000	$8,500	$7,500	$6,500	$5,500	$4,700	$4,200	$3,500	$3,000	$2,500	$2,000

Add 10% for blue and color case hardened finish.

Add 20% for original shipping carton.

* ***London Agency SAA*** – as with percussion revolvers and derringers, Colt shipped Single Action Army revolvers to England for sale through its London Agency. John Kopec, co-author of *A Study of the Colt Single Action Army Revolver*, estimates that 18% of production during the first 2 1/2 years went to England. These early guns were marked with the standard Hartford address, and most were chambered in either .450 Eley or Boxer caliber, with a 7 1/2 or 5 1/2 in. barrel. A small number were shipped with 4 3/4 in. barrels in May of 1877. According to Kenneth Moore, author of *Single Action Army Revolvers and the London Agency*, and co-author of *A Study of the Colt SAA Revolver*, Baron Von Oppen, head of Colt's London Agency, requested in Oct. 1875 that Colt change the barrel address to "14 PALL MALL, LONDON" only, in an effort to increase his sales and to prevent English customers from ordering direct from Hartford. Colt complied and sent 150 revolvers with the new barrel address in early 1876. This created a problem with English customs officials, since the guns were not made in England, they could not be marked "LONDON" only, and would not pass inspection. The London address could not be used. It is believed by Moore that these 150 Colt SAAs were the only ones marked with the London barrel address. By Jan. 1877, a compromise was reached and English customs authorized the use of the dual Hartford/London address to read "COLT'S PT. F.A. MFG. CO. HARTFORD, CT USA DEPOT 14 PALL MALL LONDON". The London proofed SAAs were usually stamped at the bottom of the barrel, and in each flute of the cylinder, and had a high quality nickel or blue finish with case hardened frame, although some all-blue examples are known. Through 1890, several thousand SAAs were sold through the London Agency.

Values for the more common English proofed SAAs with the combined Hartford/ London address are approx. 40% less than those SAAs sold during the same period in the United States. A gun with the Hartford only address would be more desirable, and one of the 150 with the London only address command substantially more than a model with the dual Hartford/London address, and perhaps more than an American counterpart. An original model with 4 3/4 in. barrel would also bring a premium. Many were reblued by the London Agency.

SAA U.S. Military, Mfg. 1873-1903

Since many of the military models listed below are frequently encountered with no original finish remaining, prices for original no condition specimens will be approx. three quarters of the 10% prices listed below. With original specimens getting harder and harder to find, many guns are now observed with major parts replacements, including barrels, cylinders, grips, etc.

Beware of restorations that are purported to be original! One expert believes that as many as 90% of Colt SAA Cavalry & Artillery models currently offered for sale, especially at gun shows, have been intentionally faked, or "enhanced" in some way. Likewise, many "questionable" guns have been consigned to the auction houses for disposal. Many have been altered in the last 40 years in all inspector serial ranges. Some have now been skillfully "aged" to look more original. When making a substantial purchase, a letter of authentication from a reliable source is suggested in addition to a factory historical letter. Also ask for a guarantee of originality in writing from the seller. No factory information is available on U.S. Cavalry revolvers below ser. no. 30,600.

Blue Book Publications, Inc. would be happy to refer you to a credible source for authenticating the military revolvers listed below (very important). While a factory letter (if possible) verifies the configuration when shipped, it does not verify originality and/or authenticity. All inquiries are treated confidentially.

Notice: Values listed on the following models in this category are for original unaltered examples only.

SINGLE ACTION ARMY (CAVALRY) - U.S. MILITARY CONTRACT

– the Colt SAA was the primary sidearm of the U.S. military forces between 1873 and 1892. While frequently called the "cavalry" model, this revolver was carried by commissioned officers in the regular army and the state militias, and issued to each man in the mounted units. A total of 37,063 were purchased by the U.S. government at an average cost of $12.50 each. Contract specifications called for 7 1/2 in. barrel, .45 Colt caliber, government blue and color case hardened finish (a softer blue color compared to the darker and more brilliant civilian finish, which required a higher polish and was therefore more expensive), and one piece, oil finished walnut grips. Each gun was stamped with the initial(s) of a U.S. ordnance principal sub-inspector and finally, with the letters "U.S." on the frame after being approved for delivery to the National Armory at Springfield, MA.

Examples displaying their original inspector's grip cartouches will command a premium. Beware of fakes! All inspector's cartouche stamps are being replicated today.

* ***Early U.S. Model SAA (Mfg. 1873 - 1875)*** – principal sub-inspectors of this early period used only the first letter of their last name to mark the revolvers which they inspected. Chronologically, they were O.W. Ainsworth (A), S.B. Lewis (L), W.W. Johnson (J), and A.P. Casey (C).

While the lower serial numbers are generally the most desirable, the small number of guns inspected by Lewis, Johnson and Casey make them harder to find and perhaps more valuable than a higher numbered Ainsworth. These guns are in the same number sequence as guns made for the civilian market up to #20,000. There are no known "U.S." marked Single Actions between serial numbers 20,000 and 30,000. According to John Kopec, arguably the most knowledgeable and authoritative U.S. Single Action researcher and co-author of the widely respected work,

A Study of the Single Action Army Revolver, the earliest known complete Ainsworth inspected Single Action is serial number "179".

Those examples displaying their original inspector's grip cartouches will command a premium. Beware of fakes! All inspector's cartouche stamps are being replicated today.

100%	98%	95%	90%	80%	70%	60%	50%	40%	30%	20%	10%

» *Ainsworth Serial Range 179 - 999 (1873)*

100%	98%	95%	90%	80%	70%	60%	50%	40%	30%	20%	10%
N/A	N/A	$112,000	$90,000	$85,000	$65,000	$60,000	$45,000	$35,000	$25,000	$18,000	$15,000

» *Ainsworth Serial Range 1,000 - 9,999 (1873-1874)*

100%	98%	95%	90%	80%	70%	60%	50%	40%	30%	20%	10%
N/A	N/A	$100,000	$90,000	$72,000	$60,000	$48,000	$36,000	$28,000	$24,500	$19,500	$14,500

Add 25% - 50% for Ainsworth inspected guns between ser. nos. 4,516 and 5,521 possibly issued to George Custer's 7th Cavalry. Probable (not proven) historical connotation will usually trump condition.

» *Ainsworth Serial Range 10,000 - 14,500 (1874)*

100%	98%	95%	90%	80%	70%	60%	50%	40%	30%	20%	10%
N/A	N/A	$90,000	$70,000	$52,000	$35,000	$25,000	$20,000	$18,000	$15,000	$9,000	$8,000

Many nickel finished SAA's are found in this range.

» *Lewis Serial Range 15,000-16,500 (1875)*

100%	98%	95%	90%	80%	70%	60%	50%	40%	30%	20%	10%
N/A	N/A	$85,000	$80,000	$56,000	$45,000	$31,000	$20,000	$15,500	$13,500	$12,000	$11,000

» *Johnson Serial Range 16,800-18,450 (1875)*

100%	98%	95%	90%	80%	70%	60%	50%	40%	30%	20%	10%
N/A	N/A	$90,000	$80,000	$56,000	$45,000	$30,000	$20,000	$15,000	$13,000	$11,000	$10,000

» *Casey Serial Range 16,400 - 19,530 (1875)*

100%	98%	95%	90%	80%	70%	60%	50%	40%	30%	20%	10%
N/A	N/A	$90,000	$75,000	$50,000	$35,000	$25,000	$18,000	$14,000	$12,000	$10,500	$9,500

More than a few Casey range guns are dual inspected, most with a "C" and a "J", but while interesting, this does not necessarily add a premium.

* ***Mid-Range U.S. Model SAA (1876 - 1887)*** – when military production resumed in the 30,000 serial range, the principal sub-inspectors during this eleven year period were John T. Cleveland (J.T.C.), Henry Nettleton (H.N.), and David F. Clark (D.F.C.). Starting in 1876, the marking procedure changed from one last name initial to two or all three of the sub-inspector's initials. Also in 1876, the third patent date was added to the left side of the frame in a third line.

» ***Cleveland Serial Range 30,690 to 35,570 (1876 - 1877)*** – these are the very first of the U.S. Cavalry models to be recorded in the Colt records and the first ones that can be lettered by the factory. Slightly more than 2,000 were delivered under government contract, and were inspected by John T. Cleveland. For some reason, a small group of these guns show the initials of Lewis Draper "L.D." stamped on the frames, instead of the normal "J.T.C." There is also an unusually high ratio of Civilian SAAs in this serial range with the condemned "C" mark on the frame, and there is existing correspondence from Colt and to the U.S. Ordnance Dept. complaining that Inspector Lt. David A. Lyle was being unduly hard to please. Perhaps Lewis Draper was a temporary replacement during this period. Regardless, this small group of "L.D." marked Single Action Cavalrys are an interesting variation and may command a slight premium.

100%	98%	95%	90%	80%	70%	60%	50%	40%	30%	20%	10%
N/A	N/A	$55,000	$50,000	$40,000	$25,000	$20,000	$16,000	$13,000	$11,000	$9,500	$8,500

Add 10% for "L.D." marked frames.

100% 98% 95% 90% 80% 70% 60% 50% 40% 30% 20% 10%

» ***Early Henry Nettleton Serial Range 36,800 - 39,880 Civilian U.S. Models (1877)*** – according to John Kopec's "Cavalry and Artillery Revolvers" there are a small group of known cavalry revolvers which were part of a large surplus of civilian SAAs which were inspected and accepted by the government. While some are Henry Nettleton inspected, most are marked with the "W" of E.C. Wheeler. It is known that Wheeler substituted for Nettleton during an illness. Regardless, this is a very small and desirable group of Cavalry SAAs and a premium is probably justified.

N/A N/A $65,000 $60,000 $44,000 $34,000 $28,000 $24,000 $20,000 $16,000 $14,000 $12,500

» ***Early David F. Clark Serial Range 41,000-42,300 (1878) & Standard Henry Nettleton Serial Range 47,000-50,600 U.S. Models (1878)***

N/A N/A $45,000 $35,000 $25,000 $20,000 $18,000 $15,000 $13,500 $12,000 $10,000 $8,500

» ***Later David F. Clark Serial Range 53,000-121,000 (Mfg. 1880 - 1887)***

N/A N/A $40,000 $30,000 $25,000 $18,000 $16,000 $15,000 $13,000 $10,000 $9,000 $8,000

* ***Rinaldo A. Carr, Serial Range 131,187-140,361 (Mfg. 1890 - 1891)*** – this was the last of U.S. Single Action production. Four thousand were inspected by Rinaldo A. Carr during this sixteen month period. As hostilities in the west subsided, demand decreased and many revolvers of this group went to state militias or were left in storage. Consequently, a higher percentage of R.A.C. inspected SAAs are found in excellent condition than those of other inspectors, and this is reflected in their value. The last of this group was shipped from the factory on April 29, 1891.

N/A $34,000 $29,000 $24,000 $20,000 $17,000 $15,000 $13,000 $11,000 $9,000 $7,200 $5,600

* ***Artillery Model SAAs*** – refers to U.S. government model SAA revolvers with 5 1/2 in. barrels, which were reworked and refinished between 1896 and 1903. In response to growing dissatisfaction with the stopping power of the newly adopted M1892 .38 LC cal. double action revolvers, the U.S. Ordnance Dept. directed Springfield Armory to recall all remaining quantities of .45 Colt Cavalry revolvers during 1893. The Colt Company refurbished approximately 1,200 of these during 1896, while the other 16,300 were reconditioned at Springfield Armory. During 1898, all of these Springfield refurbished revolver serial numbers became mixed and barrels were shortened. During this first re-work at Colt's in 1896, care was taken to match serial numbered parts, and in some instances, parts were even renumbered to match. After seeing hard use in the Spanish American War and the Philippine Insurrection, approximately 5,294 of these same guns were returned to Colt between 1900 and 1903 for refurbishing, and total refinishing. Our source estimates that 85% of these 1896 Colt refurbished revolvers were initially issued to the Rough Riders.

* ***Standard Mixed Numbers Variation***

N/A $10,000 $8,500 $8,000 $7,500 $7,000 $5,500 $4,500 $4,200 $4,000 $3,500 $3,000

Add 100% documented "Rough Rider" association.

Add 10% for Custer period frames (under #6500).

100%	98%	95%	90%	80%	70%	60%	50%	40%	30%	20%	10%

Only rarely will one be found with all the matching serial numbers (except the barrel), indicating that it had been refurbished at Colt's during 1896. (Factory letter advised). These guns will bring a premium price, and must be authenticated, as they may have been recently altered, or are simply shortened Cavalry revolvers.

A few artillery models are believed to have been redone at various government arsenals, and this could explain the existence of several known artillery revolvers with blue frames. In fact, new information recently discovered by noted Single Action specialist Dave Lanara seems to confirm that some U.S. Artillery and Cavalry models were indeed refinished at the Manila Arsenal in the Philippines with blue frames, this was due to the lack of color case hardening capabilities at that location. Regardless, the artillery model is very popular with collectors and has become one of the most studied and interesting variants of the Colt Single Action revolver.

* ***Matching Numbers in Late Inspector Ranges (DFC & RAC)***

N/A	$17,000	$15,000	$12,000	$10,500	$8,000	$7,000	$6,000	$5,200	$4,600	$4,000	$3,400

Must be authenticated.

* ***Matching Numbers in Early Inspector Ranges (A, C, J, LD, JTC, HN)***

N/A	$23,000	$21,500	$18,000	$15,000	$13,500	$11,000	$9,500	$8,000	$6,500	$5,200	$4,000

Add 20% for SAA's in the Custer ser. no. range (ser. no. 4516 - 6500).

Must be authenticated.

* ***Blued Frame Variation With Mixed Number*** – must be authenticated.

N/A	$10,000	$8,500	$7,200	$6,000	$4,600	$4,100	$3,600	$3,200	$2,800	$2,500	$2,200

* ***New York State Militia SAA*** – in 1895 before work began on the artillery models, Colt refurbished 800 SAA revolvers supplied by Springfield Armory, especially for the New York State Militia. These guns retained their 7 1/2 inch barrels and all original parts wherever possible. Replacement parts were serial numbered to match, and strangely, barrels and cylinders were given the missing first and second digits of the whole serial number where they had never before been applied. In addition to receiving a high polish blue and case hardened civilian finish, their hammers were "fire-blued" instead of being color case hardened. Since most other Cavalry models in the government's possession were cut to 5 1/2 inches shortly thereafter, these 800 are quite possibly the only remaining 7 1/2 inch SAAs that could actually have seen service on the American frontier against hostiles. Most other 7 1/2 inch Cavalry revolvers that are seen today were likely issued to state militias rather than the U.S. Army. Some are found with unit markings on their buttstraps and/or grips or with lanyard swivels. These 800 Colt revolvers therefore may have played a very significant role in the history of the Indian wars.

N/A	$28,000	$24,000	$20,000	$15,000	$13,000	$10,000	$8,000	$6,750	$5,500	$4,800	$4,000

Since New York Militia revolvers are frequently encountered with a mismatched part, the question is often asked if the mismatched part affects value. If the serial number of the mismatched part can be attributed to another known New York Militia revolver, then the answer is "only slightly". Since the serial numbers of all 800 refurbished 1895 New York Militia models are recorded in the Colt ledgers, the serial number of the mismatched part should always belong to another documented New York example. In many cases, cylinders had been inadvertently switched by a New York Trooper, or back straps were refitted onto an incorrect revolver when the New York Militia armorer fitted the lanyard swivel.

CAUTION: Unscrupulous fakers have been known to restamp the mismatched part with the "host" revolver's primary serial number.

* ***Condemned U.S. Cavalry*** – throughout military contract production, a small percentage of SAAs did not pass inspection and were condemned, receiving a large "C" stamped on the frame, just over the serial number. These guns were set aside, and later completed as civilian revolvers. They are often found with the Ordnance sub-inspector's initials, such as J.T.C., on the bottom of the frame, but will not have a "U.S." on the left side. This does not have a negative effect on the value of these guns to the collector, and they should be regarded as normal civilian revolvers with an interesting history.

REVOLVERS: SAA, 2ND GENERATION: 1956-1975 MFG.

The author wishes to express his thanks to Charles Layson, and Carol and the late Don Wilkerson for their generous contributions to the 2nd & 3rd Generation Colt SAA information.

Popular demand brought back the Single Action Army in 1956 with minor modifications, most not detectable except to experts. Serial numbers began at 0001SA, and continued to 73,000SA before the "New Model" was introduced in 1976 (ser. no. 80,000SA). Premiums are paid for rare production variances in NIB condition. It should be noted "premium niches" exist in this model as collectors are establishing premiums paid for rarer production variances (the interrelation of barrel length, caliber, frame type, finish quality, year of manufacture, and other special features). The order of desirability on standard 2nd Generation SAAs is as follows: 4 3/4 in. barrels are the most desirable, followed by 7 1/2 in., and then 5 1/2 in. Caliber desirability is as follows: .45 LC has the most demand, followed by .44 Spl., .38 Spl., and then .357 Mag. It follows that desirable calibers found with desirable barrel lengths will command healthy premiums if production was unusually low for a particular configuration. Reference books specifically on the post-war SAA are a must when determining the rarity factors on these multiple production combinations. Buntlines, Sheriff's Models, and special orders through the Custom Gun Shop are in a class by themselves, and have to be evaluated one at a time.

It is advisable to procure a factory letter when buying or selling older or recently manufactured Colt single actions (hence, guaranteeing authenticity and value credibility). These watermarked letters are based on the original factory shipping records and are available by contacting Colt Archive Properties LLC in Hartford, CT. While not totally infallible, these letters are normally very accurate. The cost to document 2nd generation

MSR	100%	98%	95%	90%	80%	70%	60%

SAA's is $100. This research can be expedited for an additional $100. This expedite service provides a verbal report within 24-48 hours and a documentation letter follows in 2-3 weeks. Additionally, premium charges apply for factory engraved guns ($50-$150), or unique shipping destinations ($50-$200). To contact the Archive Department for assistance call 1-800-962-2658, Ext. 1343. Once contacted, they will tell you what the exact historical research charge will be for the service you are requesting. The address to write to is COLT ARCHIVE PROPERTIES LLC, 1295 Blue Hills Avenue, Bloomfield, CT 06002. For a complete Archive Services price list, please refer to the Colt website at coltsmfg.com.

SINGLE ACTION ARMY (SAA, 2ND GENERATION) - .357 Mag., .38 Spl., .44 Spl., or .45 LC cal., denoted by SA suffix, 3 (Sheriff's Model), 4 3/4, 5 1/2, 7 1/2, or 12 (Buntline) in. barrel length - 5 1/2, 7 1/2, and 12 in. barrels have the one-line barrel address, and are all blue, blue/case hardened, or nickel finished. 2nd Generation SAAs have been grouped into the following 3 categories.

* ***SAA Early 2nd Generation*** - ser. no. range 0001SA to approx. 39,000SA, shipped in one-piece black box similar to pre-war box. Mfg. from 1956-65.

.45 LC cal.	$3,100	$2,500	$2,250	$1,800	$1,600	$1,350	$1,100
.44 Spl. cal.	$2,900	$2,300	$2,100	$1,600	$1,500	$1,200	$1,000
.38 Spl. cal.	$2,700	$2,100	$1,900	$1,500	$1,400	$1,100	$1,000
.357 Mag. cal.	$2,300	$1,800	$1,600	$1,400	$1,300	$1,000	$900

Add 30% for original black box in good condition.

Add 20% for original nickel finish.

Add 15% for original 4 3/4 in. barrel.

Subtract 10% for rounded "fanning, quick draw" hammer configuration, where sharp corners above the firing pin were removed so as not to scratch the shooter's palm or thumb when trying to cock and fire quickly. Guns with this type of hammer fall between serial #26,500SA (1959) and #61,900SA (1972) approximately.

The very earliest models of this group, with serial numbers under 10,000 SA, have become more desirable when found in 100% new condition, with perfect black box, brush and papers - this configuration may bring an additional 20%.

* ***SAA Mid-Range 2nd Generation*** - approx. ser. no. range 39,000SA to 70,055SA, most were shipped in a red and white, two-piece, stagecoach box, but at approx. serial range 65,XXXSA a light wood grain box was used followed by a dark wood grain box. Mfg. 1965-1973.

.45 LC cal.	$2,200	$2,000	$1,800	$1,600	$1,350	$1,150	$950
.44 Spl. cal.	$2,000	$1,850	$1,600	$1,400	$1,250	$1,000	$850
.357 Mag. cal.	$1,900	$1,700	$1,500	$1,300	$1,100	$900	$800

Add 30% for original stagecoach box.

Add 10% for original light or dark grain wood box with styrofoam inserts.

Add 10% for original nickel finish.

Add 15% for original 4 3/4 in. barrel.

MSR	100%	98%	95%	90%	80%	70%	60%

* ***SAA Late 2nd Generation*** - approx. ser. no. range 70,055SA to 73,205SA, shipped in a brown, wood grain cardboard shell with 2 styrofoam inserts. Mfg. 1973-1976.

.45 LC cal.	$2,000	$1,850	$1,650	$1,400	$1,250	$1,000	$900
.357 Mag. cal.	$1,800	$1,650	$1,450	$1,250	$1,050	$900	$800

Add 15% for original brown/styrofoam box.

Add 10% for original nickel finish.

Add 10% for original 4 3/4 in. barrel.

2nd Generation SAAs in stagecoach box w/o eagle black grips (ser. numbered under approx. 52,000SA) are more desirable than those with eagle. Also, flat-top hammers are more desirable than round top hammers found between ser. no. range 27,012SA-61,575SA (mfg. mid-1959-1972).

Colt manufactured approximately 100 screwless frames during the 1970s, and assembled approximately 50 guns at the time. The other 50 sat in the warehouse until Colt started assembling the screwless frames again during the 1990s. Most of these recent guns are engraved and in .38-40 WCF or .45 LC cal., and have either a 4 3/4 or 5 in. barrel. Typically, the engraver's name is part of the serial number. Bangor's distributed most of these guns, and in today's marketplace they are priced in the $7,500-$25,000 range.

SHERIFF'S MODEL SAA (1961 MODEL) - .45 LC cal., distinictive configuration with 3 in. barrel and no ejector rod housing, ser. no. followed by SM suffix, 503 were mfg. for Centennial Arms Corp. - 478 had a blue/case hardened finish and 25 were done in nickel.

Blue/cc finish	$2,750	$2,000	$1,750	$1,550	$1,300	$1,100	$900
Nickel finish	$7,850	$4,850	$4,200	$3,600	$3,000	$2,400	$2,100

Add 25% for original two-piece box.

Original nickel finish is very rare on this model, watch for refinishing.

BUNTLINE SPECIAL SAA (2ND GENERATION) - .45 LC cal. only, 12 in. barrel, blue/case hardened finish, rubber (early mfg.) or walnut grips. Over 3,900 mfg. 1957-1975.

	$2,000	$1,750	$1,500	$1,450	$1,350	$1,200	$1,000
Nickel finish	$3,850	$2,900	$2,500	$2,250	$1,950	$1,800	$1,650

Add 30% for original black box.

Add 10% for black hard rubber grips.

Add 150% for nickel finish with black box, 50% for nickel with later tan box.

Original nickel finish is very rare on this model, watch for refinishing.

NEW FRONTIER SAA (2ND GENERATION) - .357 Mag., .38 Spl. (rare), .44 Spl., or .45 LC cal., denoted by flat-top frame, adj. rear sight, and "NF" after the serial number, 4 3/4 (scarce), 5 1/2 (scarce), or 7 1/2 (most common) in. barrel, case hardened frame/blue finish and smooth walnut grips were standard. Approx. 4,200 mfg. 1961-1975.

	$1,400	$1,200	$1,100	$950	$850	$750	$650
.38 Spl., 5 1/2 in. bbl.	$3,750	$2,850	$2,600	$2,400	$2,200	$2,000	$1,800

MSR	100%	98%	95%	90%	80%	70%	60%

Add 15% for later brown/styrofoam box.

Add 20% for stagecoach or black box (must be in correct ser. no. range).

Add 35% for early black and gold box.

Add 50% for 4 3/4 in. barrel.

Add 25% for 5 1/2 in. barrel.

This model in .38 Spl. cal. with 7 1/2 in. barrel is very rare. NIB specimens can sell for as much as $8,750.

NEW FRONTIER BUNTLINE SAA (2ND GENERATION) - .45 LC cal. only, 12 in. barrel, flat-top frame and adj. rear sight. Approx. 72 mfg. 1962-67.

	100%	98%	95%	90%	80%	70%	60%
	$2,500	$2,190	$1,875	$1,700	$1,375	$1,125	$875

Add 50% for original black or tan box (must be serial numbered to the gun).

FACTORY ENGRAVED 2ND GENERATION SAAs - approx. 350 revolvers were factory engraved with 90% being in .45 LC cal. Values range from 75%-100% higher than non-engraved specimens, with additional premiums paid for rare styles and configurations and/or for the notoriety of the engraver. Those SAAs done by Albert Herbert, A.A. White, Robert Burt, Leonard Francolini, and Dennis Kies are probably the highest-priced examples. Always check authenticity when buying, selling, or trading engraved 2nd Generation SAAs with the Colt Archive Dept. The charge for a factory letter per engraved gun is $150. $50 will be refunded if Colt cannot provide historical documentation.

Factory engraved 2nd Generation SAAs are at least 10 times rarer than engraved 3rd Generation pistols.

REVOLVERS: SAA, 3RD GENERATION: 1976-CURRENT MFG.

After a short break in production, Colt Firearms announced the resumption of full-scale production of the Single Action on Feb. 4th, 1976, at the N.S.G.A. (National Sporting Goods Association) Bi-Centennial show in Chicago.

The "New Model Colt Single Action Army" or the "Colt Post-War Single Action Army - New Model", as it was commonly referred to at the time, is known today to collectors as the "3rd Generation Colt Single Action Army". The most significant change in the new 3rd Generation guns was the elimination of the full length, removable cylinder bushing which was no longer considered necessary with the use of modern, smokeless powder. This removal reduced the cost of manufacturing of each unit.

Production began with ser. no. 80,000SA, and reached 99,999SA in 1978. At this point, the SA suffix changed to a prefix beginning with SA01,001. Serialization reached SA99,999 during 1993, and began over, this time separating the letters SA, and starting with S02,001A.

Starting at approximately ser. no. S34,000A, Colt reintroduced the full length cylinder bushing which had been eliminated in 1976, making these current 3rd Generation Single Actions essentially the same as the 1st and 2nd Generation guns. The factory still refers to these as 3rd Generation however, and not 4th Generation, as some collectors are now calling them.

MSR	100%	98%	95%	90%	80%	70%	60%

For a listing of Colt's "P-Codes" (referring to the factory's model number designations specifying frame type, caliber, finish, and barrel length), please refer to the Colt Single Action Model Numbers section in the back of this book (located in Colt Serialization). As with 1st and 2nd Generation Single Actions, a factory letter authenticating configuration and shipping destination can be obtained by writing to: COLT ARCHIVE PROPERTIES LLC, 1295 Blue Hills Avenue, Bloomfield, CT 06002.

All 100% values on currently manufactured revolvers in this section assume NIB condition.

Please contact the Colt Custom Shop for a written quotation ($25) regarding a custom built SAA with special options/features. Their address is: Colt Manufacturing Company, Inc. P.O. Box 1868, Hartford, CT 06101, ATTN: Custom Shop.

STANDARD/CUSTOM SINGLE ACTION ARMY SAA (3RD GENERATION) – .32-20 WCF (mfg. 2005-2011), .357 Mag. (disc. approx. 1983, reintroduced 2005), .38 Spl. (reintroduced 2005-2011), .38-40 WCF (reintroduced 2005-2011), .44 Spl. (disc. approx. 1983), .44-40 WCF (disc. 2011), or .45 LC cal., 4 (disc. 1988), 4 3/4, 5 (disc. 1987), 5 1/2, or 7 1/2 in. barrel, 5 1/2 and 7 1/2 in. barrels have the one-line barrel address, fixed sights, standard finishes include full blue (disc.), color case hardened/blue or nickel (disc. 2018), plastic black eagle or walnut grips (used mostly during 1991-92) standard, current mfg. of black powder frames is available in .45 LC cal. only (see separate listing for current mfg.), most recent mfg. has blue shipping box with white slip cover. Mfg. 1976 to date. Original 1976 issue price was approx. $242.

MSR $1,799	$1,895	$1,500	$1,295	$1,195	$995	$895	$795

Add $200 nickel finish (disc. 2018).

Add 25% for original .38 Spl. cal. (disc.)

Add 10% for black powder frame mfg. pre-1996.

Add $700 for original two-piece ivory grips with screw.

Add $700 for original one-piece ivory grips w/o screw.

Add 5% for original brown box with styrofoam inserts (mfg. 1976-93).

Typically, the engraver's name is part of the serial number. Bangor's originally distributed most of these guns. In today's marketplace price range from $8,500-$25,000, depending on configuration and engraving.

The following calibers .32-20 WCF, .38 Spl., .38-40 WCF, .44-40 WCF, and .44 Spl. are available through special order from the Colt Custom Shop. Please contact the Custom Shop for availability of options and pricing.

Some Colt SAA dealers and collectors have recently commented that current NIB 3rd Generation SAAs are bringing premiums over the 100% values listed due to the custom shop not producing SAAs per indiviual order like it used to. This has resulted in a decrease in supply (especially nickel-finished SAAs), and the result is that values on these NIB specimens have gone up accordingly.

MSR	100%	98%	95%	90%	80%	70%	60%

Through 2001, Colt offered the SAA as both Standard and Custom Models. The difference is that single actions, which are further customized with engraving, special barrel lengths, stocks, etc., are packaged more elaborately because of the added value of the customizing.

Beginning 2001, all orders for SAA models are processed through the Colt Custom Shop. The 2001 Custom Shop MSR for the Custom SAA was $2,100.

Various custom order barrel lengths have been available on this model for some time.

The .357 Mag. and .44 Spl. cals. were mostly discontinued by 1983.

Colt manufactured approximately 100 screwless frames during the 1970s, and assembled approximately 50 guns at the time. The other 50 sat in the warehouse until Colt started assembling the screwless frames again during the 1990s. Most of these recent guns are engraved and in .38-40 WCF or .45 LC cal., and have either a 4 3/4 or 5 in. barrel.

To reference factory coding for the various Standard Model P (SAA) configurations, please refer to the Colt Single Action Model Numbers within the Colt Serialization section in the back of this text.

BLACK POWDER FRAME SAA (3RD GENERATION) - .45 LC cal., 4 3/4, 5 1/2, or 7 1/2 in. barrel, features old style black powder frame, standard finish is case colored frame and blue barrel/cylinder. Mfg. 1984-1995, reintroduced 2008-2018.

	100%	98%	95%	90%	80%	70%	60%
	$1,895	$1,500	$1,295	$1,195	$995	$895	$795

Last MSR was $1,799.

COLT COWBOY SAA - .45 LC cal., 4 3/4 (disc. 1999, reintroduced 2002), 5 1/2, or 7 1/2 (disc. 1999) in. barrel marked "COLT COWBOY .45 COLT" on left side, transfer bar safety, all steel construction, frame assembly done in the U.S., charcoal case colors on frame with blue metal parts, rampant Colt black composition grips similar in design to those used on 1st generation SAAs, 40 oz. Not mfg. in U.S. While advertised beginning 1998, this model was not manufactured until 1999-2003.

	100%	98%	95%	90%	80%	70%	60%
	$1,295	$995	$850	$750	$650	$550	$450

Last MSR was $670.

* ***Cowboy SAA Collection Set*** - includes SAA in .45 LC cal., with 5 1/2 in. barrel, stag (very limited) or imitation ivory (more common) grips, blue/color case hardened finish, accessories include collector's Bowie knife, silver medallion and collector's case, marked "1 of 1,000". Limited mfg. 2000 only.

	100%	98%	95%	90%	80%	70%	60%
Faux ivory	$1,250	$750	$625	$500	$425	$400	$400
Stag	$1,850	$1,625	$1,375	$1,100	$875	$700	$550

Last MSR was approx. $1,600.

MSR	100%	98%	95%	90%	80%	70%	60%

SHERIFF'S MODEL SAA (3RD GENERATION, MFG 1980-1985) - .44-40 WCF, .44 Spl., or .45 LC cal., 3 in. barrel w/o ejector rod, blue/case colored, nickel, or royal blue finish. Approx. 4,560 guns mfg. 1980-85.

.45 LC cal. (blue/CH)	$1,595	$1,150	$950	$850	$750	$600	$550
.44 Spl./.44-40 WCF	$1,495	$975	$850	$750	$675	$600	$525

Add 10% for extra convertible cylinder.

Add 10% for original nickel finish.

Add $550 for original ivory grips.

Subtract 20% for all blue finish.

* ***Sheriff's Model SAA (3rd Generation - Recent Mfg.)*** - .44-40 WCF or .45 LC (most popular) cal., 3 or 4 in. barrel w/o ejector rod, blue/case colored (disc. 2009) or nickel finish, black plastic grips. Mfg. 2008-2010.

Blue/cc finish (disc. 2009)	$1,595	$1,295	$1,195	$995	$795	$695	$595
Nickel finish (disc. 2010)	$1,695	$1,395	$1,295	$1,195	$895	$795	$695

Last MSR was $1,490 (nickel finish) in 2010.

BUNTLINE SPECIAL MODEL SAA (3RD GENERATION) - .44-40 WCF or .45 LC cal. only, 12 in. barrel, blue/case hardened finish, walnut grips.

	$1,595	$1,050	$850	$750	$650	$600	$550

Add 10% for original nickel finish.

Add $550 for original ivory grips.

NEW FRONTIER SAA (3RD GENERATION - 1978-1981 MFG.) - .357 Mag., .44-40 WCF (rare), .44 Spl., or .45 LC cal., denoted by "NF" serial suffix, 4 3/4, 5 1/2, or 7 1/2 in. barrel, blue/case hardened finish, flat-top frame, adj. rear sight, plain two-piece walnut grips. Mfg. 1978-1983.

	$1,395	$950	$825	$750	$700	$650	$600

Subtract 10% for 5 1/2 in. barrel.

Subtract 15% for 7 1/2 in. barrel.

Add 5% for original brown box with styrofoam inserts.

Serial numbers on the New Frontier started at 01001NF, but during 1980 a few New Frontiers with 5 1/2 in. barrels were produced in the 7000NF serial range, where 2nd Generation New Frontiers left off. Therefore, a 3rd Generation New Frontier will either have a ser. no. starting with "O" or will have a higher number than 7288NF with no "O" prefix.

FRONTIER SIX SHOOTER SAA (3RD GENERATION) - .44-40 WCF cal., black powder frame, 4 3/4, 5 1/2, or 7 1/2 in. barrel with "Colt Frontier Six Shooter" acid etched in a panel on the left side of barrel, similar to 1st Generation SAAs, blue (disc. 2009) or nickel finish. Mfg. 2008-2010.

Blue finish (disc. 2009)	$1,895	$1,495	$1,295	$1,095	$895	$795	$695
Nickel finish (disc. 2010)	$1,895	$1,595	$1,395	$1,195	$995	$895	$795

The last MSR on nickel finish was $1,547 (2010).

MSR	100%	98%	95%	90%	80%	70%	60%

NEW FRONTIER SAA (3RD GENERATION - RECENT MFG.) – .357 Mag. (disc. 2011), .44 Spl., or .45 LC cal., 4 3/4 (.45 LC cal. only), 5 1/2, or 7 1/2 in. barrel, royal blue/case hardened finish, flat-top frame, adj. rear sight, two-piece smooth walnut grips with medallions. Mfg. 2011-2018.

	$1,575	$1,250	$995	$850	$725	$625	$575

Last MSR was $1,899.

The following calibers .32-20 WCF, .38 Spl., .38-40 WCF, .44-40 WCF, and .44 Spl. are available through special order from the Colt Custom Shop. Please contact the Custom Shop for availability of options and pricing.

NEW FRONTIER BUNTLINE SPECIAL SAA (3RD GENERATION) – .45 LC cal. only, 12 in. barrel, flat-top frame, adj. rear sight, limited mfg. as the New Buntline Commemorative during 1979. Please refer to the Colt Commemorative section for value information.

STOREKEEPER'S MODEL SAA (3RD GENERATION - 1984-85 MFG.) – .45 LC cal. only, black powder frame, 4 in. barrel w/ejector rod, full nickel or royal blue/case hardened finish, ivory grips. Approx. 280 mfg. 1984-1985.

Blue/cc finish	$1,895	$1,650	$1,500	$1,250	$1,000	$850	$750
Nickel finish	$2,000	$1,700	$1,600	$1,300	$1,100	$900	$800

* ***Storekeeper's Model SAA (3rd Generation - 2008-2010 Mfg.)*** – .44-40 WCF or .45 LC cal., 4 in. barrel w/ejector rod, blue/case hardened (disc. 2009) or nickel (mfg. 2010) finish. Mfg. 2008-2010.

Blue/cc finish	$1,695	$1,395	$1,195	$1,095	$895	$795	$695
Nickel finish	$1,795	$1,495	$1,295	$1,195	$995	$895	$795

Last MSR was $1,490 (nickel finish) in 2010.

COLT CLASSIC SAA – .45 LC cal., 5 1/2 in. barrel only, all blue finish, uncheckered wood grips with Colt medallions, twin gold barrel bands on back of cylinder and front of barrel. Limited mfg. 2010 only.

	$1,795	$1,395	$1,295	$1,095	$995	$895	$750

Last MSR was $1,620.

HUGH O'BRIAN-WYATT EARP LIMITED EDITION – .45 LC cal., set includes one 4 3/4 in. and one 12 in. barreled Buntline SAA models, smooth walnut grips, case colored frame and hammer with polished blue barrel and cylinder, barrels are etched "Hugh O'Brian - Wyatt Earp Tribute" and backstrap features Hugh O'Brian's signature, set includes French fitted walnut case with hinged glass top and removable drawer, includes replica marshall badge, certificates signed by Hugh O'Brian and double holster Buntline special gun belt, mfg. by Frontier Gunleather, total mfg. determined by orders taken by Dec. 31, 2010.

	$4,500	$4,100	$3,600	$3,100	$2,750	$2,350	$1,900

Last MSR was $4,712.

Add $150 for holster set.

MSR	100%	98%	95%	90%	80%	70%	60%

COLT 175th ANNIVERSARY LIMITED EDITION SAA - .45 LC cal., Colt royal blue finish only, 175th Anniversary (1836-2011) Limited Edition with selective 24Kt. gold plated scroll on frame, backstrap, barrel and cylinder, black powder frame, left side of barrel is marked "1836 - 175th Anniversary - 2011", 4 3/4, 5 1/2, or 7 1/2 in. barrel, black eagle plastic grips, 175 manufactured in each barrel length 2011 only.

MSR	100%	98%	95%	90%	80%	70%	60%
	$2,500	$1,575	$1,325	$1,100	$950	$825	$700

Last MSR was $1,580.

COLT CUSTOM SHOP ENGRAVING, SAA & SEMI-AUTO, 1976-PRESENT

Prior to 1976, Colt had three factory engraving patterns - A, B, and C coverage. During 1976, they expanded the Custom Shop and a new class D pattern was added. To inaugurate the Custom Gun shop in 1976, Colt created a "Custom Edition" of deluxe engraved Model P revolvers. This custom edition was the first of many custom editions to be produced by the Custom Gun Shop over the years. The term "Custom Edition" is defined by Don Wilkerson as a group of identical revolvers assembled under the direction of the Custom Gun Shop and sold through Colt's normal distribution system. A "Custom Edition" differs from a "Special Edition" in that a special edition is a group of revolvers made per customer specifications, sold to one purchaser, and not through Colt's normal distribution system . An example of a custom edition: Twenty-five P-1970 revolvers were assembled on Custom Shop order #2622. All twenty-five .44-40 cal. Royal Blue and casehardened revolvers were assembled with unfluted cylinders and ivory stocks. This custom edition was shipped to the various Colt distributors in early 1984.

An example of a special edition: Two hundred P-1970 revolvers were ordered by the Powder Horn Gun Shop in Bozeman, Montana to commemorate the founding of the Bozeman trail. Each revolver in the edition was assembled with an unfluted cylinder and acid etched with gold leaf. All two hundred revolvers were contracted by and sold to the Powder Horn Gun Shop.

A large number of custom editions have been assembled by the Custom Gun Shop since 1976. The great majority of revolvers coming from the Custom Gun Shop are associated with either a "factory order" number or a "Custom shop" number. The end label of the shipping carton is the place where these two terms are most likely to be encountered. Custom Shop orders have varied from as few as a single revolver to as many as 100 revolvers.

The listings below represent both current and discontinued Custom Shop engraving prices for the various frame sizes, amount of engraving coverage (A = 25% coverage, B = 50% coverage, C = 75% coverage, and D = 100% coverage), and the three levels of engraving execution (i.e., Standard, Expert, and Master levels). SAAs are considered large frame, revolvers and full-size Government Models are considered medium frame, and Government Model 380s are considered small frame. Most buyers of engraved Colt SAAs today are very knowledgeable, and many of them are no longer satisfied with Standard types of patterns and styles. As a result, those engraved guns with the rarest production variances coupled with unique engraving done at an Expert or better level are currently more desireable than their counterparts with Standard engraving patterns. Colt currently employs three full-time engravers at the factory, in addition to several outside sources (at all engraving levels).

The name of the engraver is available only when ordering either the Expert or the Master level of engraving.

MSR	100%	98%	95%	90%	80%	70%	60%

CUSTOM & SPECIAL ENGRAVED SAA EDITIONS (3RD GENERATION) – beginning in 1976, with the introduction of the "New Model" SAA (3rd Generation), the Colt Custom Shop produced many custom and special edition engraved Single Army Action revolvers. According to Mr. Don Wilkerson, author of *The Post-War Single Action Revolver 1976-1986*, "the term custom edition is defined as a group of identical revolvers assembled under the direction of the Custom Gun Shop at Colt's and sold through the normal distribution system. A custom edition differs from a special edition in that special editions are a group of revolvers made up to a customer's unique specifications, and sold as a group to one purchaser...." While the exact number is not known, it is thought that approx. 3,500 SAAs have been engraved since 1976. Since each edition is unique, values vary widely, depending upon the notability of the engraver, the amount and type of coverage, and the number produced. Models listed below are recent Colt Custom Editions.

* ***SAA Engraved European Model*** – 9mm Para. cal., nickel finish only, 4 3/4 (110 mfg.), 5 1/2 (110 mfg.), or 7 1/2 (50 mfg.) in. barrel, rosewood grips with silver medallions, 40-43 oz. Mfg. 1991-92 only.

	$2,450	$1,725	$1,395	$1,195	$1,065	$855	$750

Last MSR was $1,990.

* ***SAA Engraved U.S. Model*** – .45 ACP cal., royal blue finish only, 4 3/4, 5 1/2, or 7 1/2 in. barrel, walnut grips, 40-43 oz. Mfg. 1991-92 only.

	$1,950	$1,325	$1,100	$985	$795	$675	$565

Last MSR was $1,960.

* ***SAA Old World Engravers Sampler*** – .45 LC cal., 5 1/2 in. barrel, nickel finish, buffalo horn grips, includes four unique styles of engraving. Mfg. 1997-98, reintroduced 2001-2002.

	$2,975	$2,450	$2,000	$1,740	$1,495	$1,215	$1,000

Last MSR was $3,445.

* ***Legend Rodeo/Legend Rodeo II SAA*** – disc. 1998.

	$1,950	$1,500	$1,250	$1,100	$895	$785	$630

Last MSR was $2,450.

* ***125th Anniversary Edition SAA*** – beveled cylinder, fire blue finish, "45 COLT" on left side of barrel and address on top of barrel. 1,000 mfg. 1997-2002.

	$1,600	$1,150	$825	N/A	N/A	N/A	N/A

Last MSR was $2,070.

* ***Model P w/Unsigned B Coverage Engraving*** – choice of cals. and barrel lengths, blue or nickel finish, features unsigned standard American scroll B engraving coverage. Disc. 2010.

	$2,250	$2,000	$1,750	$1,500	$1,250	$1,000	$875

Last MSR was $2,319.

Add $231 for nickel finish.

* ***Modern Masters Model P w/Signed B Coverage Engraving*** - choice of cals. and barrel lengths, blue or nickel finish, features signed standard American scroll B engraving coverage. Mfg. 2009-disc.

Last MSR on this model was $6,528.

SAA CUSTOM SHOP ENGRAVING PRICES - PRE-1997 - values below represent 1995 published SAA Custom Shop A-D engraving options before the company started separate Standard, Expert, and Master level pricing during 1997. For current Colt Custom Shop engraving prices, please refer to the "Colt Custom Shop Engraving - Current Mfg." section below.

Add $1,163 for Class "A" engraving (25% metal coverage).

Add $2,324 for Class "B" engraving (50% metal coverage).

Add $3,487 for Class "C" engraving (75% metal coverage).

Add $4,647 for Class "D" engraving (100% metal coverage).

Add an additional 13% (approx.) for Buntline engraving.

Standard Engraving was performed mostly by standard level factory engravers and engraving options generally included A-D style coverage. Typically, gold work was not performed by these engravers and specimens are mostly unsigned. Expert Engravers executed classic American style scroll, w/o gold work, and may have signed their work.

FACTORY ENGRAVED SAAs (3RD GENERATION) - the rarity of the SAA configuration in addition to the notability of the engraver will make the difference on the premiums commanded. 3rd Generation factory engraved SAAs were produced in much greater numbers than were 2nd Generation SAAs. Over 80% of engraved 3rd Generation SAAs are .45 LC caliber, the majority have 7 1/2 in. barrels, and some variation of blue finish. Grade "C" (41% of engraved mfg.) and Grade "D" (24% of engraved mfg.) dominate production.

Current MSR on a Colt SAA with signed Master Level Engraving "B" coverage is $7,061.

Use the following add-ons as general guidelines for values on factory engraved recently manufactured 3rd Generation SAAs.

Add approx. 10% for original nickel finish.

Add 25% for 4 3/4 in. barrel.

Add 15% for 5 1/2 in. barrel.

Add 10% for calibers other than .45 LC.

Add 30% for factory ivory grips.

Add 10% for original blue cardboard or plastic box.

Unfortunately, the quality of the engraving on some early Third Generation SAAs has been substandard, and as a result, these guns usually cap at approx. $2,000.

During 1978-79, Colt engraved as many as 300-500 guns on a single factory order. If the level of quality is similar to today's SAAs, the price will also be similar.

Large Frame Size: Current SAAs and M1911s

The following is a listing of current Custom Shop engraving for both SAAs and M1911s. *Other Custom Shop options are priced on request, including a wide variety of gold/silver* inlays, panel scenes, color enamel inlays, gold/silver frame outlines, etc.

Add $1,130 for A Standard engraving.

Add $1,300 for B Standard, $2,075 for B Expert (signed), or $3,725 for B Master (signed) level engraving.

Add $1,700 for C Standard, $2,878 for C Expert (signed), or $5,415 for C Master (signed) level engraving.

Add $2,000 for D Standard, $4,280 for D Expert (signed), or $6,900 for D Master (signed) level engraving.

Add 20% to large frame pricing for Buntline Models (disc.).

Medium Frame Size

Medium frame engraving was discontinued circa 1998.

Values listed reflect last published MSRs.

Add $900 for Standard A level engraving.

Add $1,200 for B Standard, $1,700 for B Expert, or $3,150 for B Master level engraving.

Add $1,400 for C Standard, $2,500 for C Expert, or $4,538 for C Master level engraving.

Add $1,600 for D Standard, $3,600 for D Expert, or $6,300 for D Master level engraving.

Small Frame Size

Factory small frame engraving was disc. 1998.

Values listed reflect last published MSRs. Subtract 20% from small frame pricing for Mustang Models.

Add $400 for A Standard, $600 for A Expert, or $800 for A Master level engraving.

Add $600 for B Standard, $800 for B Expert, or $1,000 for B Master level engraving.

Add $800 for C Standard, $1,100 for C Expert, or $1,500 for C Master level engraving.

Add $1,100 for D Standard, $1,300 for D Expert, or $1,900 for D Master level engraving.

POPULAR SAA CUSTOM SHOP SPECIAL ORDER OPTIONS

Add $329 for special barrel length, for "45 Colt" or two line address on barrel add $95, add $450 for caliber change, for custom-tuned action most recent MSR was $197, add $275 (available in .45 LC only beginning 2000) for extra regular fluted or unfluted cylinder, for extra long fluted cylinder most recent MSR was $308, add $152 for beveled front of cylinder, add $180 for fire blue package (screws, base pin, and ejector rod head), add $200 for mirror brite finish (disc.), add $1,618 for nickel finish, add $1,390 for blue/color case finish, add $1,390 for full blue finish, add $425, for gold or silver plating, last published MSR was $425, currently it's POR), add $105 for black eagle grips, add $305 for smooth walnut grips with medallions, add $275 for North American elkhorn grips (disc.), add $400 for red stag grips (disc.), add $450 for sambar stag grips (disc.), add $625 for stag grips, add $425 for buffalo horn grips, add $375 for mother-of-pearl grips (disc.), add $840 for one or two piece plain ivory grips, $425 for imitation ivory, approx. 10% for grip checkering, add $350 for scrimshaw engraving (3 initials only), add $65

MSR	100%	98%	95%	90%	80%	70%	60%

for consecutive serial numbers, add $350 for individual unique serial number, add $105 to modify and shorten ejector housing, add $55 for bullseye ejector rod head, add $359 for birdshead grips, add $400 for extra long backstrap, for extended butt frame last MSR was $400, for special length barrel add $329, to regulate barrel for accuracy add $225, for qualify screws add $84, for wide spur hammer with blue finish add $225, for wide spur hammer with nickel or hard chrome finish add $255.

While a few screwless frame SAAs have been mfg. to date (approx.100), the Custom Shop now lists this option as a standard custom order feature. Price is POR.

REVOLVERS: SAA, SCOUT MODEL

100% values below assume NIB condition. Subtract 10% without box.

FRONTIER SCOUT (Q or F SUFFIX) - .22 LR or .22 WMR (introduced after 1960) cal., "Q" or "F" suffix, blue or bright alloy frame, all blue, or duotone (bright alloy frame disc. 1961), 4 3/4 or 9 1/2 (Buntline, blue only) in. barrel, available with interchangeable cylinders after 1964, black composition or walnut grips, approx. 246,000 mfg. 1957-1970.

	100%	98%	95%	90%	80%	70%	60%
	$500	$400	$325	$250	$200	$175	$150

Add 10% for extra cylinder.

Add 20% for Buntline model (marked "BUNTLINE SCOUT .22 CAL.")

Add 25% for "Q" suffix with duo-tone finish (mfg. 1957-58 only).

Add 10% for original box.

Add 50% for walnut grips (must have factory box or letter).

FRONTIER SCOUT (K SUFFIX) - Zamac alloy frame version of "Q" Model with "K" suffix, nickel finish with walnut stocks, approx. 44,000 mfg. 1960-1970.

	100%	98%	95%	90%	80%	70%	60%
	$600	$425	$325	$250	$200	$175	$150
Scout cased pair	$1,200	$900	$750	$550	$450	$350	$320
Buntline cased pair	$1,500	$1,125	$950	$675	$575	$425	$400

Add 20% for Buntline model (marked "BUNTLINE SCOUT .22 CAL.")

Add 10% for original box.

This model used the alloy Zamac for manufacture (as opposed to aluminum in the "Q" and "F" suffix models), and specimens are 6 oz. heavier as a result.

FRONTIER SCOUT '62 (P SUFFIX) - blue finish version of "K" Model, except has "P" suffix, Staglite grips, approx. 68,000 mfg. 1962-1970.

	100%	98%	95%	90%	80%	70%	60%
	$600	$450	$375	$275	$225	$175	$160
Scout cased pair	$1,200	$900	$750	$550	$450	$350	$320
Buntline cased pair	$1,500	$1,125	$950	$675	$575	$425	$400

Add 10% for original box.

Add 20% for Buntline model (marked "BUNTLINE SCOUT .22 CAL.")

PEACEMAKER 22 SCOUT - .22 LR/.22 WMR cal., color case hardened steel frame, 4.4, 4 3/4, 6, or 7 1/2 (nicknamed Buntline Model but

MSR	100%	98%	95%	90%	80%	70%	60%

may be marked Peacemaker or Buntline) in. barrel, black composition grips, furnished with interchangeable .22 LR/.22 WMR cylinders, approx. 190,000 mfg. 1970-1977.

	$750	$600	$450	$350	$300	$200	$150

Add 20% for 4.4 in. barrel.

Add 50% for 4 3/4 in. barrel (first year of production).

Add 10% for original box.

Add 25% for single cylinder model (must have original box with model number).

Subtract 10% if without extra cylinder.

This model can be identified by its "G" or "L" ser. no. prefix.

NEW FRONTIER 22 SCOUT – similar features as Peacemaker Model, except with flat-top frame, ramp front and adj. rear sight, mfg. 1970-1977, reintroduced in 1982 without convertible .22 WMR cylinder and added crossbolt safety, all blue finish became standard in 1985, models with safety are .22 LR only, G or L (1974 only) ser. no. prefix. Mfg. disc. 1986.

	$600	$475	$350	$250	$200	$175	$150

Last MSR was $181.

Add 50% for 4 3/4 in. barrel (first year of production).

Add 25% for single cylinder model w/o safety (must have original box with model number).

Add 20% for 4.4 in. barrel.

Add 10% for original box.

Subtract 10% if w/o extra cylinder (model w/o safety only).

PISTOLS: SEMI-AUTO, DISC.

Most of the semi-auto pistol models listed in the various pistol categories can have their original configuration confirmed with a Colt factory letter. To receive a letter, write: COLT ARCHIVE PROPERTIES, LLC, 1295 Blue Hills Avenue, Bloomfield, CT 06002. The research fee for these pistols is typically either $75 or $100, depending on the model. If they cannot obtain additional information on the variation you request, they will refund $50.

Until several years ago, the Single Action Army revolver commanded the most attention among Colt handgun collectors. Since 1987, Colt Semi-Autos have been in tremendous demand and have out-accelerated many other areas of Colt collecting. Because condition and originality play such a key role in determining Colt Semi-Auto prices, many variations have had their values pushed upward to the point where it is difficult to accurately determine a realistic price, especially on those models in 98% original condition or better. As a result, some of the rarer models rarely encountered in true 100% original condition have had their values deleted since extreme rarity precludes accurate price evaluation. As always, the hardest prices to ascertain when firearms market conditions are bullish are the 98-100% values.

MODEL 1900 – .38 ACP cal., 6 in. barrel, blue, plain walnut grips - checkered hard rubber grips after S/N 2,450, high spur hammer, sight safety. Mfg. 1900-03.

N/A	$15,000	$11,000	$7,600	$5,500	$4,000	$3,000	

MSR	100%	98%	95%	90%	80%	70%	60%

Add 100% for U.S. marked 1st Army contracts (100 guns serial numbered 11-207).

Add 75% for U.S. marked Navy contracts (250 guns serial numbered 1,001-1,250).

Add 60% for U.S. marked 2nd Army contracts (200 guns serial numbered 1,501-1,700).

Subtract 30%-50% for altered sight safety (factory refinished).

This model is serial numbered approx. between 1-4,274.

Somewhere between serial number 2,200 and 2,450, Colt began altering the sights to fixed sights in the production process, shipping both types. By approx. serial number 3,300, most guns shipped were altered during production. Guns altered during production are not refinished. Altered guns below serial number 2,200 were refinished, or at least had the slides refinished.

MODEL 1902 SPORTING - .38 ACP, 6 in. barrel, blue, fixed sights, checkered hard rubber grips, no safety, high spur hammer or round hammer. Mfg. 1902-08.

N/A $5,750 $4,250 $3,250 $2,500 $1,750 $900

This model is serial numbered approx. 4,275-11,000 and 30,000-30,190.

MODEL 1902 MILITARY - .38 ACP cal., 6 in. barrel, blue, similar to 1902 Sporting, round hammer changed to spur type in 1908, checkered black hard rubber grips, lanyard swivel on bottom rear of left grip. Mfg. 1902-29.

N/A $5,750 $4,500 $3,500 $2,500 $1,500 $900

Add 30% for front slide serrations.

Add 20% with original box and instructions.

This model is serial numbered approx. 11,000-16,000 and 30,200-43,266.

MODEL 1902 MILITARY-U.S. ARMY MARKED - similar specifications to 1902 Military, only serial number range 15,001-15,200.

N/A $18,000 $15,000 $12,500 $10,000 $8,750 $6,000

MODEL 1903 POCKET HAMMER (.38 ACP) - .38 ACP cal., 4 1/2 in. barrel, blue finish standard, round or spur hammer, checkered black hard rubber grips, similar to 1902 Sporting, but 4 1/2 in. barrel, 7 1/2 in. overall. Mfg. 1903-29.

$5,000 $4,000 $2,750 $2,000 $1,250 $900 $750

Add 30% for early round hammer.

Add 20% with original box and instructions.

This model is serial numbered approx. 16,000-47,226.

MODEL 1903 POCKET (MODEL M .32 ACP) - .32 ACP cal., 3 3/4 (Types II-IV) or 4 (Type I) in. barrel, charcoal blue, checkered hard rubber grips, hammerless, slide lock and grip safeties, barrel bushing. Mfg. 1903-1946.

$1,250 $1,050 $700 $550 $450 $375 $325

MSR	100%	98%	95%	90%	80%	70%	60%

Add 20% for nickel finish (mostly w/pearl grips).

Add 60% for first model (Type I) mfg. 1903-1911 if in 100%-98% condition. If lower than 98%, add 20%.

Add 30% for Type II if in 100%-98% condition.

Add 30% with original box and instructions.

Type I - 32 ACPs have a 4 in. barrel, barrel bushing, no magazine safety, and are serial numbered 1-71,999.

Type II - 32 ACPs still retain their barrel bushing but have a 3 3/4 in. barrel and were mfg. from 1908-1910. They are serial numbered 72,000-105,050.

Type III - 32 ACPs do not have a barrel bushing and were mfg. from 1910-1926. They are serial numbered 105,051-468,096.

Type IV - 32 ACPs have the added magazine safety (of which there are both the commercial and "U.S. Property" variations). They are serial numbered 468,097-554,446.

* ***Model 1903 Parkerized*** - U.S. Property, 3 1/4 in. barrel, no barrel bushing, magazine safety, serial numbered 554,447-572,214.

	100%	98%	95%	90%	80%	70%	60%
	$2,400	$1,950	$1,200	$1,000	$850	$650	$600

Add 50% for blue U.S. Property S/N 554,447 - approx. 562,000.

Add 20% with original box and instructions.

The 100% value on this model assumes NIB condition.

* ***Model 1903 Pocket General Officer's Pistol*** - .32 ACP cal., blue (mfg. until 1942) or parkerized (mfg. started 1942) finish.

	100%	98%	95%	90%	80%	70%	60%
Parkerized	N/A	$3,000	$2,000	$1,700	$1,300	$1,050	$900
Blue finish	N/A	$3,400	$2,700	$2,300	$1,850	$1,550	$1,250

Values assume issue to a General, and there must be paperwork to link the gun to the recipient. Otherwise, these values do not apply - see U.S. Property above for applicable values.

MODEL 1905 - .45 ACP cal., 5 in. barrel, blue, fixed sights, checkered walnut grips, similar to the Model 1902 Sporting. Mfg. 1905-1911.

	100%	98%	95%	90%	80%	70%	60%
	N/A	$7,500	$5,000	$3,800	$3,000	$2,000	$1,500

Add 50% for factory slotted specimens (500 manufactured).

Add 250% for 1907 U.S. Military Contract variation (205 manufactured).

The shoulder stock option for this pistol is exceedingly rare. Depending on the condition, this accessory can add $7,500-$10,000 to the price of the gun.

MODEL 1908 POCKET (MODEL M .380 ACP) - .380 ACP cal., first issue, 3 3/4 in. barrel only, similar to Model M .32 ACP, except chambered for .380 ACP. Mfg. 1908-1940.

	100%	98%	95%	90%	80%	70%	60%
	$1,650	$1,475	$1,200	$900	$800	$700	$450

Add $100 for nickel finish.

Add 50% for factory pearl grips.

MSR	100%	98%	95%	90%	80%	70%	60%

100% values assume NIB condition. Subtract 15% if without cardboard box. Pearl grips are normally encountered with nickel finish on this model.

Type II - 380 ACPs with barrel bushing and were mfg. 1908-1910 (6,251 mfg.). They are serial numbered 1-6,251.

Type III - 380 ACPs do not have a barrel bushing and were mfg. 1910-1926. They are serial numbered 6,252-92,893.

Type IV - 380 ACPs have the added magazine safety (of which there are both the commercial and "U.S. Property" variations). They are serial numbered 92,894-134,499.

* ***Model 1908 "U.S. Property"*** - blue finish only, U.S. Property marking. Serial numbered 134,500-138,000.

	N/A	$3,000	$2,250	$1,750	$1,300	$950	$750

* ***Model 1908 General Officer's Pistol*** - .380 ACP cal., blue finish only.

	N/A	$4,000	$3,250	$2,700	$2,300	$1,950	$1,550

Values assume issue to a General, and there must be paperwork to link the gun to the recipient. Otherwise, these values do not apply - see U.S. Property above for applicable values.

VEST POCKET MODEL 1908-HAMMERLESS - .25 ACP cal., 2 in. barrel, fixed sights, checkered hard rubber grips on early models, walnut on later, 6 shot mag., magazine disconnect added on guns made after 1916. Mfg. 1908-1946.

* ***Vest Pocket Model 1908 Blue finish***

	$850	$750	$600	$500	$425	$350	$275

Add 50% for factory pearl grips.

Add 50% for NIB condition if in 95% or better condition only.

* ***Vest Pocket Model 1908 Nickel finish***

	$1,200	$1,000	$850	$650	$550	$450	$375
U.S. Property marked	$4,800	$4,000	$3,400	$2,600	$2,200	$1,800	$1,500

Add 50% for factory pearl grips.

Add 50% for NIB condition if in 95% or better condition only.

This model was also supplied with a suede purse. Add $150-$200, depending on condition.

MODEL 1909 - .45 ACP cal., straight handle design, 5 in. barrel, checkered walnut grips, approx. 22 mfg., ultra rare.

Extreme rarity factor precludes accurate price evaluation by individual condition factors. Specimens that are original and over 90% have sold for over $35,000 recently.

MODEL 1910 - .45 ACP cal., while not a production model, this gun is probably the most desirable semi-auto Colt pistol.

MSR	100%	98%	95%	90%	80%	70%	60%

PISTOLS: SEMI-AUTO, GOVT. MODEL 1911 COMMERCIAL VARIATIONS

MODEL 1911 COMMERCIAL – .45 ACP cal., 5 in. barrel, fixed sights, 7 shot mag., flat main spring housing, polished blue finish only, checkered walnut grips. Denoted by "C" preceding serial number, approx. ser. no. range C1-C138,532. Watch for fakes. Colt licensed other companies to manufacture the military variation under government contracts, 39 oz. Mfg. 1912-1925.

Most M1911 variations listed below are not as collectible if under 60% original condition. However, they are still very desirable as shooters, and values (if in original condition) will approximate the 60% prices if in good mechanical condition.

Colt Model 1911s continue to enjoy high demand as of this writing and prices continue to be strong in the 95%-100% condition factors. Be careful on the 98%+ condition specimens, especially the rarer variations. Some collectors are now requiring a potential high-dollar Model 1911 to pass a metallurgical X-ray examination before purchasing.

* ***Model 1911 High Polish Blue*** – mfg. 1912 through ser. no. 4,500.

N/A	$15,000	$12,000	$9,000	$6,500	$4,000	$2,000

* ***Model 1911 Regular Finish*** – pistols mfg. after ser. no. 4,500.

N/A	$4,100	$3,250	$2,100	$1,350	$1,100	$850

Approx. 138,532 were mfg. between 1912-1925.

PISTOLS: SEMI-AUTO, GOVT. MODEL 1911 MILITARY VARIATIONS

All pistols in this section are .45 ACP (11.25mm) cal., unless otherwise noted. Values for original 98%+ M1911 Military Models have risen considerably in recent years, and as a result, values for original mint guns can double and even sometimes triple the values of 98% condition.

Over 2,550,000 M1911 pistols were ordered for WWI and WWII by the U.S. Government, but approx. 650,000 were mfg. between 1911-1925. Those pistols with a parkerized finish will indicate post-WWI reworking, usually marked with an arsenal code (ie. AA-AUGUSTA ARSENAL, SA-SPRINGFIELD ARSENAL, RIA-ROCK ISLAND ARSENAL, etc.). Please check individual listings for values of arsenal refinished pistols.

COLT MFG. MODEL 1911 MILITARY – right side of slide marked "MODEL OF 1911 U.S. ARMY", blue finish only (NOT parkerized unless reworked).

Recent sales for original mint examples of the Model 1911 Military are as follows: $14,000 for 1912 mfg., depending on the variation (there are three), $7,000 for 1913-1915 mfg., $7,500 for 1916 mfg., $6,000 for 1917-1918 mfg. and $6,000 for 1918 later mfg. (black Army finish).

* ***Model 1911 (1912 mfg.)*** – includes three variations.

N/A	$10,000	$7,750	$6,000	$5,000	$4,000	$3,000

* ***Model 1911 (1913-1915 mfg.)***

N/A	$5,400	$4,750	$4,200	$3,600	$2,200	$1,600

Add 300% for the first 114 pistols with oversize "United States Property" marking.

Add 150% for pistols in the ser. no. range 115-2,400.

MSR	100%	98%	95%	90%	80%	70%	60%

* *Model 1911 (1916 mfg.)* - only 4,200 produced.

N/A	$5,700	$5,000	$4,200	$3,650	$2,050	$1,500

* *Model 1911 (1917-1918 early mfg.)* - early blue finish.

N/A	$4,750	$3,200	$2,050	$1,500	$1,200	$1,000

* *Model 1911 (1917-1918 mfg.)* - can be determined by black Army finish.

N/A	$4,750	$3,200	$2,050	$1,500	$1,200	$1,000

* *Model 1911 (1919-1925 mfg.)*

N/A	$4,750	$3,500	$3,000	$2,000	$1,500	$1,200

NORTH AMERICAN ARMS COMPANY - less than 100 mfg. in Quebec, Canada during 1918 only, blue finish. Be very aware of fakes, as this variation is perhaps the most desirable Colt WWI Govt. semi-auto.

N/A	N/A	$35,000	$30,000	$25,000	$20,000	$16,000

Note: a characteristic of the North American is the poor finish. The very best condition specimens will be in the 80%-90% range. All mint 100% specimens encountered in this model appear to have been refinished.

REMINGTON - UMC - over 21,500 mfg. (ser. numbered 1-21,676) in 1918-1919 only, blue finish.

N/A	$8,550	$5,500	$3,850	$3,000	$2,500	$2,000

Most mint 100% specimens encountered in this model have been refinished - be careful. Mint original pistols are currently selling as high as $8,500.

SPRINGFIELD ARMORY - approx. 30,000 mfg. 1914-1915, blue finish.

N/A	$7,550	$5,750	$3,750	$3,000	$2,500	$2,000

Mint original pistols are currently selling in the $7,500 range.

Serialization is 72,751-83,855, 102,597-107,596, 113,497-120,566, and 125,567-133,186.

Most mint 100% specimens encountered in this model have been refinished - be careful.

U.S. NAVY - over 31,000 mfg. for U.S. Navy contract between 1911-1914 in defined serial ranges, blue finish. Marked "MODEL OF 1911 U.S. NAVY" on right slide side.

N/A	$10,500	$6,000	$4,500	$3,200	$2,200	$1,500

Add 100% for specimens under ser. no. 3,500.

U.S. Navy specimens are seldom found in over 80% original condition because of the corrosive conditions encountered while at sea.

U.S. MARINE CORPS. - approx. 13,500 mfg. between 1911-13 and 1916-18 in defined serial ranges, blue finish, right side of slide marked "MODEL OF 1911 U.S. ARMY".

N/A	$7,500	$5,500	$4,500	$3,500	$3,000	$2,250

Mint original specimens are currently selling in the $13,000-$15,000 range.

MSR	100%	98%	95%	90%	80%	70%	60%

WWI BRITISH SERIES - .455 cal., serialized W19,000-W110,695, marked "CALIBRE 455", blue finish, proofed with broad arrow British Ordnance stamp. Mfg. 1915-19.

N/A	$5,750	$4,750	$2,950	$2,000	$1,200	$1,000

Subtract 30% if converted to .45 ACP cal.

Mint original specimens in this model have been selling in the $7,500 - $8,500 range.

Many WWI British-series M1911s were exported back to the U.S. following WWI and were converted to .45 ACP. Usually, a "5" has been crossed out of the original cal. designation. This model also had reworks purchased for Royal Air Force. All Government Model Colts sold in England prior to July 1915 were .45ACP with "C" serial number prefix - approx. 4200 with British War Office purchases of these being 2,200 pistols (most likely issued to Royal Flying Corps (RFC), Royal Navy Air Service, Royal Navy, Royal Horse Artillery). British Ministry of Munitions contracts for the RFC and RAF Colt Government Model .455 in. Webley & Scott Self Loading Calibre pistols with "W" prefix - total 10,500. These were marked RAF.

A.J. SAVAGE MUNITIONS CO. - mfg. slides only, blue finish, marked in middle on left side of slide with flaming ordnance bomb with "S" in center.

N/A	$3,000	$2,250	$1,750	$1,250	$1,000	$800

Mint original specimens have been selling in the $3,250 - $3,500 range.

NORWEGIAN TRIAL MODEL 1911 COLT - 11.25mm cal., approx. 300 mfg. with "C" prefix in 1913-14 and 1917, usually encountered in 90% or less condition.

N/A	$4,500	$3,750	$2,750	$2,000	$1,200	$800

These guns were ordered for Norwegian service evaluation and were mfg. by Colt in Hartford, CT.

NORWEGIAN MODEL 1912 11.25MM - 11.25mm cal., mfg. under license from Colt's during 1917, "M1912" slide designation. Approx. 95 mfg.

N/A	$8,500	$7,500	$6,000	$5,000	$4,000	$3,200

NORWEGIAN 1914 11.25MM - this model has a distinctive extended slide release, all parts should be serial numbered and have numerous matching numbers, approx. 32,850 mfg. 1918-1947, mostly military contract, commercial production was very limited. Most have been refinished.

N/A	$2,350	$1,800	$1,550	$1,300	$900	$700

Add 250% for Waffenamt Nazi mfg. (mfg. 1945 only).

Serial ranges with corresponding year of manufacture on this model are as follows: 96-600 - 1918, 601-1,150 - 1919, 1,151-1,650 (Naval Artillery) - 1920, 1,651-2,200 - 1921, 2,201- 2,950 - 1922, 2,951-4,610 - 1923, 4,611-6,700 - 1924, 6,701-8,940 - 1925,

MSR	100%	98%	95%	90%	80%	70%	60%

8,941-11,820 - 1926, 11,821-15,900 - 1927, 15,901-20,100 - 1928, 20,101-21,440 - 1929, 21,441-21,940 - 1932, 21,941-22,040 - 1933, 22,041-22,141 - 1934, 22,142-22,211 - 1936, 22,212-22,311 - 1939, 22,312-22,361 - 1940, 22,362-26,460 - 1941, 26,461-29,614 - 1942, 29,615-32,335 (Waffenamt Nazi proofed) - 1945, 32,336-32,854 - (last original production) 1947.

Nazi production of the M1914 began in 1941. Between 1941-42, approx. 7,000 pistols were mfg. without Waffenamt stampings. Nazi proofed guns (all 1945 dated) began in the mid- 29,000 serial range, and 920 were mfg. with the Nazi Eagle (ser. no. range 29615-30,534). Also, three guns were produced as prototypes for further German pistol production - they are marked M1-M2, and M3.

ARGENTINE CONTRACT MODEL 1916 - identified by the Argentine seal on top of slide, with C prefix 5 digit ser. no., from 1914-1919, Colt delivered approx. 1,000 pistols to Argentina, with the ser. no. range approx. 20001-21000.

	N/A	$3,850	$3,500	$3,150	$2,750	$2,250	$1,800

Most specimens of this model have been refinished.

RUSSIAN CONTRACT - approx. 51,000 mfg. in U.S. as commerical guns with random serial numbers approx. C23000-C89000, blue finish, identified by cyrillic inscription on left side of frame (translates to English Order). Mfg. 1916-17.

	N/A	$8,750	$4,500	$4,000	$3,250	$2,500	$2,000

Mint original specimens have been selling in the $12,500 - $15,000 range.

This contract is seldolm encountered - beware of fakes.

1911 MILITARY REWORKS - .45 ACP cal., these are pistols that the government sent back to various military arsenals for reworking, arsenals include Augusta Arsenal (AA), Springfield Armory (SA), and Rock Island Arsenal (RIA), pistols may have original parts (matching) or parts from other manufacturers (mismatched), parkerized (most common), or arsenal blue finish.

Colt Mfg.	$1,400	$1,225	$1,050	$950	$770	$625	$495
Remington UMC Mfg.	$1,800	$1,575	$1,350	$1,225	$995	$815	$625
Springfield Mfg.	$1,800	$1,575	$1,350	$1,225	$995	$815	$625

Add 15% for box and DCM papers.

Add 15% for arsenal blue finish.

Subtract 40% if mismatched.

PISTOLS: SEMI-AUTO, GOVT. MODEL 1911A1 COMMERCIAL VARIATIONS

All pistols in this section are .45 ACP cal., unless otherwise noted.

GOVERNMENT MODEL 1911A1 - commercial blue finish or parkerized, checkered walnut grips, checkered arched mainspring housing relief cuts in frame for improved trigger reach, and longer grip safety spur. As in

MSR	100%	98%	95%	90%	80%	70%	60%

the Model 1911, Colt licensed other companies to produce under govt. contract during WWII. Mfg. 1925-1970.

Most M1911A1 variations listed below are not as collectible if under 60% original condition. However, they are still very desirable as shooters, and values (if in original condition) will approximate the 60% prices if in good mechanical condition.

MODEL 1911A1 PRE-WWII COLT COMMERCIAL - "C" preceding serial number, mfg. 1925-1942. Approx. ser. no. range C138,533-C215,000.

N/A	$4,500	$3,500	$3,000	$2,500	$1,800	$1,000

Add 50% for nickel finish.

Add 20% with original box and instructions.

Add 20% for Swartz safety.

MODEL 1911A1 1946-1970 COLT COMMERCIAL - 5 in. barrel, fixed sights, "C" prefix until 1950 when changed to "C" suffix. Approx. 196,000 mfg. 1946-1970.

* ***Model 1911A1 1946-1950 Mfg.*** - "C" Prefix with serial numbers C221,000-C240,227.

N/A	$2,450	$2,150	$1,750	$1,100	$950	$700

* ***Model 1911A1 1950-1970 Mfg.*** - "C" Suffix with serial numbers 240,228C-336,169C.

N/A	$2,300	$2,050	$1,650	$1,000	$900	$700

Add 10% for nickel finish.

SUPER .38 AUTOMATIC PISTOL - identical to Govt. Model .45, except chambered for .38 Super cal., blue or nickel finish. Mfg. 1928-70.

* ***Super .38 Automatic Pistol Pre-War***

N/A	$6,000	$5,750	$3,500	$2,250	$1,700	$1,200

* ***Super .38 Automatic Pistol 2nd Model***

N/A	$2,750	$2,400	$1,800	$1,400	$1,100	$900

* ***Super .38 Automatic Pistol 3rd Model***

$2,500	$2,000	$1,800	$1,200	$900	$750	$600

* ***Super .38 Automatic Pistol 4th Model***

$2,200	$1,800	$1,600	$1,000	$800	$700	$600

* ***Super .38 Automatic Pistol CS Prefix***

$2,200	$1,800	$1,600	$1,000	$800	$700	$600

Add approx. 50% for nickel finish.

Pre-war variations are serialized below approx. 37,000.

The 2nd Model may be differentiated by noticing the heavier barrel and Rampant Colt on right side. The 3rd Model has a fat barrel with Rampant Colt on left side. The 4th Model has a thin barrel and Rampant Colt on left side.

MSR	100%	98%	95%	90%	80%	70%	60%

SUPER MATCH .38 - similar to Super .38, but hand honed action, match grade barrel, recent research indicates that 2,392 had adj. sights, 857 were supplied with fixed sights, and on 557 models the type of sights was not indicated. 4,001 mfg. 1934-1947. Examine carefully for fakes.

Buyer beware - fakes are known to exist!

The first Super Match noted is ser. no. 15550, a fixed sight model, and was shipped on Feb. 9, 1934.

The lowest serial number is 14310, and was shipped on July 10, 1934. However, two serial numbers were much lower than the expected serial number ranges. Ser. no. 2253 was shipped on June 18, 1940 and ser. no. 10312 was shipped on Sept. 25, 1935. It is unknown if these guns were roll marked Super Match, but they were noted in the Colt Records as Super Match models.

The first adj. sight Super Match is ser. no. 17091, and was shipped on Feb. 7, 1935.

The last adj. sight Super Match noted is ser. no. 35731, and was shipped on Jan. 17, 1947.

The highest ser. no. Super Match is ser. no. 35999, a fixed sight model, and was shipped on Oct. 20, 1939.

Approx. 40 were mfg. with match barrels and/or hand fitted actions, w/o mention of the Super Match markings.

Total .38 Super Match pistols recorded in the Colt shipping records is 3,961. 2,250 were noted as having adj. sight, and 831 were noted as having fixed sights.

* ***Super Match .38 Fixed sights***

N/A	$10,000	$7,500	$6,000	$4,500	$3,000	$2,000

* ***Super Match .38 Adj. sights***

N/A	$11,500	$9,000	$7,000	$5,500	$4,000	$3,000

For adj. sight values to apply, the sight must be an original factory installed Stevens sight. After market adj. sights are not applicable. Be cautious of fixed sight Super Matches converted to adj. sight. A Colt historical letter is available for this model for $100.

There were 3,909 .38 Super Matches manufactured from Feb. 16, 1934 - Jan. 17, 1947. 998 had fixed sights and 2,911 had adj. sights.

MATCH .38 AMU - .38 AMU cal. (semi-rimless .38 Spl., mfg. by Win.), this variation was mfg. by Colt from a .38 Super frame (and has .38 Super serialization) with a .38 AMU conversion kit slide, the Army took .45 frames and assembled their guns using .38 AMU kits, blue finish.

* ***Match .38 AMU Colt mfg. (unmodified)***

N/A	$3,500	$2,700	$2,200	$1,900	$1,675	$1,400

MSR	100%	98%	95%	90%	80%	70%	60%

* *Match .38 AMU Army modified*

N/A $2,250 $1,850 $1,275 $1,000 $800 $700

* *Match .38 AMU kit only*

$1,850 $1,700 $1,450 $1,150 $900 $700 $500

On this configuration, the barrel, slide, and mag. were marked ".38 AMU".

SUPER MATCH .38 MS - .38 Super cal., 1961 mfg., serial numbered 101MS - 855MS, 754 total mfg, same configuration as the .38 AMU.

$5,500 $4,500 $3,500 $2,700 $2,000 $1,500 $1,300

1968-1969 BB TRANSITIONAL - denoted by BB prefix on serial number.

$3,100 $2,750 $2,100 $1,500 $1,000 $800 $700

.45 ACP TO .22 LR CONVERSION UNIT - consists of slide assembly, barrel, bushing, floating chamber, ejector, recoil spring and guide, fitted with Stevens adj. rear sight from 1938 to 1947 and Colt Master adj. sight from 1947 to 1954.

$650 $600 $550 $425 $350 $275 $200

* *.45 ACP to .22 LR Conversion Unit U Prefix* - has "U" prefix on top of slide.

$2,000 $1,800 $1,650 $1,275 $1,050 $825 $600

* *.45 ACP to .22 LR Conversion Unit Marine Corps* - should have pre-war Marine Corps documentation.

$2,500 $2,275 $2,100 $1,925 $1,475 $1,225 $950

.22 LR TO .45 ACP CONVERSION UNIT - converted service Ace .22 to .45 ACP cal. Mfg. 1938-1942. Very rare - 112 mfg.

$6,500 $5,000 $4,000 $3,000 $2,250 $1,500 $1,100

Add 50% for original box and instructions.

These units have "U" prefixed serial numbers on top of slide. Watch for fakes!

PISTOLS: SEMI-AUTO, GOVT. MODEL 1911A1 MILITARY VARIATIONS

All pistols in this section are .45 ACP (11.25mm) cal., unless otherwise noted. Values for original 98%+ M1911A1s have risen considerably in recent years, and as a result, values for original mint guns can double and even sometimes triple the values of 98% condition. Inspect carefully for arsenal reworks (so marked by proofing, normally on left side of frame above or behind trigger), and reparkerizing.

COLT MFG. MODEL 1911A1 MILITARY - approx. 438,527 mfg. between 1924- 1945, ser. nos. 700,000 - on up, right side of frame marked "M1911A1 U.S. ARMY", bright blue finish up to approx. ser. no. 780,000, parkerized finish after that. - standard military finish (WWII mfg.).

N/A $4,500 $3,850 $2,900 $2,200 $1,500 $1,000

Add 200% for 1937 Navy (S/N 710,001 - 712,345) Blue.

MSR	100%	98%	95%	90%	80%	70%	60%

1937 Navy variations with blue finish are currently selling in the $1,000 - $7,000 range, depending on original condition.

Add 250% for 1938 Army (S/N 712,350 - 713,645) Blue.

1938 Army variations with blue finish are currently selling in the $1,500 - $9,000 range, depending on original condition.

Add 200% for 1939 Navy (S/N 713,646 - 717,281) Blue.

1939 Navy variations with blue finish are currently selling in the $1,000 - $7,000 range, depending on original condition.

Early 1911A1 military models with bright blue finish are currently selling in the $1,000 - $7,000 price range, depending on condition.

Add 150% for Blue guns outside these serial ranges.

Add 150% for 1942 Navy (S/N 793,658 - 797,639) Parkerized.

Add 25-50% for Schwartz safety variation depending on condition.

A large grouping of over 7,000 Commercial 1911A1s was transferred to the U.S. government. These pistols had their commercial serial numbers crudely removed (in ser. range 860,000 - 866,000) and re-stamped with a new military serial number. Some of these guns are unusual as the frames and slides have been cut for the Schwartz safety.

* *Model 1911A1 General Officer's Pistol*

N/A	$7,000	$6,000	$4,500	$3,500	$2,100	$1,600

Values above assume issue to a General, and there must be paperwork to link the gun to the recipient.

DRAKE NATIONAL MATCH - Drake made slides only for use by the U.S. Army Marksmanship Unit to allow assembly of match guns.

N/A	$2,000	$1,700	$1,400	$1,000	$850	$700

GOVERNMENT NATIONAL MATCH REWORKS - assembled by government armorers, all parts marked "NM", parkerized finish. Most will be "S.A." marked.

N/A	$2,000	$1,700	$1,400	$1,000	$850	$700

Add 25% for Air Force pistols marked "AFPG" on slide.

These pistols were made specifically for the U.S. shooting team at Camp Perry.

ITHACA - .45 ACP cal., 7 shot mag., 5 in. barrel, parkerized finish, approx. 369,129 mfg. 1943-1945 in Ithaca, NY, ser. no. ranges 856,405-916,404, 1,208,674-1,279,673, 1,441,431-1,471,430, 1,743,847-1,890,503, 2,075,104-2,134,403, and 2,619,014-2,693,613.

N/A	$2,200	$1,800	$1,500	$1,200	$1,100	$800

Add 20% for original shipping carton.

UNION SWITCH AND SIGNAL - approx. 55,000 mfg. 1943 only in Swissvale, PA, ser. no. range 1,041,405-1,096,404. Sandblast and blue finish.

N/A	$6,100	$5,100	$4,000	$3,300	$2,200	$1,600

MSR	100%	98%	95%	90%	80%	70%	60%

REMINGTON RAND - approx. 1,086,624 mfg. 1943-1945 in Syracuse, NY, ser. no. ranges 916,405-1,041,404, 1,279,649-1,441,430, 1,471,431-1,609,528, 1,743,847-1,816,641, 1,890,504-2,075,103, 2,134,404-2,244,803, and 2,380,014-2,619,013. Parkerized finish.

$2,500 $2,250 $2,000 $1,650 $1,200 $1,000 $900

Add 20% for original shipping carton (watch for fakes).

SINGER MFG. CO. - 500 mfg. 1941 in Elizabeth, NJ, ser. no. range S800,001-S800,500. Blue finish with plastic grips.

N/A N/A $65,000 $50,000$40,000 $32,500 $24,000

The Singer 1911A1 variation is one of the most sought-after Colt models. In recent years, values have increased significantly, and as a result, some fakes have emerged. Most specimens are now recognized by ser. no. and be very cautious when contemplating a purchase. Some collectors unsure of authenticity are now requiring X-ray testing to determine originality (slide restampings, ser. no. changes, etc.).

GENERAL OFFICER'S PISTOL (M15) - standard military finish, issued by Rock Island Arsenal to Generals.

$7,500 $6,500 $5,500 $4,000 $3,200 $2,800 $2,200

MEXICAN CONTRACT - mfg. approx. 1921-27 with "C" prefix ser. nos., frames marked "EJERCITO MEXICANO", most surviving examples show much use.

N/A $3,800 $2,900 $1,900 $1,400 $1,100 $900

BRAZILIAN CONTRACT

N/A $4,800 $3,000 $2,200 $1,700 $1,350 $1,000

ARGENTINE CONTRACT MODEL 1927 - serial numbered 1-10,000 under the mainspring housing and on the top of slide (should be matching), must have Argentine crest and "Model 1927" on right side of slide, external serial number applied to top of slide by the Argentine Arsenal, most have been Arsenal refinished.

$1,500 $1,300 $1,100 $900 $800 $600 $500

Add 75% if original finish.

ARGENTINE MFG. - in 1927, the Argentina Arsenal "DGFM-FMAP" began manufacturing the Model 1911A1. The slide marking is two lines and reads "EJERCITO ARGENTINO SIST.COLT.CAL. 11.25mm MOD.1927", these guns were made in Argentina under license from Colt, with Colt machinery, and with help from Colt engineers, and are known as Model 1927 Systema Colt.

$1,400 $1,200 $1,000 $800 $700 $600 $500

Add 50% if original finish.

Add 20% for Argentine Navy "ARMADA NACIONAL" (small shipments between 1912-1948). Markings vary on different types.

Add 30% for Air Force markings ("AERONAUTICA ARGENTINA" and winged crest).

MSR	100%	98%	95%	90%	80%	70%	60%

This variation is not to be confused with the Ballester Molina/Rigaud Models (sold by Hispano Argentino Fábrica de Automóviles S.A., in Buenos Aires, Argentina - also known as the HAFDASA). Please refer to the Hispano Argentino Fábrica de Automóviles S.A. section.

ARGENTINE SERVICE MODEL ACE - .22 LR cal., conversion of the 1927 Argentine Contract Model, bottom right side of slide is marked "TRANSE A CAL .22 POR EST. VENTURINI S.A." Originally imported during 1996, this model was arsenal refinished and most pistols were in the 70%-95% condition range.

	$1,050	$900	$700	$650	$600	$550	$525

1911A1 MILITARY REWORKS - .45 ACP cal., these are pistols that the government sent back to various military arsenals for reworking, arsenals include Augusta Arsenal (AA), Springfield Armory (SA), and Rock Island Arsenal (RIA), pistols may have original parts (matching) or parts from other manufacturers (mismatched), finish is generally parkerized, but some pistols will have original finish with arsenal markings.

Colt Mfg.	$1,400	$1,225	$1,050	$950	$775	$625	$495
Remington Mfg.	$1,200	$1,050	$900	$815	$675	$550	$425
Ithaca Mfg.	$1,200	$1,050	$900	$815	$675	$550	$425
US & S Mfg.	$1,800	$1,575	$1,350	$1,225	$995	$815	$625
Singer Mfg.	N/A	$10,000	$8,000	$6,500	$5,250	$4,000	$3,500

Add 15% for box and DCM papers.

Add 100% if arsenal marked but with original finish.

Subtract 20% for mismatched slide and frame.

PISTOLS: SEMI-AUTO, ACE MODELS, 1931-1947 MFG.

COMMERCIAL ACE - .22 LR cal., similar to Government .45 ACP, but in .22 LR cal., 4 3/4 in. barrel, blue, adj. sights, checkered walnut grips, almost 11,000 mfg. (ser. no. range 1-10,935) 1931-41 and 1947.

	N/A	$4,500	$3,500	$2,500	$2,000	$1,500	$1,200

Add 20% for original box and instructions.

SERVICE MODEL ACE - .22 LR cal., 5 in. barrel, blue or parkerized finish, similar to .45 ACP National Match except for caliber, has floating chamber to simulate .45 ACP recoil, limited mfg. 1935-1945.

	N/A	$7,500	$6,000	$4,500	$3,250	$2,500	$2,000

Add 20% for original box and instructions.

Subtract 30% for parkerized finish.

Add 25% for models shipped to the U.S. Coast Guard (short production run, rarely seen).

This variation is marked "SERVICE MODEL" on left frame, serial numbers have "SM" prefix and have ranges to approx. 13,800. Other markings such as "U.S. PROP'Y" or "R.S." (inspectors' marks) have also been observed on this model, and can add a premium if original condition is 95% or more.

MSR	100%	98%	95%	90%	80%	70%	60%

PISTOLS: SEMI-AUTO, NATIONAL MATCH MODELS - PRE-WWII

NATIONAL MATCH – .45 ACP cal., similar to Government Model, except has hand-honed action, match grade barrel, blue or nickel finish, stamped "National Match" on right side of slide. There were a total of 4,813 National Matches manufactured between Feb. 9, 1932 - Sept. 16, 1941, serial numbered C162997-C204640. 3,339 had fixed sights, and 1,474 had adj. sights.

Add 20% with original box and instructions.

The first National Match and lowest ser. no. C162997, a fixed sight model, was shipped on Jan. 7, 1932.

The last National Match, ser. no. C200288, a fixed sight model, was shipped on Feb. 22, 1942.

The highest ser. no. is C204671, an adj. sight model, and was shipped on Aug. 20, 1941.

Of the total 4,813 National Match pistols, 1,474 were noted as having adj. sights, and 3,339 were noted as having fixed sights.

There were 45 nickel National Match models, four were engraved and two were inscribed.

There were 47 engraved National Match models, four of them nickel and eight with gold inlays.

There were fifteen inscribed National Match models, two of them nickel.

* ***National Match Fixed sights***

N/A	$13,500	$11,000	$9,000	$7,000	$4,750	$3,650

* ***National Match Adj. sights***

N/A	$16,500	$14,000	$11,500	$8,750	$5,750	$3,950

For adj. sight values to apply, the sight must be an original factory installed Stevens sight. After market adj. sights are not applicable. Be cautious of fixed sight National Match models that have been converted to adj. sight.

A Colt historical letter is available for this model for $100.

PISTOLS: SEMI-AUTO, NATIONAL MATCH MODELS - WWII & POST-WWII

Add 10% for NIB condition on discontinued models listed below.

Unless noted otherwise, all National Match models listed in this section will have "National Match" stamped on the left side of the slide.

NATIONAL MATCH – .45 ACP cal., match grade barrel, royal blue finish, new design bushing, beveld barrel bushing and recoil spring plug, flat or arched (mfg. approx. 1959-64) mainspring housing, long trigger w/adj. overtravel stop, hand fitted slide with enlarged ejection port, adj. target sights, gold medallions in grips, "NM" suffix. Mfg. 1957-1970.

$3,000	$2,300	$1,700	$1,125	$800	$650	$600

Note: This model was the first Gold Cup National Match Model manufactured following WWII.

MSR	100%	98%	95%	90%	80%	70%	60%

MKII/MKIII NATIONAL MATCH MID-RANGE - .38 Spl. Mid-Range Wadcutter cal., similar to National Match, except chambered for .38 Spl. Mid-Range Wadcutter, "MR" suffix. Mfg. 1961-1971.

	$2,000	$1,600	$1,200	$1,000	$800	$700	$600

Colt had problems with the original barrels of the Gold Cup .38 Mid-Range. The MKII was the first revision (very scarce), and the MKIII was the final revision.

MKIV/SERIES 70 GOLD CUP NATIONAL MATCH - 9mm Para. (rare) or .45 ACP cal., flat mainspring housing, Colt blue finish accurizer barrel and bushing, adj. trigger, target hammer, solid rib, Colt-Elliason rear sight. Mfg. 1970-1983.

	$2,100	$1,750	$1,550	$1,050	$800	$700	$600

Add 25% for satin nickel if in 98% or better condition.

MKIV/SERIES 70 GOLD CUP 75TH ANNIVERSARY NATIONAL MATCH - similar to Gold Cup, except was mfg. as a Camp Perry commemorative, 200 mfg. 1978 only.

	$1,650	$1,400	$1,200	$1,000	$750	$650	$550

MKIV SERIES 80 GOLD CUP NATIONAL MATCH - .45 ACP cal., 5 in. barrel, flat mainspring housing, 7 or 8 shot mag., accurizer barrel and bushing, wide grooved adj. target trigger, target hammer, solid rib, Colt-Elliason rear sight, 39 oz. Mfg. 1983-1996.

	$1,200	$1,000	$850	$700	$600	$550	$500

Last MSR was $937.

In 1992, this model was updated to accept an 8 shot mag. During 1997, this updated model was designated the Gold Cup Trophy.

* ***MKIV Series 80 Stainless Gold Cup National Match*** - similar to Gold Cup, only manufactured from stainless steel, matte finish. Mfg. late 1986-1996.

	$1,100	$950	$800	$650	$600	$550	$500

Last MSR was $1,003.

Add $200 for "Ultimate" bright stainless steel finish.

Add 10% for NIB condition.

* ***Gold Cup MKIV Series 80 Elite IX Gold Cup National Match*** - 9mm Para. cal., stainless steel and blue, marked "GCNM" on right side, and "ELITE IX - 9mm Luger" on left side, "IX" prefix in ser. no. Approx. 750 mfg. in 1989.

	$2,500	$1,900	$1,500	$1,150	$900	$700	$675

Add 10% for NIB condition.

* ***Gold Cup MKIV Series 80 .38 Super Elite National Match*** - two-tone gun (stainless steel frame and blue slide), special edition by AcuSport. Mfg. 1987.

	$1,800	$1,400	$1,100	$900	$675	$550	$400

MSR	100%	98%	95%	90%	80%	70%	60%

* ***Gold Cup MKIV Series 80 .45 ACP Super Elite National Match*** - Mfg. circa 1987.

	$1,800	$1,400	$1,100	$900	$675	$550	$400

* ***Gold Cup MKIV Series 80 Bullseye National Match*** - .45 ACP cal., hand-built, tuned, and adjusted by Colt's custom gunsmiths for precise match accuracy, includes factory-installed Bo-Mar sights, equipped with carrying case and 2 extra mags. Mfg. 1991-92.

	$1,700	$1,400	$1,200	$950	$800	$700	$650

Last MSR was $1,500.

* ***Gold Cup MKIV Series 80 National Match Presentation*** - .45 ACP cal., similar to regular Gold Cup Series 80 National Match, except has a deep blue mirror bright finish accented by custom jeweled hammer, trigger, and barrel hood. Supplied with oak and velvet custom case. Mfg. 1991-92.

	$1,500	$1,200	$1,000	$900	$850	$750	$550

Last MSR was $1,195.

GOLD CUP TROPHY NATIONAL MATCH (MODEL O) - .45 ACP cal., flat mainspring housing, 7 (disc.) or 8 shot mag., accurizer barrel and bushing, flat-top slide, adj. aluminum trigger, target hammer, Bo-Mar rear sight, checkered black wrap-around rubber grips, shipped with test target, 39 oz. Mfg. 1997-2010.

	$1,200	$1,000	$800	$700	$600	$500	$450

Last MSR was $1,053.

This model replaced the MKIV/Series 80 Gold Cup National Match in 1997, and is only available from the Colt Custom Shop.

GOLD CUP NATIONAL MATCH O SERIES 70 - 9mm Para. (new 2018) or .45 ACP cal., 5 in. National Match barrel, fully adj. Bomar style rear sight, spur hammer, drilled wide target trigger, lowered and flared ejection port, rounded slide top, blue finish, wrap-around rubber grips with Colt medallions, 37 oz. New 2015.

MSR $1,299	$1,125	$995	$875	$800	$700	$600	$550

GOLD CUP NATIONAL MATCH O SERIES 80 - .45 ACP cal., 5 in. National Match barrel, features fully adj. Bomar style rear sight, spur hammer, drilled wide target trigger, lowered and flared ejection port, rounded slide top, blue finish, wrap-around rubber grips with Colt medallions, 37 oz. Mfg. 2012-mid-2015.

	$1,075	$975	$875	$800	$700	$600	$550

Last MSR was $1,217.

PISTOLS: SEMI-AUTO, CUSTOM SHOP ENGRAVING PRICING, PRE-1991

Values below represent pre-1991 factory semi-auto Custom Shop A-D engraving options, before they started separate Standard, Expert, and Master level pricing (1997). It should also be understood that, in most cases, the quality of the engraving and notoriety of the engraver can be as important as the amount of coverage. Small Frame Engraving Options: includes Mustang, .380 ACP Government, Detective Special, and Diamondback models. Medium Frame Engraving Options: includes .45 ACP Gold Cup, Government Model, Officer's ACP, Python, Combat Commander, King Cobra, Trooper MKV, Lawman MKV, and Delta Elite models. Special engraving/options include inlays, seals, custom grips, and lettering. Prices were quoted upon request. Smooth ivory grips were $215 extra (1990 retail). Beginning in 1991, Colt began shipping all models in a distinctive blue plastic carrying case/shipping container. Please refer to the "SAA & Semi-Auto Colt Custom Shop Engraving - 1976-Present" listing earlier in this section for current semi-auto engraving options and pricing. Semi-auto custom-order quotations from Colt are available at $25 each (deductible from work order).

Add $776-$969 for Class "A" Engraving (1/4 Metal Coverage) depending on frame size.

Add $959-$1,199 for Class "B" Engraving (1/2 Metal Coverage) depending on frame size.

Add $1,426-$1,783 for Class "C" Engraving (3/4 Metal Coverage) depending on frame size.

Add $1,814-$2,289 for Class "D" Engraving (Full Metal Coverage) depending on frame size.

Add 7% for 6 in. barrel, 14% for 8 in. barrel, or 25% for stainless steel construction.

PISTOLS: SEMI-AUTO, CURRENT CUSTOM SHOP ENGRAVING PRICING

The following Colt Custom Shop engraving options apply to M1911 variations only.

Add $1,130 for A Standard engraving.

Add $1,300 for B Standard, $2,075 for B Expert (signed), or $3,725 for B Master (signed) level engraving.

Add $1,700 for C Standard, $2,878 for C Expert (signed), or $5,415 for C Master (signed) level engraving.

Add $2,000 for D Standard, $4,280 for D Expert (signed), or $6,900 for D Master (signed) level engraving.

PISTOLS: SEMI-AUTO, SINGLE ACTION, RECENT/CURRENT MFG.

Factory Colt abbreviations used on its price sheets are as follows: B - blue, BPF - black powder frame, BRS - Bomar rear sights, BSTS - bright polished stainless steel, CARS - Colt adjustable rear sight, CC/B - colored case/blue, CCBS - Colt Champion Bomar style sight, CCES - Colt Champion Elliason style sights, CER - Cerakote, FDE - Flat Dark Earth, F-H - Front Heinie sight, FOA - Fiber optic front, adj. rear, FOB - Fiber Optic Front, Bomar Style Rear, FXS - fixed sights, GE - gold enhancement, HC - hard chrome, IBFDE - Ion Bond FDE finish, L/W - lightweight, M - matte black, MP - Magpul accessories, NBRFFO - Novak Black Rear Front Fiber Optic, NM - National Match, NNS - Novak Night Sights, R - accessory rail, SE - semi-automatic enhanced, STS - stainless steel, TT - Two Tone, WDS - white dot sights, WDC - white dot carry, and WDCN - white dot carry Novak sights.

Some Series 80 pistols, including Gold Cups and Defenders with slanted slide serrations, polished ejection port, and beavertail safety are more desirable than standard models without these features. See individual models for pricing.

MSR	100%	98%	95%	90%	80%	70%	60%

JUNIOR COLT POCKET MODEL - .22 S or .25 ACP cal., 2 1/4 in. barrel, blue, checkered walnut grips, made by Astra in Spain 1958-1968.

.22 Short	$375	$350	$275	$250	$200	$180	$150
.25 ACP	$350	$325	$250	$225	$175	$160	$140

Add 10% for nickel finish.

A very few conversion kits were offered for this model. They are rare and asking prices are $250-$325 if in mint condition.

COLT AUTOMATIC CALIBER .25 - .25 ACP cal., mfg. by Firearms International for Colt 1970-1973.

	$350	$325	$250	$225	$175	$160	$140

COMMANDER (PRE-70 SERIES) - 9mm Para, .38 Super, or .45 ACP cal., 4 1/4 in. barrel, full size grips, Colt alloy frame and mainspring housing. Mfg. 1950-1969.

9mm Para.	$1,850	$1,425	$1,125	$1,000	$900	$700	$600
.38 Super/.45 ACP	$1,800	$1,400	$1,125	$1,000	$900	$700	$600

Add 10% if NIB.

* ***Commander General Officer's Pistol M1969*** - there were two shipments of the M1969 pistol. One was on 3/18/1969 to the Arsenal and were serialized 327248C, 327337C, 327338C, and 327673C. The second shipment was sent to military exchange in care of Robert Tremont on 5/2/1969, and were serialized CS-001868, CS-002019, CS-002023, CS-002027, CS-02248, and CS-002770.

	$8,000	$7,500	$7,000	$6,000	$5,000	$4,000	$3,250

.38 SPECIAL/.45 ACP KIT GUNS - .38 Spl. or .45 ACP cal., left side slide marking includes either "COLT .38 SPEC. KIT", or "COLT .45 ACP KIT", these kit guns were designed to be used for competitive target shooting, and many of the guns were shipped without sights, with the buyer providing the sights of his/her choice, kit guns can be found with a myriad of various target sights. Approx. serial no. range is 00100-01164. Production began in 1964, and fewer than 400 of the .38 Spl. Kit Guns were mfg. by 1970. It is estimated that approx. 1,050 .45 ACP Kit Guns were mfg. by the end of 1970.

	$2,300	$2,000	$1,500	$1,100	$800	$650	$550

This model is also known as the Gil Hebard Model and is basically a .38 AMU.

SERIES 70 LIGHTWEIGHT COMMANDER - 7.65mm (.30 Luger), 9mm Para, .38 Super, or .45 ACP cal., 4 1/4 in. barrel, full size grips, this model is denoted by a "CLW" prefix. Mfg. 1970-83.

9mm Para.	$1,650	$1,100	$800	$700	$600	$500	$450
.38 Super/.45 ACP	$1,500	$1,000	$775	$675	$575	$500	$450
7.65mm	$2,600	$2,000	$1,575	$1,250	$995	$875	$750

Add 10% for NIB condition.

MSR	100%	98%	95%	90%	80%	70%	60%

500 Lightweight Commanders were mfg. in 7.65mm cal. during 1971. While most of these were mfg. for export trade, 5 were sold in the U.S.

SERIES 70 COMBAT COMMANDER - 9mm Para., .38 Super, or .45 ACP cal., similar to Series 70 Lightweight (LW) Commander, except has steel frame, blue or satin nickel (scarce) finish. Mfg. 1971-1980.

	$1,300	$1,125	$900	$800	$675	$610	$500

Add 10% for NIB condition.

Add 10% for satin nickel finish if in 98% condition or better.

GOVERNMENT MODEL MKIV/SERIES 70 - .45 ACP, .38 Super, 9mm Para., or 9mm Steyr cal., 5 in. barrel, checkered walnut grips/medallion. Series 70 models were serial numbered with "SM" prefixes (approx. 3,000 mfg.), "70G" prefixes 1970-76, "70L" and "70S" prefixes also (see Serialization section for more information), "G70" suffixes 1976-80, "B70" suffixes 1979-81, and "70B" prefixes 1981-83. Mfg. 1970-83.

Blue finish	$1,450	$1,200	$995	$800	$650	$525	$425
Nickel finish	$1,800	$1,550	$1,200	$900	$775	$600	$500

Add 10% if in NIB condition, 20% for NIB with early two-piece box.

Add 10% for .38 Super, 9mm Para., or 9mm Steyr cal. if in 100% condition.

Add 10% for satin nickel finish if in 98% condition or better.

9mm Steyr was made for export to Europe only. However, a few specimens have found their way into the United States. Prices for NIB specimens are in the $1,000 range.

* ***Series 70 Combat Govt.*** - .45 ACP cal., bluish-black metal finish, features modifications for combat shooting, forerunner to the Combat Elite.

	$1,400	$1,200	$1,000	$850	$775	$700	$650

Add 10% for NIB condition.

* ***Government Model MKIV/Series 70 Conversion Unit*** - converts .45 ACP to .22 LR, mfg. 1954-84 with either Accro adj. rear or fixed sight.

Adj. Sight	$600	$550	$400	$350	$300	$250	$200
Fixed Sight	$700	$600	$450	$375	$300	$250	$200

Add 50% for conversion units in bright nickel finish (very scarce). Must be accompanied by original box w/nickel label.

GOVERNMENT MODEL SERIES 70 (NEW MFG.) - .45 ACP cal., single action, patterned after the original Series 70 pistol, 5 in. barrel, spur hammer, high-profile fixed sights, checkered diamond pattern rosewood grips, arched mainspring housing, high polish blue finish, 37 oz. New 2018.

MSR $899	$775	$650	$575	$500	$450	$415	$375

1991 SERIES GOVERNMENT MODEL SERIES 70 MODEL O - .45 ACP cal., patterned after the original Series 70 pistol, 5 in. barrel, high polish blue finish, fixed sights. Mfg. from the Custom Shop 2002-2016.

	$875	$750	$650	$575	$500	$375	$325

Last MSR was $899.

MSR	100%	98%	95%	90%	80%	70%	60%

* *1991 Series Government Model Series 70 Model O Stainless* – .45 ACP cal., similar to Series 70 Model O except is stainless steel. Mfg. 2005-2016.

	$850	$725	$625	$525	$450	$395	$350

Last MSR was $979.

POST-WAR ACE SERVICE MODEL – .22 LR cal., similar specifications to previous pre-WWII manufacture, blue (most common) or electroless nickel Custom Shop finish, "SM" prefix (most common) or "B 70" suffix, approx. 30,000 mfg. between 1978-1989.

Blue finish	$2,000	$1,750	$1,250	$1,000	$650	$525	$425

Add 10% for NIB condition.

This model is serial numbered approx. SM14,001-SM43,830.

GOVERNMENT MODEL MKIV/SERIES 80 – .38 Super, 9mm Para. (disc. 1992), 9x23mm Win. (mfg. 1997 only), or .45 ACP (disc. 1996) cal., single action, 5 in. barrel, 7 or 8 (new 1992) shot mag. in .45 ACP, approx. 38 oz., firing pin safety, checkered walnut (pre-1991 mfg.) or rubber combat style grips with medallion (new 1991). Production started in 1983 with ser. no. FG01000.

* *Government Model MKIV/Series 80 Blue Finish* – this finish was disc. in 1997.

	$975	$825	$675	$600	$525	$500	$450

Last MSR was $600.

Add 10% for 9mm Para. (disc. 1992) cal.

Add 10% for NIB condition.

* *Government Model MKIV/Series 80 Nickel Finish* – .45 ACP (disc. 1986) or .38 Super (disc. in 1987) cal.

	$1,000	$775	$725	$625	$550	$500	$450

Last MSR was $735.

Add 10% for NIB condition.

* *Government Model MKIV/Series 80 Satin Nickel & Blue Finish* – with Colt-Pachmayr grips. Disc. 1986.

	$1,000	$850	$750	$650	$575	$500	$450

Last MSR was $557.

Add 10% for NIB condition.

* *Government Model MKIV/Series 80 Stainless Steel* – 9mm Para. (mfg. 1991-92), .38 Super (new 1990), .40 S&W (new 1992), or .45 ACP cal. Disc. 1998.

	$995	$875	$725	$650	$575	$525	$475

Last MSR was $813.

Add 10% for 9mm Para. (disc. 1992) cal.

Add 10% for NIB condition.

MSR	100%	98%	95%	90%	80%	70%	60%

* ***Government Model MKIV/Series 80 "Ultimate" Bright Stainless Steel*** – .38 Super (new 1991) or .45 ACP cal., high polish stainless finish. Mfg. 1986-96.

	$1,400	$1,200	$1,000	$800	$700	$625	$550

Last MSR was $863.

Add 10% for NIB condition.

* ***Government Model MKIV/Series 80 Limited Class Model .45 ACP*** – .45 ACP cal., designed for tactical competition, includes parkerized matte finish, lightweight composite trigger, ambidextrous safety, upswept beavertail grip safety, beveled magwell, accurized, includes signed target. Mfg. 1994-97.

	$1,000	$850	$750	$650	$575	$500	$450

Last MSR was $936.

* ***Government Model MKIV/Series 80 Custom Compensated Model .45 ACP*** – .45 ACP cal., designed for serious competitive shooting, blue slide with full profile BAT Compensator, Bo-Mar rear sight, flared funnel magwell. Mfg. by Custom Shop 1994-98.

	$2,000	$1,600	$1,350	$1,100	$975	$850	$725

Last MSR was $2,428.

MODEL M1911A1 CUSTOM TACTICAL GOV'T - LEVEL I – .45 ACP cal., designed for tactical competition, Commander style hammer, beveled/contoured magwell, nylon flat mainspring housing, ambidextrous safety, long nylon trigger with overtravel stop, available in Officer's or Commmander's length. Mfg. 1998-2001.

	$995	$900	$800	$600	$525	$450	$400

Last MSR was $730.

In late 1999, this model was redesignated the Model O Custom Tactical Gov't.

* ***Model M1911A1 Custom Tactical Gov't. Model - Level II*** – similar to Level I, except has Videcki long aluminum trigger with overtravel stop, Heinie fixed combat sights, Colt match grade barrel bushing, high-ride grip safety with palm swell, double diamond stocks. Mfg. 1998-2001.

	$1,100	$950	$825	$625	$550	$475	$425

Last MSR was $935.

* ***Model M1911A1 Custom Tactical Gov't. Model - Level III*** – similar to Level II, except has Bo-Mar adj. rear sight, super match hammer. Mfg. 1998-2001.

	$1,250	$995	$875	$675	$595	$525	$450

Last MSR was $1,350.

COMBAT GOVERNMENT SERIES 80 – .45 ACP cal., dark matte metal finish, features modifications for combat shooting, successor to the Series 70 Combat Govt. Mfg. 1983-1998.

	$950	$800	$650	$550	$475	$450	$400

Add 10% for NIB condition.

MSR	100%	98%	95%	90%	80%	70%	60%

* ***Combat Elite Series 80*** – .38 Super or .45 ACP cal., similar to Gold Cup, only with wraparound rubber grips, beveled magwell, stainless steel frame with carbon steel slide, and Accro adj. sighting system. Mfg. 1986-1996.

	$1,300	$1,100	$875	$750	$575	$525	$450

Last MSR was $895.

Note: Colt has issued a factory recall on the safety for this model sold after March 2007 in the following ser. no. range: CG10000E-CG11293E. These pistols must be returned to Colt's factory for part(s) replacement.

COMBAT GOVERNMENT SERIES 80 CONVERSION UNIT – converts Series 80 Govt. Model only to .22 LR or 9mm Para., mfg. 1984-86, 1995, and 1998, with Accro adj. rear sight.

9mm Para.	$725	$650	$500	$400	$325	$250	$200
.22 LR (mfg. 1984-86)	$750	$650	$500	$400	$325	$250	$200
.22 LR (mfg. 1995, rare)	$775	$675	$525	$425	$325	$250	$200

Last MSR was $305 for .22 LR (mfg. 1984-86).

* ***Colt Ace II Conversion Unit*** – similar to above, except features an aluminum slide and barrel w/o floating chamber, does not have hold open feature. Mfg. 1998.

	$350	$295	$275	$225	$190	$175	$150

COMBAT TARGET MODEL SERIES 80 – .45 ACP cal. only, 5 in. barrel, adj. sights, matte finish. Mfg. 1997 only.

	$1,000	$875	$750	$650	$450	$425	$400

Last MSR was $768.

* ***Combat Target Model Stainless Series 80*** – similar to Combat Target Model, except stainless steel finish. Mfg. 1997 only.

	$995	$900	$800	$650	$525	$450	$400

Last MSR was $820.

SPECIAL COMBAT GOVERNMENT MODEL O (COMPETITION SERIES 80) – .38 Super (mfg. 2005-2017) or .45 ACP cal., competition model, blue (disc.), two-tone (new 2004), or hard chrome (disc. 2017) slide and frame, 5 in. throated barrel, supplied with two 8 shot mags., flared magwell, flared ejection port, cut-out hammer, skeletonized trigger, Bo-Mar rear and Clark dovetail front sight, custom tuning, polished ramp, shipped with certified target. Mfg. by the Custom Shop. New 1992.

MSR $2,199	$1,925	$1,700	$1,450	$1,300	$1,100	$900	$700

SPECIAL COMBAT GOVERNMENT CARRY MODEL O (SERIES 80) – .45 ACP cal., 5 in. throated barrel, flared ejection port, skeletonized trigger, custom tuning, blue or royal blue (disc.), hard chrome (disc.), or two-tone (disc.) finish, bar-dot-bar (disc. 2000) or Novak (new 2009) night sights, and ambidextrous safety. Mfg. 1992-2000, reintroduced 2009.

MSR $2,099	$1,775	$1,450	$1,125	$950	$775	$675	$575

MSR	100%	98%	95%	90%	80%	70%	60%

SPECIAL COMBAT GOVERNMENT CMC MARINE MODEL O - .45 ACP cal., full size with 5 in. National Match stainless steel barrel, front and rear slide serrations, features Desert Tan cerakote finish, stainless steel frame and slide, Novak night sights with Trijicon inserts, serrated grip straps with lanyard loop, aluminum trigger, unique patterned grips, G10 composite grips, lower Picatinny rail, includes Pelican case with two 7 shot mags, cleaning kit, and test target. Mfg. for United States Marine Corps by the Custom Shop, limited civilian availability. Mfg. 2013-2015.

	$2,600	$2,100	$1,750	$1,200	$775	$675	$575

Last MSR was $2,149.

SPECIAL COMBAT GOVERNMENT - .45 ACP cal., 5 in., 8 shot, 3-hole aluminum trigger, Bomar adj. rear sight, Novak front sight, lowered and flared ejection port, 38 1/2 oz. Mfg. 2017 only.

	$1,850	$1,650	$1,450	$1,300	$1,100	$900	$700

Last MSR was $2,099.

LIGHTWEIGHT COMMANDER - 9mm Para. (disc. 2018) or .45 ACP cal., 4 1/4 in. barrel, 8 or 9 (disc. 2018) shot, dual spring recoil system, black anodized aluminum receiver, blued carbon steel slide, vertical front strap serrations, white dot carry Novak sights, undercut trigger guard, upswept beavertail grip safety, custom Colt logo Black Cherry G10 grips, 29.4 oz. New 2016.

MSR $999	$850	$700	$575	$475	$425	$400	$375

COMMANDER LIGHTWEIGHT SERIES 80 - 9mm Para, .38 Super, or .45 ACP cal., 4 1/4 in. barrel, similar to Government Model, except shorter and lighter alloy frame, fixed sights, round spur hammer, 27 1/2 oz. Mfg. 1983-97.

	$1,050	$800	$650	$575	$525	$475	$450

Last MSR was $735.

Add 10% for .38 Super or 9mm Para. (disc.) cals.

Some pistols are marked "Super Lite Commander - .38 Super - " on left side, and "Lightweight Commander Model" on right side. There may be an "M" on magazine floorplate, with the Colt logo.

COMBAT COMMANDER SERIES 80 - .38 Super (disc.), 9mm Para. (disc. 1992), or .45 ACP cal., similar to Lightweight, except has steel frame.

* ***Combat Commander Series 80 Blue Finish*** - disc. 1996.

	$1,050	$800	$650	$500	$450	$425	$400

Last MSR was $735.

Add 10% for 9mm Para. (disc.) or .38 Super (disc.) cal.

* ***Combat Commander Series 80 Blue Slide/Stainless Steel Receiver*** - .45 ACP cal., two-tone matte finish, upswept grip safety, lightweight perforated trigger, black Hogue grips, 8 shot mag., 35 oz. Mfg. 1998 only.

	$800	$650	$550	$525	$500	$475	$450

Last MSR was $813.

MSR	100%	98%	95%	90%	80%	70%	60%

* *Combat Commander Series 80 Stainless Steel* - .38 Super (mfg. 1992-97) or .45 ACP cal. Mfg. 1990-98.

	$850	$675	$550	$475	$450	$425	$400

Last MSR was $813.

* *Combat Commander Series 80 Satin Nickel* - disc. 1986.

	$975	$800	$675	$625	$575	$550	$475

Last MSR was $550.

* *Combat Commander Series 80 Gold Cup Commander* - .45 ACP cal., features custom shop alterations including heavy duty adj. target sights, beveled magwell, serrated front strap, checkered mainspring housing, wide grip safety, and Palo Alto wood grips. Mfg. 1991-93.

	$2,000	$1,750	$1,400	$1,050	$825	$700	$600

Last MSR was $936.

* *Combat Commander Series 80 Gold Cup Commander Stainless* - stainless variation of the Gold Cup Commander. Mfg. 1992-disc.

	$2,000	$1,750	$1,400	$1,050	$825	$700	$600

Last MSR was $949

COMMANDING OFFICER'S LIGHTWEIGHT - 9mm Para. cal., 3 1/2 in. barrel, Officer slide, lightweight commander frame, three-dot sights, Officer's Model extended grip safety, round combat commander hammer, matte black finish, black pebble rubber grips with gold medallions, 500 mfg. by the Custom Shop.

	$1,395	$1,075	$825	$700	$575	$500	$450

COMPETITION PISTOL - 9mm Para. (disc. 2018), .38 Super (limited mfg.), or .45 ACP cal., full size Government model, 5 in. National Match barrel, 8 or 9 shot, dual spring recoil system, Novak adj. rear and fiber optic front sights, undercut trigger guard, upswept beavertail grip safety, custom blue Colt logo G10 grips, 36 oz. New 2016.

MSR $949	$815	$675	$600	$500	$450	$400	$350

Add $50 for .38 Super cal. (disc.).

* *Competition Pistol Stainless Steel* - 9mm Para., .38 Super, or .45 ACP cal., full size Government model, 5 in. National Match barrel, 8 or 9 shot, stainless steel construction, undercut trigger guard, Novak adj. rear and fiber optic front sights, G10 checkered blue grips, upswept beavertail grip safety became available in 2018 (not available in 38 Super cal.), dual spring recoil system, stainless steel or blue titanium finish, 36 oz. New 2016.

MSR $999	$850	$750	$650	$575	$525	$500	$465

Add $50 for .38 Super cal.

CONCEALED CARRY GOLD CUP COMMANDER - .45 ACP cal., 4 1/4 in. barrel, stainless steel with hard chrome finish, gold cup features including adj. sights, trigger, and match barrel, rosewood grips, designed by Joe Pittenger for the Colt Custom Shop during 2001. 15 pistols were mfg. with serial numbers CC001JP-CC015JP. Mfg. 2001 only.

	$2,700	$2,200	$1,850	$1,500	$900	$750	$650

MSR	100%	98%	95%	90%	80%	70%	60%

OFFICER'S ACP MODEL SERIES 80 - .45 ACP cal. only, 3 1/2 in. barrel, 34 oz., 6 shot mag., short version of the Government Model. Mfg. 1985-disc.

* ***Officer's ACP Model Series 80 Blue Finish*** - disc. 1996.

	$850	$700	$600	$500	$400	$350	$300

Last MSR was $735.

* ***Officer's ACP Model Series 80 Matte Blue Finish*** - disc. 1991.

	$850	$750	$650	$550	$450	$425	$400

Last MSR was $625.

* ***Officer's ACP Model Series 80 Stainless Steel*** - matte stainless steel finish. Mfg. 1986-97.

	$850	$750	$650	$550	$450	$425	$400

Last MSR was $813.

Add $200 for "Ultimate" bright stainless steel finish (mfg. 1987-1996).

* ***Officer's ACP Model Series 80 Lightweight*** - similar to Officer's ACP, except has alloy frame and weighs 24 oz. Mfg. 1985-1997.

	$900	$800	$700	$600	$500	$475	$425

Last MSR was $735.

* ***Officer's ACP Model Series 80 Concealed Carry*** - .45 ACP cal., features matte stainless steel slide with matte blue aluminum alloy receiver, 7 shot mag., black contoured Hogue grips, upswept beavertail grip safety, lightweight perforated trigger, 26 oz. Mfg. 1998 only.

	$1,200	$1,000	$800	$700	$500	$450	$400

Last MSR was $813.

* ***Officer's ACP Model Series 80 Satin Nickel*** - disc. 1985.

	$950	$850	$750	$650	$550	$500	$450

Last MSR was $513.

* ***General Officer's ACP Model Series 80*** - bright stainless steel with rosewood grips, special edition. Disc. 1996.

	$1,750	$1,500	$1,250	$900	$675	$550	$425

Last MSR was $750.

DEFENDER SERIES MODEL O - 9mm Para., .40 S&W (mfg. 1999 only) or .45 ACP cal., 3 in. barrel with 3-dot (disc.) or white dot carry Novak sights, 7 shot mag., rubber wrap-around grips with finger grooves, lightweight perforated trigger, blue or stainless steel slide and frame - frame finished in matte stainless, firing pin safety, 22 1/2 oz. New 1998.

MSR $999	$875	$695	$575	$475	$425	$375	$325

Note: Colt has issued a factory recall on the safety for this model sold after March 2007 in the following ser. no. range: DR33036 - DR35948 X. Colt will send you a new recoil spring assembly kit that includes the Guide Pad to replace in your pistol.

MSR	100%	98%	95%	90%	80%	70%	60%

DEFENDER PLUS - .45 ACP cal., similar to Defender Model O, except has aluminum frame and 8 shot mag. Mfg. 2002-2003.

	$875	$775	$700	$625	$575	$550	$475

Last MSR was $876.

COLT CONCEALED CARRY - .45 ACP cal., 3 in. barrel, aluminum frame with steel slide, Series 80 firing pin safety system, checkered double diamond walnut grips, front strap serrations, 25 oz. Mfg. 2007.

	$800	$725	$650	$575	$500	$450	$400

Last MSR was $885.

XSE (XS) SERIES MODEL O - .45 ACP cal., 4 1/4 or 5 in. barrel, stainless brushed finish, front and rear slide serrations, checkered double diamond rosewood grips, 3-dot (disc.) or white dot carry Novak sights, new roll marking and enhanced tolerances, extended ambidextrous thumb safeties. New 2000.

* ***XSE Series Model O Government*** - 9mm Para. (new 2015) or .45 ACP cal., 5 in. barrel, blue (new 2002) or stainless brushed (SS Model) finish, 8 shot mag., 36 oz. Disc. mid-2015.

	$925	$775	$675	$575	$475	$400	$350

Last MSR was $1,104.

* ***XSE Series Model O Lightweight Government*** - .45 ACP cal., 5 in. barrel, features lightweight aluminum alloy frame, blue finish, carbon steel slide, 8 shot mag., 27 oz. Mfg. 2012-mid 2015.

	$925	$775	$675	$575	$475	$400	$350

Last MSR was $1,104.

* ***XSE Series Model O Combat Elite*** - .45 ACP cal., 5 in. barrel, two-tone finish (brushed stainless steel receiver/blued carbon steel slide), 8 shot, combat hammer with elongated slot, white dot carry Novak sights, skeletonized trigger, checkered rosewood grips with Colt logo. Mfg. 2009-2017.

	$935	$795	$675	$575	$475	$425	$375

Last MSR was $1,099.

Note: Colt has issued a recall for ser. nos. CG10000E - CG11293E X due to a problem with the safety and/or guide pad. Improper hardness may cause the safety or guide pad to crack and might not prevent the gun from an accidental firing. Please contact Colt directly if you have one of the pistols - recall@colt.com.

* ***XSE Series Model O Concealed Carry Officers SS*** - features lightweight aluminum alloy frame, 4 1/4 in. barrel and 7 shot mag. Limited mfg. 2000 only.

	$1,000	$900	$700	$600	$500	$450	$400

Last MSR was $750.

MSR	100%	98%	95%	90%	80%	70%	60%

* ***XSE Series Model O Commander SS*** - .45 ACP cal., features 4 1/4 in. barrel, 8 shot mag., brushed stainless steel receiver and slide, 33 1/2 oz. Disc. mid-2015.

	$925	$775	$675	$575	$475	$400	$350

Last MSR was $1,104.

* ***XSE (XS) Series Model O Lightweight Commander SS*** - .38 Super (disc. 2011), 9mm Para. (new 2015), or .45 ACP cal., features lightweight aluminum alloy frame, 4 1/4 in. barrel, brushed stainless steel slide, cerakote, 8 shot mag., 27 oz. Disc. mid-2015.

	$925	$775	$675	$575	$475	$400	$350

Last MSR was $1,104.

Early production first series XS Series Lightweight Commander pistols manufactured during 2000 became the XSE Series Lightweight Commander SS pistols during 2001.

RAIL GUN SERIES MODEL O - 9mm Para. (mfg. 2016-2017) or .45 ACP cal., dual recoil spring system, 5 in. National Match stainless steel barrel, 8 or 9 (disc. 2017) shot mag., 3-hole aluminum trigger, Novak white dot sights, diamond checkered rosewood grips, upswept beavertail grip safety, Series 80 firing pin safety, Picatinny rail underneath frame in front of trigger guard, wide slide serrations, stainless, two-tone (disc.), or Cerakote (mfg. 2011-2016) finish, 40 oz. Mfg. 2009-2018.

	$1,025	$895	$725	$625	$525	$450	$395

Last MSR was $1,199.

Add $50 for Cerakote finish (mfg. 2011-2016).

* ***Rail Gun Model O Cerakote Stainless*** - .45 ACP cal., 5 in. barrel, 7 shot mag., Desert Tan Cerakote finish, includes blue plastic pistol case. Mfg. 2015-2016.

	$1,475	$1,225	$1,025	$875	$775	$675	$575

Last MSR was $1,699.

* ***Rail Gun M45A1 Close Quarter Battle*** - .45 ACP cal., 5 in. barrel, 7 shot mag., IonBond FDE finish, night sights, includes blue plastic pistol case. New 2017.

MSR $1,699	$1,475	$1,225	$1,025	$875	$775	$675	$575

* ***Rail Gun Model O Commander Stainless Steel*** - .45 ACP cal., features 4 1/4 in. barrel, 8 shot mag., brushed stainless steel receiver and slide, features Picatinny rail in front of trigger guard, 33 1/2 oz. Limited mfg. 2015 only.

	$1,025	$895	$725	$625	$525	$450	$395

Last MSR was $1,198.

* ***Rail Gun Model O Lightweight Commander Stainless Steel*** - .45 ACP cal., features 4 1/4 in. barrel, 8 shot mag., black anodized frame with blue steel slide, diamond patterned checkered walnut grips, features Picatinny rail in front of trigger guard and skeletonized trigger, 33 1/2 oz. Limited mfg. 2015 only.

	$1,025	$895	$725	$625	$525	$450	$395

Last MSR was $1,198.

MSR	100%	98%	95%	90%	80%	70%	60%

* ***Rail Gun Model O Lightweight*** - .45 ACP cal., 5 in. barrel, 8 shot mag., black anodized frame with blue steel slide, diamond patterned checkered walnut grips, features Picatinny rail in front of trigger guard and skeletonized trigger, 33 1/2 oz. Limited mfg. 2015 only.

	$1,025	$895	$725	$625	$525	$450	$395

Last MSR was $1,198.

COMBAT UNIT RAIL GUN - 9mm Para. or .45 ACP cal., 5 in. National Match barrel, 8 or 9 shot, blackened stainless steel receiver and slide, undercut trigger guard, Novak night sights, custom Gray Colt logo G10 grips, upswept beavertail grip safety, dual spring recoil system, checkered front strap, 40 oz. Limited mfg. 2016 only.

	$1,295	$1,050	$900	$775	$650	$550	$450

Last MSR was $1,499.

GOLD CUP NATIONAL MATCH MKIV/SERIES 80/MODEL O - please refer to the listings for Gold Cup National Match models under Pistols: Semi-Auto, National Match Models - WWII and Post-WWII.

GOLD CUP TROPHY STAINLESS - 9mm Para. (new 2018), .38 Super (new 2019), or .45 ACP cal., stainless steel, 5 in. barrel, Bomar style sights, round top slide and wraparound black synthetic grips, matte finish, 39 oz. New 1997.

MSR $1,699	$1,495	$1,275	$1,050	$875	$650	$475	$375

Add $50 for .38 Super cal.

GOVERNMENT 1911A1 GOLD CUP ACE .22 LR CAL. - .22 LR cal., 5 in. barrel, SA, fully adj. rear sight, w/o rail, 12 shot mag. only, Commander-style hammer, black checkered rubber wrap-around grips with diamond patterns, black anodized zinc alloy finish, manual and beavertail grip safeties, checkered front grip strap, skeleton trigger, 36 oz. Mfg. by Umarex GmbH in Germany under license from Colt beginning 2012, and currently distributed by Walther Arms.

MSR $499	$425	$365	$325	$295	$260	$230	$200

GOVERNMENT MODEL O (1991 SERIES/MKIV SERIES 80) - 9mm Para. (disc. 2001, reintroduced 2015-2016) or .45 ACP cal., 5 in. barrel, similar to original WWII issue pistols with government issue parkerized matte (disc.) or blue finish, fixed sights, checkered rosewood double diamond wood (blue only) or checkered black composite grips, 7 shot mag., early guns were marked Colt M1991A1 on left side of slide, 38 oz., includes brown molded case. New 1991.

MSR $799	$725	$600	$500	$400	$350	$325	$295

Add $93 for Custom Government Model in .45 ACP cal. with blue steel and low profile combat sights (mfg. 2013 only).

Add 15% for 9mm Para. cal.

This model is serialized consecutively with the last batch of Govt. military models manufactured during 1945.

MSR	100%	98%	95%	90%	80%	70%	60%

* ***Government Model O Stainless Steel (1991 Series)*** – .45 ACP or 9mm Para. cal., 5 in. barrel, matte stainless steel frame and slide, black checkered grips, white dot sights. Mfg. 1996-2016.

	$750	$650	$550	$450	$395	$350	$325

Last MSR was $879.

GOVERNMENT MODEL O (1991 SERIES) – .38 Super cal., 5 in. barrel, M1911 (bright stainless only) or M1911A1 style frame, Govt. Model, blue, 3-dot sights, checkered rubber or double diamond walnut (bright stainless only) grips, 9 shot mag., beveled magwell. Mfg. 2003-2009, reintroduced 2011-2016.

	$850	$725	$625	$550	$495	$450	$350

Last MSR was $849.

* ***Government Model O .38 Super Stainless*** – similar to Government Model O .38 Super, except is available in stainless steel. Disc. 2009, reintroduced mid-2015-2016.

	$925	$825	$700	$600	$425	$400	$375

Last MSR was $929.

* ***Government Model O Super Bright Stainless*** – .38 Super or .45 ACP (new 2018) cal., bright polished stainless steel only. Mfg. by Colt Custom Shop. New 2003.

MSR $1,549	$1,500	$1,350	$1,100	$900	$650	$550	$450

Subtract $50 for .45 ACP cal.

CQB GOVERNMENT MODEL O – .45 ACP cal., 5 in. National Match barrel, 8 shot mag., stainless steel construction with grey Cerakote frame finish and black Cerakote slide finish or FDE Cerakote frame and black DLC slide finish (new 2019), custom tune trigger, Novak low mount carry night sights, G10 grips, lower Picatinny rail, dual recoil spring system, 42 oz.

MSR $2,199	$1,925	$1,700	$1,450	$1,300	$1,100	$900	$700

CUSTOM COMPETITION O SERIES – .45 ACP cal., 5 in. National Match target barrel, 8 shot mag., fully blended magwell, stainless steel construction w/grey Cerakote frame finish and black Cerakote slide finish, competition trigger, green fiber optic front sight, adj. Bomar style rear sights, gray/black G10 grips, front and rear slide serrations, 25 LPI front strap checkering, 42. oz. New 2018.

MSR $2,499	$2,175	$1,875	$1,550	$1,300	$1,125	$925	$750

COMBAT COMMANDER MODEL O (1991 SERIES COMMANDER/ MKIV SERIES 80) – 9mm Para. (disc., reintroduced 2015) or .45 ACP cal., 4 1/4 in. barrel, full size grip, 7 shot mag., parkerized finish, blued carbon steel receiver and slide, 36 oz. Mfg. 1993-2005, reintroduced 2007.

MSR $999	$850	$700	$575	$475	$425	$400	$375

MSR	100%	98%	95%	90%	80%	70%	60%

» ***Combat Commander Stainless Steel (1991 Series Commander SS)*** – .45 ACP cal., similar to Combat Commander Model O, except is stainless steel. Mfg. 1999-2005, reintroduced 2007-2016.

	$800	$675	$550	$475	$425	$400	$375

Last MSR was $929.

COMBAT ELITE COMMANDER – 9mm Para. or .45 ACP cal., steel Commander frame, 4 1/4 in. barrel, 9 shot mag., Novak night sights, G10 half checkered black grips with scallop, Series 80 upswept beavertail grip safety, 25 LPI checkering, Two-Tone Elite (stainless steel and black) finish. New late 2018.

MSR $1,399	$1,200	$1,050	$925	$825	$725	$625	$525

COMBAT ELITE DEFENDER – 9mm Para. or .45 ACP cal., stainless steel frame and slide, 3 in. barrel, 7 shot mag., Novak night sights, G10 half checkered black grips with scallop, Series 80 upswept beavertail grip safety, 25 LPI checkering, polished slide flats, Two-Tone (stainless steel and black) Elite finish. New late 2018.

MSR $1,399	$1,200	$1,050	$925	$825	$725	$625	$525

COMBAT ELITE GOVERNMENT – 9mm Para. or .45 ACP cal., steel frame, 5 in. National Match barrel, 7 shot mag., Novak night sights, G10 half checkered black grips with scallop, Series 80 upswept beavertail grip safety, 25 LPI checkering, dual recoil spring system, Two-Tone (stainless steel and black) Elite finish. New late 2018.

MSR $1,399	$1,200	$1,050	$925	$825	$725	$625	$525

1991 SERIES OFFICER'S COMPACT (MKIV SERIES 80) – similar to Model M1991 Commander, except has 3 1/2 in. barrel, 6 shot mag., 34 oz. Mfg. 1992-1999.

	$600	$500	$425	$400	$375	$350	$325

Last MSR was $556.

» ***1991 Series Officer's Stainless Compact*** – similar to Model M1991A1 Officer's Compact, except is stainless steel. Mfg. 1999 only.

	$800	$725	$650	$500	$475	$450	$400

Last MSR was $610.

NEW AGENT SA MODEL O – 9mm Para. (disc. 2012) or .45 ACP cal., 3 in. barrel, Series 80 firing pin safety system, hammerless, 7 shot mag., double diamond slim fit or Crimson Trace (new 2012) grips, black anodized aluminum frame, blue finish, beveled magwell, skeletonized trigger, snag free trench style sights, front strap serrations, captive recoil spring system. Mfg. 2008-mid-2015.

	$925	$795	$650	$550	$450	$400	$350

Last MSR was $1,078.

Add $288 for Crimson Trace Lasergrips (new 2012).

Add 10% for 9mm Para. cal. (disc. 2012).

MSR	100%	98%	95%	90%	80%	70%	60%

Note: Colt has issued a factory recall on the safety for this model sold after March 2007 in the following ser. no. range: GT01001-GT04505 XX. These pistols must be returned to Colt's factory for part(s) replacement.

GUNSITE MODEL O - .45 ACP cal., M1911 style frame, Series 70 firing pin safety system, 4 1/4 (Commander configuration) or 5 in. barrel, checkered thin rosewood grips, blue or stainless steel, many shooting features are included, such as serrated flat mainspring housing, Gold Cup front strap serrations, Heinie front and Novak rear sights, two 8 shot Wilson mags., McCormick hammer and sear, slide marked with Gunsite logo. Mfg. 2003-2005.

	$1,300	$1,100	$900	$775	$700	$625	$575

Last MSR was $1,400.

M1911 MODEL O SERIES 70 - .45 ACP cal., 5 in. barrel, accurate reproduction of the Model 1911 U.S. military sidearm, original style checkered walnut grips, carbonia blue finish, 7 shot mag., original WWI roll marks, original style packaging (cardboard box with wax paper), 4,400 were scheduled for mfg. by the Custom Shop, 38 oz. Mfg. 2003-2009.

	$1,600	$1,250	$900	$750	$575	$475	$425

Last MSR was $990.

Note: Colt has issued a recall for ser. nos. 4597WMK - 5414WMK X due to a problem with the safety and/or guide pad. Improper hardness may cause the safety or guide pad to crack and might not prevent the gun from an accidental firing. Please contact Colt directly if you have one of the pistols - recall@colt.com.

M1911A1 WWII REPLICA MODEL O - .45 ACP cal., 5 in. barrel, incorporates pre-Series 70 firing pin safety system, accurate reproduction of the Model 1911A1 U.S. military sidearm, original style composite grips, parkerized finish or stainless steel construction, 7 shot mag., original WWII roll marks, lanyard loop on arched serrated mainspring housing, wide spur hammer, safety and slide stop with original serrations, 38 oz., original style packaging (cardboard box with wax paper), approx. 4,000 mfg. by the Custom Shop. Mfg. 2001-2004.

	$1,600	$1,250	$900	$750	$575	$500	$450

Last MSR was $940.

Colt has issued a factory recall on the safety for this model sold after March 2007 in the following ser. no. range: 4597WMK-5414WMK. These pistols must be returned to Colt's factory for part(s) replacement.

MSR	100%	98%	95%	90%	80%	70%	60%

M1911 SERIES 70 WWI MODEL 1918 REPLICA - .45 ACP cal., 5 in. barrel, accurate reproduction of the Model 1911 U.S. military sidearm manufactured during 1918, featuring black finish, original WWI roll marks, limited mfg. by the Custom Shop. Mfg. 2008-2009.

	$1,400	$1,100	$950	$825	$600	$525	$450

Last MSR was $990.

Colt also offered this model in a Presentation Grade with blue or nickel finish and unsigned A engraving coverage - MSRs ranged from $2,278 - $2,378.

Note: Colt has issued a factory recall on the safety for this model sold after March 2007 in the following ser. no. range: 1001WW1-3431WW1X. These pistols must be returned to Colt's factory for part(s) replacement.

GOVERNMENT MODEL 1911A1 .22 CAL. - .22 LR cal., patterned after the Colt Post War Ace Service Model, features 5 in. barrel, checkered diamond patterned rubber grips, half-cock mechanism, all steel construction, 10 or 12 shot mag., standard 1911A1 model with removable front and drift adj. rear sight, single slide serrations, 36 oz. Mfg. by Umarex in Germany beginning 2011 and distributed by Walther Arms.

MSR $399	$350	$300	$265	$225	$200	$185	$175

This model is also available in a Gold Cup variation - please refer to the listing in the Pistols: Semi-Auto, National Match Models - WWII & Post-WWII category.

GOVERNMENT MODEL 1911A1 .22 CAL. RAIL GUN - .22 LR cal., similar to Government Model 1911 .22 cal., except has lower Picatinny rail on frame, double slide serrations, skeleton trigger, low mount 3-dot combat style sights, beavertail grip safety and Commander style hammer, black or FDE (new 2013) finish, 36 oz. Mfg. by Umarex in Germany beginning 2011 and imported/distributed by Walther Arms.

MSR $449	$385	$325	$285	$240	$215	$195	$185

Add $50 for FDE finish (new 2013).

This model is also available in a Gold Cup variation - please refer to the listing in the Pistols: Semi-Auto, National Match Models - WWII & Post-WWII category.

M1911ANVII 100th ANNIVERSARY - .45 ACP cal., features 100th Anniversary of the M1911 with gold accents including slide banners, "Colt" and prancing stallion on rear sides of slide, royal blue metal finish, smooth cocobolo grips with 100th Anniversary gold plated medallions, includes walnut display case, serial numbers beginning with 19110001. 750 mfg. 2011 only.

	$2,150	$1,775	$1,525	N/A	N/A	N/A	N/A

Last MSR was $2,295.

MSR	100%	98%	95%	90%	80%	70%	60%

M1911ANVIII 100th ANNIVERSARY - .45 ACP cal., based on Colt 1911A1 mfg. in 1918, custom military roll marks on frame and slide, brushed blue finish, walnut double diamond grips, special edition 100th Anniversary packaging, serialization begins with 00011911. Mfg. limited to all orders placed by Nov. 30, 2011.

$1,300 $1,150 $900 N/A N/A N/A N/A

Last MSR was $1,150.

M1911 100th ANNIVERSARY CUSTOM SHOP - .45 ACP cal., 4 variations featuring either A, B, C, or D coverage standard engraving, gold inlayed serial number and "1911-2011" on slide, blue finish. 100 mfg. total in all four engraving patterns, mfg. 2011 only.

* ***M1911 100th Anniversary Custom Shop w/A Engraving*** - .45 ACP cal., featuring Custom Shop A coverage standard engraving. Mfg. 2011 only.

$2,450 $2,100 $1,750 N/A N/A N/A N/A

Last MSR was $2,640.

* ***M1911 100th Anniversary Custom Shop w/B Engraving*** - .45 ACP cal., featuring Custom Shop B coverage standard engraving. Mfg. 2011 only.

$2,675 $2,275 $1,875 N/A N/A N/A N/A

Last MSR was $2,900.

* ***M1911 100th Anniversary Custom Shop w/C Engraving*** - .45 ACP cal., featuring Custom Shop C coverage standard engraving. Mfg. 2011 only.

$2,995 $2,550 $2,100 N/A N/A N/A N/A

Last MSR was $3,265.

* ***M1911 100th Anniversary Custom Shop w/D Engraving*** - .45 ACP cal., featuring Custom Shop D coverage standard engraving. Mfg. 2011 only.

$3,200 $2,875 $2,475 N/A N/A N/A N/A

Last MSR was $3,535.

DELTA ELITE (1987-1996 MFG.) - 10mm cal., 5 in. barrel, black neoprene grips, high profile 3-dot sights, blue finish, 8 shot mag., 38 oz. Mfg. 1987-96.

$925 $750 $625 $600 $500 $475 $450

Last MSR was $807.

* ***Delta Elite First Edition (1991 Mfg.)*** - features laser engraving with gold-fill, smooth wood grips, includes presentation case. 500 mfg. 1991 only.

$1,050 $850 $675 $625 $525 $500 $450

* ***Delta Elite Stainless Steel*** - matte stainless steel finish. Mfg. 1989-96.

$925 $725 $625 $600 $575 $550 $525

Last MSR was $860.

Add $78 for "Ultimate" brite stainless steel finish (disc. 1993).

* ***Delta Elite First Edition (1988 Mfg.)*** - features stamped lettering on slide, ebony grips, and do not have display case. 1,000 mfg. 1988 only.

$1,150 $900 $725 $650 $550 $500 $450

MSR	100%	98%	95%	90%	80%	70%	60%

DELTA ELITE - 10mm cal., single action, 5 in. barrel, 8 shot mag., stainless steel or two-tone (TT suffix, new 2018) frame, Novak (new 2016) white dot sights, diamond laser cut cocobolo grips with trademark Colt logo on both grips, upswept beavertail grip safety (new 2016), extended thumb safety (new 2016). New 2008.

MSR $1,199	$1,025	$875	$725	$625	$525	$425	$375

Add $100 for lower Picatinny rail (new 2017).

DELTA GOLD CUP STAINLESS - 10mm cal., target variation, includes Accro adj. rear sight and trigger (serrated also), wraparound combat grips. Mfg. 1989-93, re-released 1995-96.

	$1,200	$1,000	$800	$700	$650	$575	$525

Last MSR was $1,027.

* *Delta Gold Cup Blue* - similar to Delta Gold Cup Stainless, except has blue finish. Mfg. 1991 only.

	$950	$825	$750	$675	$600	$550	$500

Last MSR was $870.

.380 GOVERNMENT MODEL SERIES 80 - .380 ACP cal. only, single action, 3 1/4 in. barrel, 7 shot mag., fixed sights, composition stocks, 21 3/4 oz. Mfg. 1983-1997.

* *.380 Government Model Series 80 Blue Finish* - finish disc. in 1997.

	$725	$600	$550	$500	$450	$400	$350

Last MSR was $474.

* *.380 Government Model Series 80 Nickel Finish* - bright polish nickel finish with white composite grips. Disc. 1994.

	$775	$675	$600	$500	$450	$400	$350

Last MSR was $504.

* *.380 Government Model Series 80 Coltguard Finish* - employs a high-strength electroless matte nickel finish. Mfg. 1986-89.

	$750	$650	$575	$500	$450	$400	$350

Last MSR was $406.

* *.380 Government Model Series 80 Stainless Steel* - mfg. 1989-97.

	$700	$600	$500	$450	$425	$400	$350

Last MSR was $508.

GOVT. POCKETLITE L.W. - similar to .380 Series 80 Govt. Model, except frame is mfg. with alloy, blue or nickel/stainless (mfg. 1992-93) finish only, black composition grips, 14 3/4 oz. Mfg. 1991-97.

	$750	$650	$525	$450	$400	$350	$325

Last MSR was $462.

Add 15% for nickel/stainless finish (disc. 1993).

MSR	100%	98%	95%	90%	80%	70%	60%

* ***Govt. Pocketlite Teflon Nickel/Stainless*** - similar to Govt. Pocketlite L.W., except has combination of Teflon nickel, stainless steel finish. Mfg. 1997-98.

$725 $600 $500 $400 $350 $300 $275

Last MSR was $508.

MUSTANG - similar to .380 Series Govt., except has 2 3/4 in. barrel, single action, 5 or 6 (new 1992) shot mag., blue finish only, 18 1/2 oz. Mfg. 1986-1998.

$825 $700 $575 $475 $375 $300 $275

Last MSR was $462.

* ***Mustang Nickel finish*** - bright polish nickel finish with white composite grips. Mfg. 1987-94.

$900 $750 $650 $525 $425 $350 $300

Last MSR was $504.

* ***Mustang Stainless Steel*** - stainless steel variation of the Mustang. Mfg. 1990-97.

$700 $650 $600 $550 $500 $395 $295

Last MSR was $508.

* ***Mustang Coltguard finish*** - employs a high-strength electroless matte nickel finish. Mfg. 1987.

$975 $825 $700 $600 $500 $400 $350

Last MSR was $406.

MUSTANG LITE - .380 ACP cal., SA only, 2 3/4 in. barrel, 6 shot mag., black tactical polymer grip frame with ribbed grip straps and tactical profile, brushed stainless steel slide, firing pin safety block, Commander style hammer, solid aluminum trigger, lowered ejection port, 12 1/2 oz. New 2015.

MSR $599 $500 $425 $360 $315 $275 $235 $200

MUSTANG PLUS II - .380 ACP cal. only, 2 3/4 in. barrel, blue finish, black composition grips, 7 shot mag., 20 oz. Mfg. 1988-96.

$775 $650 $550 $475 $400 $350 $275

Last MSR was $462.

This model has the full grip length of the .380 Government Model.

* ***Mustang Plus II Stainless Steel*** - stainless steel variation of the Mustang Plus II. Mfg. 1990-1998.

$700 $600 $550 $475 $400 $350 $275

Last MSR was $508.

MUSTANG POCKETLITE L.W. - similar to Mustang, except has aluminum alloy receiver and stainless slide, blue (disc. 1997) or nickel/stainless finish, black composite grips, 12 1/2 oz. Introduced 1987.

$775 $650 $525 $450 $375 $325 $300

Last MSR was $462.

MSR	100%	98%	95%	90%	80%	70%	60%

* ***Mustang Pocketlite L.W. Nickel/Stainless Steel Finish*** – similar to Mustang Pocketlite, except has nickel finish frame and stainless steel slide. Mfg. 1991-96.

	$800	$700	$550	$450	$375	$325	$300

Last MSR was $493.

* ***Mustang Pocketlite Teflon Nickel/Stainless*** – similar to Mustang Pocketlite L.W., except has combination of Teflon nickel, stainless steel finish. Mfg. 1997-99.

	$775	$650	$525	$450	$375	$325	$300

Last MSR was $508.

* ***Mustang Pocketlite L.W. Lady Elite*** – features hard chrome receiver, blue slide with silver painted rollmark, finger extension mag., soft carrying case, limited mfg. 1995-96.

	$775	$650	$525	$450	$375	$325	$300

Last MSR was $612.

* ***Mustang Pocketlite L.W. Nite Lite .380*** – .380 ACP cal., features bar-dot night sight, Teflon coated alloy receiver with stainless slide, finger extension mag., includes carrying case. Mfg. 1994 only.

	$775	$650	$525	$450	$375	$325	$300

Last MSR was $577.

MUSTANG POCKETLITE, CURRENT MFG. – .380 ACP cal., SA only, 2 3/4 in. barrel, 7 shot mag., firing pin safety block, commander style hammer, solid aluminum trigger, lowered ejection port, brushed stainless steel slide with electroless nickel finished frame, black composite grips with Colt medallions, 12 1/2 oz. New 2012.

MSR $699	$595	$475	$415	$325	$275	$225	$200

MUSTANG XSP – .380 ACP cal., 2 3/4 in. barrel, 6 shot mag., textured polymer grip frame with ribbed front and back straps, ambidextrous safety, black stainless steel slide, fixed front and rear sights, wide slide serrations, squared off trigger guard, lower 3/8 in. integrated accessory rail, hard chrome small parts, matte black finish, 12 oz. Mfg. mid-2013-mid 2015.

	$575	$475	$425	$350	$295	$250	$225

Last MSR was $672.

Add $125 for Mustang XSP First Edition.

PISTOLS: SEMI-AUTO, DOUBLE ACTION - RECENT MFG.

DOUBLE EAGLE SERIES 90 I & II – 9mm Para. (mfg. 1991 only), .38 Super (mfg. 1991 only), .45 ACP, or 10mm (disc. 1993) cal., double action semi-auto that operates on the Browning/Colt short recoil, pivoting link locking system used by the Govt. Model, 5 in. barrel, matte stainless steel only, 3-dot sighting system or Accro adj. rear sight (disc. 1994), checkered synthetic Xenoy grips, 8 shot mag. (9 shot in 9mm

MSR	100%	98%	95%	90%	80%	70%	60%

Para. or .38 Super cal.), decocking lever, squared off combat trigger guard, 39 oz. Mfg. 1990-96.

	$850	$650	$500	$430	$375	$315	$270

Last MSR was $727.

Add $100 for 9mm Para. or .38 Super cal. Add $20 for 10mm cal. Add 10% for NIB condition.

The first edition (1,000 mfg. in 1989) on this model did not have a decocking lever - MSR was $916.

* ***Double Eagle Combat Commander*** – .40 S&W (new 1992) or .45 ACP cal., 4 1/4 in. barrel, 8 shot mag., white dot sights, 36 oz. Mfg. 1991-96.

	$850	$650	$500	$430	$375	$315	$270

Last MSR was $727.

Add 100-200% for X serial number guns.

* ***Double Eagle Officer's Model*** - .45 ACP cal., 3 1/2 in. barrel, 8 shot mag., 35 oz. Mfg. 1991-disc.

	$850	$650	$500	$430	$375	$315	$270

Last MSR was $727.

* ***Double Eagle Officer's Lightweight Model*** – .45 ACP cal. only, 3 1/2 in. barrel, alloy frame with blue finish only, white dot sights, 25 oz. Mfg. 1991-93.

	$850	$650	$500	$400	$365	$330	$295

Last MSR was $696.

ALL AMERICAN MODEL 2000 – 9mm Para. cal. only, double action semi-auto, roller-bearing mounted trigger allowing double action only trigger pull every shot, recoil operated rotary action featuring integral locking lugs similar to the military M16 rifle, hammerless, 4 1/2 in. barrel, matte finished steel slide and polymer receiver, 15 shot mag., 3-dot sighting system, ambidextrous mag. release, black synthetic checkered grips, internal striker block safety, checkered trigger guard and front grip strap, 29 oz. Manufacturing difficulty forced discontinuance and design and tooling were returned to Reed Knight. Mfg. 1991-93.

* ***Model 2000 - Polymer Frame***

	$750	$650	$525	$450	$375	$325	$275

Last MSR was $575.

Add 10% for NIB condition.

This model could also be converted to a shorter version using a 3 3/4 in. barrel/bushing kit (no tools or other components were needed - $75 retail during 1993 only).

* ***Model 2000 - Aluminum Frame*** – similar to polymer Model 2000, except frame is aluminum, serial numbered RK00001-RK03000 to commemorate the designer (Reed Knight). Mfg. 1993.

	$850	$700	$550	$465	$375	$325	$275

Last MSR was $575.

Add 10% for NIB condition.

MSR	100%	98%	95%	90%	80%	70%	60%

PONY SERIES 90 - .380 ACP cal., double action only, 2 3/4 in. barrel, bobbed hammer, 6 shot mag., stainless construction, brushed finish, fixed sights, black composition grips, 19 oz. Mfg. 1997-1998.

	$725	$650	$550	$450	$350	$300	$275

Last MSR was $529.

* *Pony Series 90 Pocketlite Lightweight* - .380 ACP cal., similar to Pony Series 90, except utilizes aluminum and stainless steel construction, brushed finish, 13 oz. Mfg. 1997-1999.

	$750	$675	$550	$450	$350	$300	$275

Last MSR was $529.

POCKET NINE - 9mm Para. cal., double action only, 2 3/4 in. barrel, aluminum frame, ultra slim profile, 6 shot mag., matte/brushed stainless steel, wraparound rubber grips, 3-dot sights, 17 oz. Mfg. 1999 only.

	$1,100	$925	$800	$700	$600	$500	$400

Last MSR was $615.

COLT Z40 - .40 S&W cal., DAO, alloy frame, double column mag., firing pin safety, 3-dot sights, blue finish with black checkered synthetic grips and silver trigger, straight backstrap, marked "Colt Z40" on top of slide, while approx. 750-800 pieces were mfg. 1998-99 by CZ for a Colt subcontract, they were never shipped, and as a result, very few have made it into the U.S. to date from the Czech Republic.

	$800	$750	$700	$600	$550	$525	$500

NEW AGENT DAO MODEL O - .45 ACP cal., DAO, 3 in. barrel, Series 80 firing pin safety system, hammerless, 7 shot mag., double diamond slim fit grips, black anodized aluminum frame, blue finish, beveled magwell, snag free trench style sights, front strap serrations, captive recoil spring system. Mfg. 2008-2013.

	$900	$775	$675	$550	$450	$400	$350

Last MSR was $1,041.

Note: Colt has issued a recall for ser. nos. GT01001 - GT04505 X X due to a problem with the safety and/or guide pad. Improper hardness may cause the safety or guide pad to crack and might not prevent the gun from an accidental firing. Please contact Colt directly if you have one of the pistols - recall@colt.com.

1991 SERIES GOVERNMENT MODEL O LIGHTWEIGHT - .45 ACP cal., 5 in. barrel, DAO, features black anodized aluminum receiver with blued carbon steel slide, checkered double diamond slim fit grips, 7 shot mag., blue finish, white dot sights. Mfg. 2011-2013.

	$925	$800	$700	$600	$500	$425	$375

Last MSR was $1,068.

PISTOLS: SEMI-AUTO, .22 CAL. - WOODSMAN SERIES & VARIATIONS

The publisher wishes to once again express his thanks to Major (ret.) Robert J. Rayburn for his continued generous contributions of information regarding the Colt Woodsman Series.

The Colt Woodsman was made for 62 years, and included a multitude of variations/options in models, sights, barrels, grips, markings, etc. Many of the variations are quite scarce and desirable, but generally known only to specialized collectors. The following price guidelines are for standard production models, and only for those specimens in unmodified, factory original condition.

Internally at Colt the pre-Woodsman, Woodsman, Challenger, Huntsman, and Targetsman are collectively referred to as the "Model S", since they are all built on the S frame. Casually "Woodsman" is often used to include all the various models.

Over 690,000 Woodsmans with variations were mfg. 1915-1977.

Factory engraved and special order Woodsmans are relatively rare and very desirable. Prices can fluctuate greatly, and auctions can sometimes be the only source of supply for these rarely encountered pistols. Note: 100% "as new" 1st Series Colt Woodsmans with box and accessories are almost always locked up in existing collections and are not sold except when an entire collection is liquidated. Since the demand exceeds the supply, the price of such pristine items has been rising rapidly. The older or rarer versions in such condition can sell for double or even triple the price of a 98% gun. In the listings in this section, 100% means exactly that - absolutely perfect in every way, without a single blemish or the slightest trace of blue wear or thinning on the pistol itself. Such perfect examples can still be found for some versions. For others, where such condition is rarely, if ever, encountered, market values are too volatile to be listed in the 100% column.

In this section the condition percentage does not consider accoutrements such as box, papers, or tools. Such items have grown in importance in recent years and the value assigned by collectors varies greatly depending on age, rarity and condition. For a common variety late model, the original box might add $40-$50. For a relatively rare and early Pre-WWII model, a pristine factory original box with original papers and tools might add $1,000 or even more.

BEWARE: With the Internet and the online auction sites that cater to collectors, recently manufactured fake boxes and papers have proliferated. These are sometimes advertised as modern reproductions, but all too often they are not honestly described. The unscrupulous sellers often obscure the truth by strongly implying that their product is original "new old stock" without ever actually saying that it is factory original or "correct" for the pistol listed on the label.

Three different barrel profiles were used with the 1st Series pre-Woodsman and Woodsman. Those manufactured between 1915-1922 had a thin, lightweight barrel commonly referred to as a pencil barrel (approx. serial range 1-31,000). The medium barrel, with a somewhat larger diameter, was introduced in 1922 and was retained until the 90,000 serial range (approx. mfg. 1922-1934). The pencil barrel and medium barrel both had a step-down just forward of the receiver to reduce the barrel diameter. The tapered barrel, used from 1934 until the end of production in 1947 (serial range approx. 90,000-187,423), did not have the step-down. Instead, it was gradually tapered down for the full length of the barrel.

PRE-WOODSMAN - .22 LR cal., 6 5/8 in. barrel, 10 shot mag., blue only, bottom mag. release, checkered wood grips, adj. front and rear sights, this model was officially named "Colt Automatic Pistol, Caliber .22 Target

MSR	100%	98%	95%	90%	80%	70%	60%

Model", magazine base has 2-line legend "CAL .22" "COLT". Standard *velocity ammo. only. Approx. 54,000 mfg. 1915-1927.*

	$2,450	$1,775	$1,050	$675	$450	$325	$300

Add 10% for pencil barrels (1915-1922 mfg. only, ser. nos. below 31000).

BEWARE: Because the early guns were used with corrosive ammo, many of them developed bad bores and have since been refitted with later barrels.

This model was manufactured to use standard velocity ammunition only (not high speed). Colt did offer a conversion kit for high velocity ammunition after the transition to high velocity in 1931.

WOODSMAN 1ST SERIES - .22 LR cal., 10 shot mag., blue only, bottom mag. release, checkered wood grips, marked "The Woodsman" on receiver, adj. sights, mfg. from 1927-1947, total production was approx. 112,000.

Note: Guns made prior to 1931 were designed for standard velocity .22 LR ammunition only. The new style main spring housing, designed for high velocity ammunition, began appearing at approx. ser. no. 80,000 and was completely phased in by approx. ser. no. 85,000. Later guns, INCLUDING ALL PISTOLS MADE AFTER WWII, were designed for high velocity ammunition.

151 factory engraved First Series Woodsmans were manufactured pre-WWII. The breakdown is 126 Target models, 14 Sport models, and 11 Match Target models. Values depend on engraving type/ coverage and original condition.

* ***Woodsman Sport Model*** - 4 1/2 in. barrel, this model was introduced in 1933.

	$2,200	$1,700	$1,100	$650	$450	$350	$300

Add 10% for adj. front sight (available beginning 1937).

Add 50% for medium weight barrel (1933-34 mfg. only), and an additional 50% for semi-circular "half moon" front sight (1933 mfg. only).

The vast majority of this model came with a fixed front sight, rounded at the front and serrated ramp at the rear.

Approx. serial range of the First Series Sport is 86,105-187,423 from 1933 to 1947.

* ***Woodsman Target Model*** - 6 5/8 in. barrel.

	$2,100	$1,400	$800	$450	$325	$300	$275

Note: Colt discontinued the 1st series in 1947. These guns are quite different from the 2nd series started later in 1947. Both the front and rear sights are adjustable.

WOODSMAN 1ST SERIES MATCH TARGET - .22 LR cal. only, 6 5/8 in. heavy barrel, commonly called "Bullseye" Match Target, mfg. 1938-44, production totaled around 16,000. Difficult to find in mint condition. Values listed assume original one-piece extended walnut grips.

	$3,800	$2,900	$1,800	$1,100	$950	$900	$850

MSR	100%	98%	95%	90%	80%	70%	60%

In the lower conditions, much of the value derives from the original walnut "Elephant Ear" stocks. The value of the stocks, in excellent original condition, can actually exceed the value of a lower condition gun. The extended plastic stocks, as used on the military version of the Match Target, will fit on any 1st Series Colt Woodsman. Because the plastic military stocks are readily available and inexpensive, they are often used as replacements for lost or broken original stocks. They are not to be confused with the one piece "Elephant Ear" stocks.

The correct magazine on this model has a 3-line legend "COLT WOODSMAN", "CAL. 22 L.R.", and "MATCH TARGET MOD".

* ***Woodsman 1st Series Match Target "U.S. Property" Marked*** - approx. 4,000 Match Target Woodsmans were sold to the U.S. Army and U.S. Navy during WWII. Most have serial numbers above MT12500, although some were shipped out of sequence with lower numbers. The wartime guns had elongated plastic stocks and standard blue finish, although some of them are now parkerized as the result of arsenal refinishing or other non-factory modifications. They are marked with either "US PROPERTY" or the ordnance wheel with crossed cannon, as well as the initials of the govt. inspector. Some also have additional markings.

	N/A	$3,000	$2,100	$1,200	$925	$750	$575

Since the military models have two-piece plastic grips, rather than the "Elephant Ear" stocks, the values in the lower condition categories are lower than those for the standard civilian model.

Check parkerized finish carefully for originality on this variation, as some "recent parkerizing" has been observed.

WOODSMAN 2ND SERIES - .22 LR cal. only, automatic slide stop and hold open, push button mag. release on this model is located on the left side of frame, ColtMaster rear sight was introduced during 1953, Coltwood plastic grips (mfg. 1947-1950) or injection molded plastic grips (mfg. 1950-1955), total production on all 2nd Series was (not including the Challenger) approx. 146,000, serialization has "S" suffix. Mfg. 1947-1955.

* ***Woodsman 2nd Series Sport Model*** - 4 1/2 in. barrel.

	$1,500	$1,300	$1,000	$800	$600	$500	$350

* ***Woodsman 2nd Series Target Model*** - 6 in. barrel.

	$1,400	$1,120	$1,000	$750	$500	$400	$325

* ***Woodsman 2nd Series Match Target Model*** - this model is not marked Woodsman on the gun. It is marked MATCH TARGET.

4 1/2 in. heavy bbl.	$1,950	$1,600	$1,050	$850	$700	$450	$425
6 in. heavy bbl.	$1,600	$1,400	$900	$700	$600	$400	$375

CHALLENGER MODEL - similar to Woodsman 2nd Series, only with fixed sights, without automatic hold open, and bottom mag. release, plastic grips, 4 1/2 and 6 in. barrels, mfg. 1950-1955 with total production reaching approx. 77,000.

	$895	$750	$550	$375	$325	$250	$225

MSR	100%	98%	95%	90%	80%	70%	60%

WOODSMAN 3RD SERIES - .22 LR cal. only, automatic slide stop and hold open, black plastic grips (mfg. 1955-60) or walnut grips (1960-77), 3rd Models can be differentiated from 2nd Models by their bottom mag. release. Total production of all 3rd series Woodsman models (not including the Huntsman or Targetsman) exceeded 100,000, serialization has "S" suffix. Mfg. 1955-1977.

* ***Woodsman 3rd Series Sport Model*** - 4 1/2 in. barrel.

	$995	$895	$700	$450	$350	$300	$275

* ***Woodsman 3rd Series Target Model*** - 6 in. barrel.

	$895	$795	$550	$400	$350	$300	$275

* ***Woodsman 3rd Series Match Target Model*** - 4 1/2 or 6 in. heavy barrel. This model is not marked Woodsman on the gun.

	$1,450	$1,275	$875	$500	$400	$350	$325

Add $200 for a 4 1/2 in. barrel if condition is 95% or better.

HUNTSMAN MODEL - .22 LR cal. only, 4 1/2 and 6 in. barrels, fixed sights and no automatic hold open, black plastic grips to serial number 141094-C; walnut grips after that cutoff. Mfg. 1955-1977 with total production reaching over 100,000.

	$795	$650	$500	$350	$275	$250	$225

The Huntsman is very similar to the Challenger Model, except is built on a 3rd series frame.

* ***Huntsman Model S Master Series*** - approx. 400 Model S Masters were sold in 1983. This was a parts clean-up by Colt, using Huntsman frames leftover from the last days of production. They were equipped with automatic slide stop and Elliason rear sight, gold etching on the slide, and a French fitted walnut case marked "1 of 400". Approx. 285 had straight, non-tapered Huntsman barrel, while the remainder had the tapered Woodsman Sport barrel with pinned front sight.

Huntsman barrel	$1,600	$995	$600	N/A	N/A	N/A	N/A
Woodsman barrel	$1,800	$900	$700	N/A	N/A	N/A	N/A

Above values assume original walnut case included. Values for this model in 98%-60% original condition are hard to compute, as most are mint or new.

TARGETSMAN MODEL - similar to the Huntsman, except has adj. rear sight and thumbrest on left grip, 6 in. barrel only, approx. 65,000 mfg. 1959-1977.

	$850	$695	$495	$395	$275	$250	$225

CADET - .22 LR cal., 4 1/2 in. barrel, stainless steel, 10 shot mag., predecessor to the Colt 22 Model, originally introduced in 1994, fixed sights, this model was disc. by 1995 because of litigation involving the trademarked model name and only protypes are known to exist, 33 1/2 oz.

Extreme rarity precludes acurrate pricing on this model.

MSR	100%	98%	95%	90%	80%	70%	60%

COLT 22 FIRST EDITION - .22 LR cal., 4 1/2 inch VR barrel, stainless steel or black anodized stainless steel, 10 shot mag., one-piece black Pachmary rubber grips, 33 1/2 oz. Mfg. 1994

	$600	$450	$400	$300	$225	$180	$155

An early version of the COLT 22 was called the "First Edition" Colt 22. It was available with either stainless steel or black hard chromed barrel. Marked First Edition 22 on slide. All had low serial numbers and could be ordered as matching serial number cased pairs, for example "00005PH" and "PH00005". A very small number were Colt Custom Shop engraved.

COLT 22 - .22 LR cal., 4 1/2 in. VR barrel, stainless steel, fixed sights, 10 shot mag., one-piece black Pachmayr rubber grips, 33 1/2 oz. Mfg. 1994-1998.

	$550	$425	$350	$275	$165	$140	$120

Last MSR was $248.

COLT 22 TARGET - .22 LR cal., 6 in. VR barrel with full length grooved sight rib, adj. rear sight, 40 1/2 oz. Mfg. 1995-1999.

	$600	$450	$400	$300	$165	$140	$120

Last MSR was $377.

100%	98%	95%	90%	80%	70%	60%	50%	40%	30%	20%	10%

REVOLVERS: DOUBLE ACTION

Most of the double action revolvers listed can have their original configuration confirmed with a Colt factory letter. To receive a letter, write: COLT ARCHIVE PROPERTIES, LLC, 1295 Blue Hills Avenue, Bloomfield, CT 06002. The research fee for these revolvers is typically either $75 or $100, depending on the model. If they cannot obtain additional information on the variation you request, they will refund $50. The Models 1877 and 1878 were the only fixed cylinder DA models made by Colt.

Prices on top condition Colt DAs have continued to rise steadily, particularly for correctly boxed/cased guns. Be aware of ill-matched, wrong, or fake vintage boxes or grips being mated to an unmatched gun. Original boxes and grips will enhance the values of all Colt DAs.

MODEL 1877 (RAINMAKER) - .32 Colt cal., otherwise similar to the Model 1877 Lightning. Approx. 300 mfg. from 1877-1909. Rare.

$4,800	$3,600	$2,400	$2,200	$1,800	$1,200	$1,075	$925	$850	$775	$675	$575

Ejectorless versions, fitted also with a long, knurled cylinder pin will bring a 10%-15% premium, depending on condition.

This model has a fragile mechanism - values are for working guns.

The "Rainmaker" name was used by dealers in period promotions, not by Colt.

MODEL 1877 (LIGHTNING) - .38 Colt cal., 1 1/2, 2, 2 1/2, 3, 3 1/2, 4, 4 1/2, 5, or 6 in. barrels without ejector, 4 1/2, 5, 6, 7, or 7 1/2 in. barrels with ejector, 6 shot double action, long cylinder fluting, blue finish with case hardened frame and hammer, full nickel plating also available. Over 166,000 mfg. from 1877-1909.

$4,500	$3,500	$2,000	$1,800	$1,600	$1,000	$900	$775	$700	$650	$575	$500

100%	98%	95%	90%	80%	70%	60%	50%	40%	30%	20%	10%

Subtract approx. 10% for nickel plating.

Ejectorless versions, fitted also with a long, knurled cylinder pin will bring a 10%-15% premium, depending on condition.

Also, an etched barrel will command a 10%-15% over a roll marked barrel, depending on condition.

Add 10% for 1st and 2nd year production examples or others with factory special or carved grips.

This model has a fragile mechanism - values are for working guns.

The "Lightning" and Thunderer names were used by dealers in period promotions, not by Colt.

MODEL 1877 (THUNDERER) – .41 Colt cal. only, otherwise same general specifications as Model 1877 Lightning.

$4,750	$3,750	$2,250	$2,100	$1,675	$1,125	$975	$850	$750	$700	$600	$500

Add 10% for 1st and 2nd year production examples or others with factory special grips.

MODEL 1878 DA – .32-20 WCF (scarce), .38 Colt (approx. 40 mfg.), .38-40 WCF, .41 LC (scarce, 308 mfg.), .44 Russian, .44 S&W, .44-40 WCF (Colt Frontier Six Shooter), .45 LC, .450 Eley, .455 Eley, or .476 Eley cal., 2 1/2 (scarce), 3, 3 1/2, or 4 in. barrels without ejector, 4 3/4, 5 1/2, 7 1/2, 8, 8 1/2, 9, 10, or 12 in. with ejector. Mfg. 1878-1905. Over 51,000 made.

$6,000	$5,500	$5,000	$4,250	$3,750	$2,950	$2,150	$1,500	$950	$850	$750	$700

Add 15% for 3 1/2 or 4 in. barrel. Front of frame must be checked to verify authenticity of a Sheriff's Model.

Approximately 80% of production for this model was in .44-40 WCF and .45 LC cals.

This model in .44-40 WCF was called the Colt Frontier, and this inscription is either acid etched or roll marked on the barrel. On the acid etched variation, the first few (approx. 3-500 and some later) .45 cal. guns shipped, especially to B. Kittredge were also acid etched "Omnipotent" and this represents the only non-caliber etching other than CFSS ever done by the Colt factory. An authentic Omnipotent ("All Powerful") will bring about a 30-50% premium over the same gun without the marking, especially in blue.

This model has an action that is weaker than that of the SAA, and should be carefully inspected to make sure the cylinder turns and locks up properly. Since original parts are scarce, at least $750 must be deducted for a non-working action.

Many original 1878 barrels have "found their way" on the front end of a SAA frame since the barrels are interchangable. Because of this, many "original" Model 1878 DAs may have an incorrect and/or later SAA Colt barrel attached. Watch yourself here! Also, scarce calibers should be verified with factory letter.

100%	98%	95%	90%	80%	70%	60%	50%	40%	30%	20%	10%

MODEL 1902/1904 (PHILIPPINE CONSTABULARY) - .45 LC cal., a variation of the Model 1878, except has oversized trigger guard and long trigger, 6 shot standard 1878 type cylinder with long flutes, pinched frame, 6 in. barrel, blue finish, hard rubber grips, many have been arsenal refinished.

* ***1902 Constabulary*** – 5,000 mfg., with a smaller number actually issued by the U.S. Army to the Philippine Constabulary (Police) Force (not to be confused with the Philippine Scouts, which were part of the U.S. Army), markings: "R.A.C." on left side of frame, 1902 date on right side of frame near grips, large "U.S." on right side of frame below cylinder, hard rubber grips, but some examples also show period correct wooden grips, perhaps from confirmed arsenal or Colt reworks.

N/A	N/A	$4,650	$3,650	$2,900	$2,200	$1,900	$1,800	$1,700	$1,600	$1,400	$1,300

Subtract 50% for arsenal or Colt refinish.

* ***1904 Constabulary Purchase*** – rare variation, approx. 50 more revolvers were delivered to the Army in 1904 within the 51,000 ser. no. range, use unknown, but assumed as Constabulary replacements with same overall configuration as 1902 version, last four digits of ser. no. are on the loading gate and cylinder, military inspection marks, plain wood grips.

Price at approx. 10% above the equivalent 1902 production model.

This is a gun sold to the military that was not assigned a U.S. model number, so technically it is a 'contract purchase' variation, not a unique model.

REVOLVERS: DOUBLE ACTION, SWING OUT CYLINDER

Most of the double action revolvers listed can have their original configuration confirmed with a Colt factory letter. To receive a letter, write: COLT ARCHIVE PROPERTIES, LLC, 1295 Blue Hills Avenue, Bloomfield, CT 06002. The research fee for these revolvers is typically either $75 or $100, depending on the model. If they cannot obtain additional information on the variation you request, they will refund $50.

In Oct. of 1999, Colt announced that all double action revolvers would be discontinued, including any custom shop manufacture. After over 120 years of continuous production, the series of swing out double action revolvers finally ended. As a result, interest and prices for this discontinued revolver configuration have increased greatly in recent years, even on recently discontinued models/configurations. For a few years starting in 2002, the Colt Custom Shop produced both the Anaconda and the Python Elite, but both have also since been discontinued. Prices on top condition Colt DAs have continued to remain strong, particularly for correctly boxed/cased guns.

The Snake guns - Pythons, Diamondbacks, Cobras, Boas, Anacondas, and Vipers are currently undergoing so much demand that N/As have replaced many 100% condition factors due to volatile and unpredictable pricing/sales. On most of these recently manufactured Snake guns, NIB or nearly new examples are more readily available compared to Colt Pre-WWII revolvers. It is highly recommended that on short barreled snake guns with nickel finishes a factory letter be procured before buying/selling. Be wary/

100%	98%	95%	90%	80%	70%	60%	50%	40%	30%	20%	10%

cautious of ill-matched/wrong vintage boxes and/or non-original grips. Also, reproduction box end labels and convincing repro boxes for Colt revolvers are now being made. Original, correct boxes and grips will enhance the values of all Colt DAs.

2 or low 3 digit serial number revolvers will always carry a substantial premium, regardless of condition.

MODEL 1889 "NAVY" (NEW NAVY DA, MODEL OF 1889) - .38 Short and Long Colt, and .41 Short and Long Colt cal., 3, 4 1/2, and 6 in. barrel, blue (military and civilian) or nickel (civilian only) finish, wood (U.S.Navy) or hard rubber (civilian) grips with the world "Colt" in oval at top. The first solid frame, swing out cylinder - recognizable by no visible locking latches - unless later converted to 1895 action. Cylinder rotates counter-clockwise, sideplate is also on the right-hand side of frame, Colt produced approx. 31,000 mfg. 1889-1894, 1st 5,000 were ordered by U.S. Navy, with some additional Navy orders later in production - hence name. Serial number is on the butt. US Navy versions (6 in. bbl. ONLY), also include Navy markings.

N/A	$2,750	$2,250	$1,950	$1,550	$1,250	$850	$700	$550	$425	$350	$300

Add 40% for 3 in. barrel (civilian models only). Subtract $100-$200 for broken hard rubber grips or broken action.

Add 65%-100% for U.S. Navy Contract (ser. no. 1-5,000, and in some later ser. no. blocks), U.S.N. on butt (.38 LC cal. only), depending on condition. Beware of fakes.

Note: Nearly all US Navy Military 1889 Navy issues were later converted to 1895 type actions. Unconverted Navy-marked specimens w/o notched cylinders will bring a premium, but must be authenticated by an expert - Fakes and re-assembled guns are common.

There was also no mass updating of civilian 1889 revolvers. Real, unmolested civilian 1889 Colt DAs should appear with the older and original 1889 action, not with any modified actions or updated features.

For later (post 1884) US Navy DA 38s, see below under civilian New Navy Guns.

US ARMY MODELS 1892, 1894, 1896, 1901, 1903 (DA 38 "NEW ARMY" - US ARMY ISSUED MODELS) - The US Army then followed Navy in adopting a modern 38 DA revolver. Based on Navy use, Army model has 2nd set of locking notches added to cylinder. 1892 and later DAs all look similar to 1889 Navy, except with double cylinder notches, double locking bolts, and shorter flutes, more square cyl. release thumb catch. Plain uncheckered wood grips (Army contract military issue models only). All Military models are all cal. 38 only and blue only. US Army military issue models include Model of 1892, Model of 1894, Model of 1896, Model of 1901, and Model of 1903. 1903 and 1901 models were made and survived in greater quantity and so are worth less than earlier models. Most military models have been altered, refinished, reworked

100%	98%	95%	90%	80%	70%	60%	50%	40%	30%	20%	10%

or otherwise altered, which reduces value. Technical alterations by the Army itself - such as cylinder-open lock bolt and lanyard rings added later were part of this evolution. Most alterations reduce value, but a few are sought after (similar to finding a correct SAA Artillery model) . Unaltered examples of Models of 1892, 1894 and 1896 bring a premium. US Models 1901 and 1903 are common. Values below are only for US issued specimens marked on butt "US ARMY MODEL OF xxxx"; with original wood military grips, original barrel and with US Army military markings on the butt completely intact.

N/A $2,150 $1,750 $1,350 $900 $650 $500 $425 $350 $225 $195 $175

Add 100% for unaltered Models of 1892 or 1894 (consult expert). Add 20% for Model of 1896 if w/o lanyard ring.

Subtract 90% for guns with butt markings removed. (very common - it seems a lot of these were "borrowed" from the government, and the butt or entire gun then reblued-usually very poorly.)

Subtract 75% for late factory/armory rebuilt versions of early models. Consult expert sources for details.

Subtract 90% on any U.S. marked gun if the barrel length is other than 6 in., or for altered/damaged sights, target sights added, etc. All U.S. Army issue models had 6 inch barrels, standard fixed sights, and are .38 caliber only.

Subtract 25% for Army military models if original U.S. Army wood grips with cartouche are missing.

MODEL 1892 & 1895 "NEW ARMY & NEW NAVY" - CIVILIAN & US NAVY VERSIONS – similar to 1889 Navy, but double cylinder notches, double locking bolts, and shorter flutes, square cyl. release thumb catch, hard rubber grips, .32-20 WCF (uncommon) added in 1905, .38 Short and Long Colt, and .41 Short and Long Colt cal., 3, 4 1/2, and 6 in. barrel, blue or nickel finish. Mfg. 1892-1907.

N/A $1,650 $1,150 $700 $500 $400 $300 $275 $250 $225 $195 $175

Add $100-$750 for U.S.N. markings, depending on condition.

Add 40% for 3 in. barrel (civilian only).

Subtract $100-$200 for broken hard rubber grips or broken action.

After about 1894, US Navy Colt 38 DA models were based on standard civilian (1895) Colt models with 6 in. barrels (only), and include civilian style serial numbers and hard rubber "Navy" grips; also with Navy marks, and both civilian and Navy numbers on the butt. Models made before 1898 will bring a premium. Late models of all types made after about 1903 begin to show transitional details moving towards the later Army Special model. Serial numbers for all New Army DA & New Navy DA are on the butt, not in the yoke. Numbers on yoke, latch etc. are always assembly numbers. Civilian New Navy grips have "COLT" in oval. Civilian New Army grips have the Rampant Colt.

NEW ARMY & NEW NAVY DA38 models after about 1894:

Much confusion ensues after about 1894 since in commercial production, both "NEW NAVY" civilian & NEW ARMY" civilian arms also have the dual notch system. The only difference between commercial examples was the type of hard rubber grips. "NEW NAVY" grips have only the word COLT, but no image of the rampant colt.

To add confusion, while the US Army continued to contract for special production with wooden grips and serial number markings different from commercial guns, the US NAVY after about 1894 simply purchased batches of specially produced and inspected commercial style guns. These include normal commercial markings and the regular hard rubber "New Navy" grips. Colt then included the Navy inspection markings (tridents or stars at various times) and US Navy markings on the butt. So US Issue Navy guns from about 1894 until 1903 have a commercial serial number in the commercial location on the butt, but are clearly marked as US Navy Models as well. (Because of this similarity to commercial prod'n, US Navy fakes are known to exist. Consult references and note the orientation of US Navy markings).

* ***Models 1892, 1894, 1895, 1896, 1901, 1903*** – these were all civilian variations of the Model 1892, military model (.38 Long Colt only) and values are shown above for these civilian guns.

OFFICER'S MODEL (FIRST ISSUE) – .38 Spl. or .38 Long Colt cal., 6 in. barrel, cylinder rotates counter-clockwise and sideplate is on right-hand side of frame, adj. front - adj. rear sights, high luster blue, flat-top, last patent date 1901. Mfg. 1904-08.

100%	98%	95%	90%	80%	70%	60%	50%	40%	30%	20%	10%
N/A	$1,700	$1,350	$950	$775	$625	$550	$495	$395	$325	$275	$250

OFFICER'S MODEL (SECOND ISSUE) – .32 Colt or .38 Spl. cal., 4, 4 1/2, 5, 6, or 7 1/2 in. barrel, cylinder rotates clockwise, high luster blue through 1916, adj. front - adj. rear sights, checkered walnut grips, deep set medallions in grips were standard from 1913-1923. Mfg. 1908-1926. Last patent date July 4, 1905.

100%	98%	95%	90%	80%	70%	60%	50%	40%	30%	20%	10%
N/A	$1,700	$1,350	$900	$775	$600	$525	$495	$395	$325	$275	$250

Add 100% for .32 Colt cal. in 6 or 7 1/2 in. barrel in .32 Colt cal. (rare).

Add 100% for rare 4, 4 1/2, or 5 in. barrels.

Beware of "cut-offs" and check patent date locations and the front sight and its location carefully.

OFFICER'S MODEL TARGET (THIRD ISSUE) – similar design to the Second Issue, .22 LR cal. was added beginning 1930, heavy barrel was introduced in 1935. Mfg. 1927-1949. Last patent date Oct. 5, 1926.

100%	98%	95%	90%	80%	70%	60%	50%	40%	30%	20%	10%
N/A	$1,300	$1,000	$700	$550	$475	$400	$325	$300	$275	$250	$225

Add 10% for .22 LR cal. (mfg. started 1930).

Add 50% for .32 Colt cal. (mfg. 1939-1941, w/heavy barrel, and production estimates are 800-1,500 units).

Add 100% for 4 or 5 in. barrel.

For all short barrel Officers Models, beware of "cut-offs", and check patent date locations and the front sight and its location carefully.

100%	98%	95%	90%	80%	70%	60%	50%	40%	30%	20%	10%

MODEL 1905 MARINE CORPS - .38 Short or Long cal., similar to New Navy Second Issue, except has a round butt, checkered wood grips w/o medallion, and 6 in. barrel only. Mfg. 1905-1909 in approx. ser. no. range 10,001-10,926, about 926 mfg., 812 were for government contract, and 114 were commercial.

N/A	$3,350	$2,950	$1,950	$1,725	$1,425	$1,250	$1,000	$895	$795	$695	$595

Add 30% for Military issue marked "USMC" on butt (ser. nos. 1-812). Beware of fake USMC markings.

ARMY SPECIAL MODEL - .32-20 WCF, .38 (various), or .41 Colt cal., 4, 4 1/2, 5, and 6 in. barrels, hard rubber grips standard through 1923 - checkered wood with medallions beginning about 1924, blue finish, fixed sights, rounded checkered cylinder release thumb catch, smooth trigger, has heavier frame than New Navy, approx. ser. no. range 291,000-540,000, last patent date on barrel was July 4, 1905. Mfg. 1908-27.

N/A	$1,150	$950	$700	$575	$425	$295	$275	$250	$225	$200	$175

Add 35% for nickel finish.

Subtract $75-$200 if hard rubber grips are chipped or badly worn.

NEW SERVICE MODEL - .38 Spl., .357 Mag., .38-40 WCF, .44-40 WCF, .44 Russian, .44 Spl., .45 ACP, .45 LC, .450 Eley, .455 Eley, or .476 Eley cal., 4, 5, or 6 in. barrels in .357 Mag. and .38 Spl., 4 1/2, 5 1/2, and 7 1/2 in. barrel in all others, blue or nickel finish, bright blue finish was used through circa 1916, originally hard rubber grips (until approx. late '20s), with later guns having walnut grips with medallions. Mfg. 1898-1942.

Rare cals. (.450 and .476 Eley cals.) and 4 in. barrels will command premiums over values listed below.

Subtract $150 for broken, damaged, or heavily worn grips.

New Service revolvers with smoothbore barrel prices can range $6,500-$10,000+, depending on original condition.

New Service Models marked "NEW SERVICE 45 COLT" in .45 ACP cal. with shorter cylinder for rimmed cartridge are rare. All early New Service models (first type) have flat latches. Later models (second type) have rounded cylinder latches.

Approx. 356,000 Colt New Service revolvers were mfg., but only approx. 122,800 were Commercial variations. 95% were mfg. with blue finish, while 5% were nickel plated (approx. 6,140 revolvers). Colt also mfg. a very limited number (probably less than 10) of New Service revolvers with smoothbores. When encountered, it is important to get a Colt factory letter confirming the smoothbore barrel.

* *New Service Model Commercial*

N/A	$2,950	$2,750	$2,200	$1,800	$1,525	$1,150	$900	$775	$675	$500	$400

Add 35% for nickel finish.

Add 10%-15% for "Early Model" (aka First Variation) with flat cylinder latch and

100%	98%	95%	90%	80%	70%	60%	50%	40%	30%	20%	10%

non-tapered barrel profile; made up to approximately sn 21,000 to 23,000.

Add 40% for factory pearl, ivory, or FDL walnut grips, if in perfect condition.

Add 15% for some less common calibers/markings such as "44 Russian" or .44 Russian and Special.

Add 15% or more for short barrel length of 4 1/2 inches or other short lengths; each if documented by factory letter.

* ***New Service Model 1909 Army Model***

N/A $3,400 $2,900 $2,450 $1,850 $1,700 $1,100 $900 $800 $700 $575 $500

* ***New Service Model RNWMP & RCMP Model*** – .45 LC or .455 Eley cal., contract for Royal Canadian Northwest Mounted Police.

N/A $1,750 $1,375 $1,200 $925 $850 $775 $680 $590 $510 $435 $375

* ***New Service Model 1909 Navy Model*** – shortest production run of the Model 1909 variations.

N/A $3,500 $2,900 $2,450 $1,850 $1,700 $1,100 $900 $800 $725 $650 $525

* ***New Service Model 1909 - USMC***

N/A $3,650 $3,200 $2,750 $2,250 $1,875 $1,525 $1,250 $975 $850 $775 $675

* ***New Service Model 1917 Army***

$1,900 $1,600 $1,400 $1,125 $925 $775 $625 $525 $455 $390 $335 $295

* ***New Service Model 1917 Civilian/Commercial (1917 C/CM)*** – .45 ACP cal., 5 1/2 in. barrel only, last patent date is Oct. 5, 1926, checkered walnut grips with medallions, left side of barrel marked "COLT MODEL 1917 AUTO CTGE". Approx. 1,000 mfg. during 1932, serialized 335,000-336,000.

$1,500 $1,275 $1,050 $850 $650 $525 $450 $415 $385 $350 $325 $295

* ***New Service Model 1917 Civilian/Commercial (Parts Model)*** – .38-40 WCF, .44-40 WCF, or .45 LC cal., 4 1/2 or 5 1/2 in. barrel, hard rubber grips, or checkered walnut with medallions, last patent date is July 4, 1905, approx. 1,000 mfg. serialized 336,450- 337,500.

$1,375 $1,050 $925 $800 $625 $495 $415 $380 $360 $330 $300 $275

* ***New Service Model Target*** – similar to New Service Model, flat-top frame, hand-honed action and adj. front - adj. rear sights, 6 (scarce) or 7 1/2 in. barrel, square butt, round butt available after 1930, checkered grip straps, checkered walnut grips with medallion after 1913, blue or nickel (scarce) finish. Approx. 3,400 mfg. 1900-1940.

N/A $3,300 $2,775 $2,300 $1,850 $1,500 $1,250 $900 $750 $635 $550 $460

Add 40% - 60% for 6 in. barrel, depending on original condition.

Add 25% for flat latch "Old Models" with original high polish finish.

Approx. 1,000 were mfg. in .45 LC, 960 in .455 Eley, 700 in .44 Russian, 500 in .44 Spl., and 80 in .45 ACP cal.

* ***New Service Model Shooting Master*** – various cals. from 38 Spl. through .45 LC, 6 in. barrel, checkered walnut grips with Colt Medallion, machined grip straps, trigger, hammer, and ejector rod head, round or square butt, approx. 3,500 mfg. in ser. no. range 333,000-350,000.

100%	98%	95%	90%	80%	70%	60%	50%	40%	30%	20%	10%

» ***New Service Model Shooting Master .38 Spl.*** – approx. 2,500 mfg.

N/A	$2,500	$1,950	$1,750	$1,500	$1,150	$950	$650	$550	$525	$500	$475

» ***New Service Model Shooting Master .357 Mag.*** – approx. 500 mfg.

N/A	$3,000	$2,800	$1,950	$1,700	$1,475	$1,300	$1,100	$995	$850	$750	$650

» ***New Service Model Shooting Master .45 ACP or .45 LC cals.*** – approx. 156 mfg. in .45 LC and 250 mfg. in .45 ACP cal.

N/A	N/A	$4,850	$3,750	$3,250	$2,500	$2,050	$1,675	$1,350	$1,000	$750	$600

» ***New Service Model Shooting Master .44 Spl. cal.*** – approx. 94 mfg.

N/A	N/A	$4,900	$4,050	$3,500	$3,000	$2,500	$2,000	$1,575	$1,250	$1,000	$850

The Shooting Master could be ordered with a square butt after 1933.

OFFICIAL POLICE PRE-WAR - .32-20 WCF (disc. 1942), .38-200 (British), .41 Long (disc. 1930), .38 Spl., or .22 LR (introduced 1930 - 4 or 6 in. barrel only, 4 in. scarce) cal., blue finish, 6 shot, round (very scarce) or square butt, 2, 4, 5, or 6 in. barrels, checkered walnut grips, fixed sights, last patent date on barrel was Oct. 5, 1926. Mfg. 1927-1946.

$1,150	$950	$750	$525	$465	$425	$285	$250	$225	$200	$185	$165

Add 100% for round butt with factory verified letter (very rare).

Add 15% for nickel finish.

Add 20% for .22 LR cal.

OFFICIAL POLICE POST-WAR - .22 LR or .38 Spl. cal., 2, 4, 5, or 6 in. barrel, Coltwood plastic grips 1947-1954 - checkered walnut thereafter, fixed sights, no patent dates on barrel. Mfg. 1947-69.

$950	$800	$625	$500	$335	$275	$215	$195	$175	$165	$145	$125

Add 25% for nickel finish.

Add 100% for .22 LR cal.

The 2 in. barrel in .38 Spl. cal. is scarce. .22 LR cal. was available with 4 or 6 in. barrel only.

MARSHAL MODEL – .38 Spl. cal., 2 (less common) or 4 in. barrel, round butt, differentiated by "M" suffix and "COLT MARSHAL" on barrel, about 2,500 mfg. 1954-1956 in approx. ser. no. range 833350-M through 845320-M.

N/A	$1,950	$1,750	$1,000	$850	$600	$475	$425	$385	$360	$275	$250

Add 60% for 2 in. barrel.

Add 50% for nickel finish.

COMMANDO MODEL – .38 Spl. cal., 2 in. (less common), 4 in. (common), or 6 in. (rare) barrel, should have plastic grips, parkerized finish, about 50,000 mfg. 1942-1945, 32 oz., marked "COLT COMMANDO" on barrel, last patent date on barrel was Oct. 5, 1926.

N/A	$1,650	$1,400	$1,175	$950	$800	$675	$525	$450	$350	$300	$275

Add 15% for 2 in. barrel.

100%	98%	95%	90%	80%	70%	60%	50%	40%	30%	20%	10%

OFFICIAL POLICE MKIII - .38 Spl. cal., 4, 5, or 6 in. barrels, no patent dates on barrel. Mfg. 1969-75.

* *Official Police MKIII Blue finish*

$650 $550 $500 $475 $385 $350 $325 $300 $285 $270 $150 $125

* *Official Police MKIII Nickel finish*

$750 $650 $550 $475 $385 $350 $325 $300 $285 $270 $150 $125

METROPOLITAN MK III - .38 Spl. cal., similar to Official Police, except heavier 4 in. barrel only, blue finish. Mfg. 1969-72.

$650 $550 $450 $350 $275 $250 $225 $210 $190 $175 $165 $155

OFFICER'S MODEL SPECIAL (FOURTH ISSUE) - .22 LR or .38 Spl. cal., 6 in. barrel, blue, similar to Third Issue, only heavier non-tapered barrel, new style hammer and "Coltmaster Sight", checkered plastic grips, no patent dates on barrel. Mfg. 1949-52.

$1,525 $1,225 $1,125 $750 $625 $475 $400 $325 $275 $250 $225 $195

Add $75 for .22 LR cal.

OFFICER'S MODEL MATCH (FIFTH ISSUE) - .22 LR, .22 WMR (approx. 850 mfg.), or .38 Spl. cal., 6 in. barrel, single (rare) or double action, tapered heavy barrel, nickel finish is scarce in this model, wide spur hammer, Accro sight, large target grips (walnut). Mfg. 1953-1969.

$1,500 $1,175 $975 $750 $650 $500 $400 $350 $300 $275 $250 $225

Add $75 for .22 LR cal.

Add 50% for nickel finish verified with factory letter.

* *Officer's Model Match (Fifth Issue) .22 Mag.* - .22 WMR cal., approx. 850 mfg.

N/A $2,400 $1,900 $1,750 $1,500 $1,100 $800 $700 $600 $550 $500 $450

* *Officer's Model Match Single Action Only* - limited mfg., must have accompanying factory letter.

$1,925 $1,900 $1,250 $1,100 $950 $900 $700 $650 $600 $550 $475 $475

OFFICER'S MODEL MATCH MK III (SIXTH ISSUE) - .38 Spl. cal. only, 6 in. shrouded VR barrel, wide spur hammer, Accro sights, target grips. 496 mfg. 1969-1971 only.

N/A $2,450 $1,950 $1,600 $1,200 $775 $700 $650 $600 $550 $475 $475

NEW POCKET - .32 Short and LC, or .32 Colt New Police cal., 2 1/2, 3 1/2, 5, or 6 in. barrel, first modern swing out DA, rubber grips, blue or nickel finish, round butt, last patent date on barrel was Nov. 6, 1888. Mfg. 1893-1905.

$1,450 $1,300 $975 $725 $525 $400 $300 $250 $215 $190 $170 $165

Subtract $75-$100 for chipped hard rubber grips (commonly found on this model).

POCKET POSITIVE (FIRST ISSUE) - similar to New Pocket, except has round butt and positive lock feature, also chambered for .32 Colt, .32 S&W, or .32 Colt New Police cal., last patent date on barrel was July 4, 1905. Mfg. 1905-27.

$1,350 $1,100 $750 $675 $525 $350 $325 $295 $275 $210 $185 $175

100%	98%	95%	90%	80%	70%	60%	50%	40%	30%	20%	10%

Add 20% for NIB.

Add 15%-20% for nickel finish.

Add 15% for 90%+ condition early transitional guns that are double marked with "NEW POCKET" on frame.

Subtract $75-$100 for chipped hard rubber grips (commonly found on this model).

POCKET POSITIVE (SECOND ISSUE) – similar to Pocket Positive First Issue, except available in 2 in. barrel, stippled and matted top strap, last patent date on barrel was Oct. 5, 1926. Mfg. 1927-1940.

100%	98%	95%	90%	80%	70%	60%	50%	40%	30%	20%	10%
$1,350	$1,100	$750	$650	$525	$350	$325	$295	$275	$210	$185	$175

Add 20% for NIB.

Add 15%-20% for nickel finish.

Add 15%-20% for 2 in. barrel.

Subtract $75-$100 for chipped hard rubber grips (commonly found on this model).

NEW POLICE – .32 Colt and .32 Colt New Police cal., 2 1/2, 4, and 6 in. barrels, fixed sights, same frame as New Pocket, except larger square butt gripstraps, rubber grips, last patent date on barrel was Nov. 6, 1888. Mfg. 1896-1907.

100%	98%	95%	90%	80%	70%	60%	50%	40%	30%	20%	10%
$1,350	$975	$750	$525	$400	$300	$225	$200	$175	$160	$150	$145

Add 25% for nickel finish.

Subtract $25-$50 for chipped hard rubber grips (commonly found on this model).

NEW POLICE TARGET – .32 Colt cal., 6 in. barrel, blue, late models use New Police frame, but include transitional improvements from later Police Positive Target Model (First Issue), last patent date on barrel was Nov. 6, 1888. Approx. 5,000 mfg. 1897-1907.

100%	98%	95%	90%	80%	70%	60%	50%	40%	30%	20%	10%
N/A	$1,950	$1,650	$1,200	$925	$725	$625	$450	$375	$350	$300	$275

POLICE POSITIVE (FIRST ISSUE) – .32 Colt, .32 New Police, .38 New Police, or .38 S&W cal., 2 1/2 in. (.32 cal., only), 4, 5, or 6 in. barrel, improved "positive lock" version of the New Police, hard rubber grips standard through 1923, square butt, checkered walnut grips became standard 1924, denoted by 1905 last patent date and smooth top strap. Mfg. 1907-27.

100%	98%	95%	90%	80%	70%	60%	50%	40%	30%	20%	10%
$1,000	$750	$650	$450	$375	$300	$275	$250	$225	$170	$165	$160

Add 15%-20% for nickel finish.

Add 10% for 90%+ condition early transitional guns that are double marked with "NEW POLICE" on frame.

Subtract $75-$100 for chipped grips.

POLICE POSITIVE (SECOND ISSUE) – similar to Police Positive First Issue, except has 1926 last patent date, serrated top strap, and slightly heavier frame, walnut grips standard. Mfg. 1928-1947.

100%	98%	95%	90%	80%	70%	60%	50%	40%	30%	20%	10%
$1,000	$750	$650	$455	$375	$300	$275	$250	$200	$170	$165	$160

Add 10% for .38 cal.

POLICE POSITIVE TARGET MODEL (FIRST ISSUE, MODEL "G") – .22 LR, .22 WRF, .32 Colt, or .32 New Police cal., 6 in. barrel, blue, adj. sight,

100%	98%	95%	90%	80%	70%	60%	50%	40%	30%	20%	10%

hard rubber grips standard through 1923, checkered walnut grips thereafter, last patent date on barrel was July 4, 1905, 22 oz. Mfg. 1907-1925.

$1,300	$1,100	$850	$575	$475	$425	$395	$375	$350	$325	$295	$275

Add 40% for .32 cal.

POLICE POSITIVE TARGET MODEL (SECOND ISSUE, MODEL "C") – similar to First Issue, except has slightly heavier frame and a last patent date of Oct. 5, 1926, blue finish, but a few were also mfg. in nickel, 26 oz. Mfg. 1926-41.

$1,200	$1,000	$775	$575	$475	$425	$395	$375	$350	$300	$270	$250

Add 40% for .32 cal.

Add 100% for nickel - extremely rare - must be verified by factory letter.

POLICE POSITIVE SPECIAL (FIRST ISSUE) – .32-20 WCF, .32 New Police, .38 New Police, or .38 Spl. cal., 4, 5, or 6 in. barrels, has a square butt and longer frame and cylinder to handle .38 Special and .32-20 WCF, fixed sights, frame longer to permit longer cylinder, denoted by 1905 last patent date on top of barrel, longer frame and smooth top strap, rubber grips. Mfg. 1907-27.

$900	$850	$550	$450	$375	$275	$250	$225	$200	$185	$175	$165

POLICE POSITIVE SPECIAL (SECOND ISSUE) – similar to Police Postitive Special (First Issue), except has 1926 last patent date on top of barrel, wood grips only, smooth (early mfg.) or checkered (later mfg.) trigger, and serrated top strap. Mfg. 1928-46.

$900	$850	$550	$450	$375	$275	$250	$225	$200	$185	$175	$165

CAMP PERRY MODEL – .22 LR cal., 8 in. (less common) or 10 in., Officer's Model frame modified to accept a flat single shot chamber. The model name was stamped on the left side of the chamber, the only single shot Colt on a revolver frame, last patent date on barrel was Oct. 5, 1926. 2,488 mfg. 1926-1941.

N/A	$2,350	$1,950	$1,500	$1,250	$975	$815	$745	$650	$495	$425	$365

Add 35% for 8 in. barrel.

BANKER'S SPECIAL – 2 in. barrel, blue, square butt standard through 1933, round butt standard 1934-40, last patent date on barrel was Oct. 5, 1926. Mfg. 1926-40.

* ***Banker's Special .38 cal.*** – available in .38 Colt Police Positive (New Police) or .38 S&W cal.

N/A	$1,850	$1,250	$900	$875	$625	$475	$275	$235	$200	$185	$165

Add 45% for nickel finish.

* ***Banker's Special .22 LR cal.***

N/A	$2,500	$1,850	$1,650	$1,100	$750	$650	$550	$475	$425	$385	$355

Add 30%-50% for nickel finish, depending on original condition.

COURIER – .22 S, L, or LR or .32 New Police (S&W) cal., double action, 6 shot, 3 in. barrel. Approx. 3,053 mfg. 1953-1956.

$1,500	$1,200	$950	$750	$550	$475	$425	$395	$350	$325	$295	$260

100%	98%	95%	90%	80%	70%	60%	50%	40%	30%	20%	10%

Add 10% for .22 cal.

Even though fewer .22 cal. Couriers were mfg. than Banker's Specials, the Banker's Specials are still more desirable, as they are of pre-war quality, and are less frequently encountered in 95-100% condition.

Some .32 New Police (S&W) cal. models can be found with alloy or steel cylinders.

AIRCREWMAN - .38 Spl. cal., double action, aluminum frame and cylinder, 2 in. barrel, 11 oz., fixed sights, checkered walnut grips overlapping at top of frame, inset with silver Air Force medallions, mfg. 1951 mostly.

N/A	$3,700	$2,750	$2,100	$1,700	$1,350	$1,075	$950	$850	$750	$675	$595

Approx. 1,200 mfg. within ser. no. range 2,900LW-7,775LW. Most were ordered destroyed. Perhaps less than 25 have survived.

BORDER PATROL (FIRST ISSUE) - .38 Spl. cal., double action, 6 shot, 4 in. heavy barrel, should have plastic grips, 400 mfg. during 1952 only in 823,000 ser. no. range.

N/A	$2,500	$1,500	$1,400	$1,125	$995	$875	$775	$675	$595	$525	$475

This model is built on the Official Police Model frame.

DETECTIVE SPECIAL PRE-WAR (FIRST ISSUE) - .38 Spl. cal., 2 in. barrel, blue, wood grips, square butt standard through 1932, round butt standard beginning 1933, last patent date on barrel was Oct. 5, 1926. Mfg. 1927-1946.

$2,350	$1,950	$1,725	$1,500	$1,300	$975	$795	$575	$400	$300	$250	$225

Add 20% for nickel finish.

Add 20% for square butt (early production only). Must be verified by factory letter and by ejector rod, since Police Positive Special (Second Issue) looks like a Detective Special.

DETECTIVE SPECIAL POST-WAR (SECOND ISSUE) - .32 NP, .38 NP, or .38 Spl. cal., 2 or 3 (scarce) in. barrel, can be distinguished from First Issue by 1/8 in. deeper frame (measured from hammer to bottom of frame behind trigger guard), plastic grips 1947-1954, wood grips 1955-1965, wraparound wood grips 1966-1972. Mfg. 1947-1972.

$1,450	$1,250	$950	$800	$550	$400	$275	$225	$210	$200	$190	$180

Add 20% for nickel finish.

Add 15% for 3 in. barrel.

There are four variations of the model - a pre-war design with post-war ser. nos., a "Transition" variation (late 1947-1952, with blue pre-war frame, late 1948-1952 have Coltwood grips), polished long grip frame (mfg. 1953-1966, round grip frame), and short grip frame (mfg. 1966-1972, walnut grip panels).

100%	98%	95%	90%	80%	70%	60%	50%	40%	30%	20%	10%

COBRA (FIRST ISSUE) - .22 LR, .32 Colt N.P., .38 Colt N.P., or .38 Spl. cal., first issue, 2, 3 (.22 LR cal. only), or 4 (square butt on early model, later models had round butt) in. barrel, blue or nickel finish, similar to Detective Special, only alloy frame and available in .22 LR, very early guns had plastic grips with silver medallions, changed to plastic w/o medallions, and finally changed to wood grips. Mfg. 1950-72.

100% values on the following Cobra models have been intentionally omitted, as ascertaining accurate values is very difficult and not predictable.

For definitive information on Cobras and variations, please refer to the new book *Seven Serpents - The History of Colt's Snake Guns* by Gurney Brown. Visit bluebookofgunvalues.com for more information, sample pages, and how to order. A few were shipped with factory installed hammer shroud.

* ***Cobra First Issue Blue Finish***

N/A	$1,250	$950	$800	$650	$450	$375	$325	$300	$275	$250	$200

Add 20%-40% for .22 LR cal.

Add 15%-25% for .38 cal. with 3 in. barrel.

* ***Cobra First Issue Nickel Finish***

N/A	$1,000	$850	$800	$750	$650	$575	$500	$425	$375	$300	$250

Add 30% for .22 LR cal.

Add 25% for .38 cal. with 3 in. barrel.

AGENT (FIRST ISSUE) - .38 Spl. cal., similar to Cobra first issue, except shorter grip frame. Mfg. 1962-1972.

$900	$800	$600	$400	$275	$235	$200	$190	$180	$170	$160	$150

COBRA (SECOND ISSUE) - .38 Spl. cal., similar to Cobra first issue, except shrouded ejector rod. Mfg. 1973-81.

100% values on the following Cobra models have been intentionally omitted, as ascertaining accurate values is very difficult and not predictable.

For definitive information on Cobras and variations, please refer to the book *Seven Serpents - The History of Colt's Snake Guns* by Gurney Brown. Visit bluebookofgunvalues.com for more information, sample pages, and how to order. A few were shipped with factory installed hammer shroud.

* ***Cobra Second Issue Blue Finish***

N/A	$850	$750	$600	$525	$450	$375	$325	$300	$275	$250	$200

Add 30% for .22 LR cal.

Add 25% for .38 cal. with 3 in. barrel.

* ***Cobra Second Issue Nickel Finish***

N/A	$1,150	$850	$800	$750	$650	$575	$500	$425	$375	$300	$250

Add 20%-40% for .22 LR cal.

Add 15%-25% for .38 cal. with 3 in. barrel.

MSR	100%	98%	95%	90%	80%	70%	60%

COMBAT COBRA – .357 Mag. cal., 2 1/2 in. barrel, special edition for Lew Horton with "CC" prefix and stainless steel construction. Mfg. 1986-1987.

	N/A	$4,150	$3,750	$2,450	$1,950	$1,800	$1,500

100% values have been intentionally omitted, as ascertaining accurate values is very difficult and not predictable.

For definitive information on Cobras and variations, please refer to the new book *Seven Serpents - The History of Colt's Snake Guns* by Gurney Brown. Visit bluebookofgunvalues.com for more information, sample pages, and how to order.

COBRA (NEW MFG.) – .38 Spl.+P cal., 2 in. barrel, 6 shot, matte finished stainless steel or two-tone (new 2019), red fiber optic front sight, Hogue stippled custom rubber grips with finger grooves, linear leaf main spring design allows smooth trigger pull, 25 oz. New 2017.

MSR $699	$625	$550	$500	$450	$400	$350	$300

Blue Book Publications selected this model as one of its Top 10 Industry Awards from all the new firearms at the 2017 SHOT Show.

* ***Cobra TT (Two-Tone)*** – .38 Spl.+P cal., 2 in. barrel, black DLC cylinder, 6 shot, brass bead front sight and Frame Trench rear sight, Hyena Brown G10 grips, LL2 Linear Leaf mainspring design, matte stainless steel finish. New 2019.

MSR $749	$650	$575	$515	$450	$400	$350	$300

* ***Bright Cobra*** – .38 Spl.+P cal., steel frame, 2 in. barrel, 6 shot, brass bead front sight, Frame Trench rear sight, black composite grips with Colt logo, LL2 Linear Leaf mainspring design, high polish finish. New 2019.

MSR $1,299	$1,075	$950	$850	$750	$650	$550	$450

NIGHT COBRA (NEW MFG.) – .38 Spl. +P cal., DAO, 2 in. barrel, 6 shot, stainless steel construction w/matte black DLC coating, bobbed hammer, Tritium front night sight, black synthetic VC G10 grips, linear leaf main spring design allows smooth trigger pull, 25 oz. New 2018.

MSR $899	$775	$650	$550	$475	$415	$375	$325

Blue Book Publications selected this model as one of its Top 10 Industry Awards from all the new firearms at the 2017 SHOT Show.

KING COBRA (OLDER MFG.) – .357 Mag. cal., blue metal, black neoprene round butt grips, 2 1/2 (new 1990), 4, or 6 in. solid rib barrel only, white outline rear sight, approx. 42 oz. (4 in. barrel). Mfg. 1986-92.

4 or 6 in. barrel	N/A	$1,950	$1,700	$1,450	$1,200	$950	$800
2 1/2 in. barrel	N/A	$3,500	$2,650	$2,000	$1,500	$1,100	$900

Last MSR was $410.

100% values have been intentionally omitted, as ascertaining accurate values is very difficult and not predictable.

For definitive information on Cobras and variations, please refer to

MSR	100%	98%	95%	90%	80%	70%	60%

the new book *Seven Serpents - The History of Colt's Snake Guns* by Gurney Brown. Visit bluebookofgunvalues.com for more information, sample pages, and how to order.

KING COBRA STAINLESS (OLDER MFG.) - .357 Mag. cal., stainless steel construction, black neoprene round butt grips, 2 (mfg. 1988-94), 4, 6, or 8 (mfg. 1990-94) in. solid rib barrel, white outline rear sight, approx. 36 oz. (2 1/2 in. barrel). Mfg. late 1986-92, production resumed 1994, disc. 1998.

	MSR	100%	98%	95%	90%	80%	70%
4 or 6 in. barrel	N/A	$2,100	$1,750	$1,450	$1,150	$950	$825
2 1/2 or 8 in. barrel	N/A	$2,500	$2,250	$1,975	$1,450	$1,050	$850

Last MSR was $485.

100% values have been intentionally omitted, as ascertaining accurate values is very difficult and not predictable.

For definitive information on Cobras and variations, please refer to the new book *Seven Serpents - The History of Colt's Snake Guns* by Gurney Brown. Visit bluebookofgunvalues.com for more information, sample pages, and how to order. A collector's note from Gurney Browns research: There were approx. 200 8 in. vent rib barreled King Cobra revolvers assembled using left over barrels from the Whitetailer production run with standard King Cobra markings. These revolvers WILL NOT letter from Colt as having a VR barrel. Small premiums may exist.

* ***King Cobra "Ultimate" Bright Stainless (Older Mfg.)*** - similar to King Cobra, except for bright stainless steel, 2 1/2 (new 1990), 4, 6, or 8 (new 1991) in. barrel. Mfg. 1988-92.

MSR	100%	98%	95%	90%	80%	70%
N/A	$2,850	$2,650	$2,200	$1,700	$1,300	$925

Last MSR was $470.

KING COBRA (CURRENT MFG). - .357 Mag. cal., stainless steel frame, 3 in. barrel, 6 shot, brass bead front sight, Hogue overmolded grips, brushed stainless steel finish, 28 oz. New 2019.

MSR	100%	98%	95%	90%	80%	70%	60%
MSR $899	$775	$650	$550	$475	$415	$375	$325

100%	98%	95%	90%	80%	70%	60%	50%	40%	30%	20%	10%

AGENT L.W. (SECOND ISSUE) - .38 Spl. cal., similar to First Issue, except shrouded ejector rod, matte finish since 1982. Mfg. 1973-1991.

100%	98%	95%	90%	80%	70%	60%	50%	40%	30%	20%	10%
$800	$625	$525	$425	$325	$275	$230	$200	$190	$180	$170	$160

Last MSR was $260.

DETECTIVE SPECIAL (THIRD ISSUE) - .38 Spl. cal., similar to Second Issue, shrouded ejector rod, 2 or 3 (scarce) in. barrel, integral long serrated ramp front sight, wraparound wood grips. Mfg. 1973-1986.

100%	98%	95%	90%	80%	70%	60%	50%	40%	30%	20%	10%
$975	$850	$750	$550	$475	$385	$350	$295	$200	$195	$185	$175

Last MSR was $429.

Add $100 for nickel finish. Add 15% for 3 in. barrel.

Add $600 for Class A engraving if in 98% condition or better.

100%	98%	95%	90%	80%	70%	60%	50%	40%	30%	20%	10%

COMMANDO SPECIAL - .38 Spl. cal., similar to Detective Special with steel frame, shrouded ejector rod, 2 in. barrel, matte parkerized finish, rubber grips. Mfg. 1984-86.

N/A	$750	$500	$400	$325	$295	$265	$235	$200	$190	$170	$150

Last MSR was $260.

POLICE POSITIVE SPECIAL (THIRD ISSUE) - .38 Spl. cal., similar to Detective Special Second Issue, except 4, 5, or 6 in. barrel. Mfg. 1947-76.

$750	$500	$400	$295	$250	$225	$200	$190	$180	$170	$160	$150

POLICE POSITIVE SPECIAL (FOURTH ISSUE) - .38 Spl. cal., shrouded ejector rod housing, steel frame, blue or nickel finish. Mfg. 1977-78.

$800	$600	$450	$300	$235	$210	$200	$190	$180	$170	$160	$150

Last MSR was $400.

Add 15% for nickel finish.

MSR	100%	98%	95%	90%	80%	70%	60%

POLICE POSITIVE MK V (FIFTH ISSUE) - .38 Spl. cal., full shrouded 4 in. barrel, steel frame, blue finish, rubber grips. Mfg. 1994-95.

	$600	$500	$400	$250	$195	$180	$165

100%	98%	95%	90%	80%	70%	60%	50%	40%	30%	20%	10%

VIPER MODEL - .38 Spl. cal., similar to Police Positive Special (Fourth Issue), alloy frame, 4 in. barrel, shrouded ejector rod housing. Mfg. 1977 only - rare.

N/A	$4,000	$3,650	$2,950	$2,450	$1,825	$1,550	$1,350	$1,100	$995	$850	$750

Add 50% for nickel finish.

100% values have been intentionally omitted, as ascertaining accurate values is very difficult and not predictable.

For definitive information on Vipers and variations, please refer to the new book *Seven Serpents - The History of Colt's Snake Guns* by Gurney Brown. Visit bluebookofgunvalues.com for more information, sample pages, and how to order.

DIAMONDBACK .22 CAL. - .22 LR or .22 WMR (rare) cal., 2 1/2 (scarce in .22 LR), 4, or 6 in. VR barrel, blue or nickel (more desireable) finish, adj. sights, steel frame, checkered walnut grips. Mfg. 1966-1991.

100% values on the following Diamondback models have been intentionally omitted, as ascertaining accurate values is very difficult and not predictable.

Note: .22 WMR cal. is rare, and values are difficult to accurately ascertain. Buyer beware - fakes do exist! Diamondbacks have risen in value so much that higher value guns based upon finishes, barrel length, etc. should be accompanied by a factory letter verifying details. Some guns were manufactured in electroless nickel also.

For definitive information on Diamondbacks and variations, please refer to the new book *Seven Serpents - The History of Colt's Snake Guns* by Gurney Brown. Visit bluebookofgunvalues.com for more information, sample pages, and how to order.

100%	98%	95%	90%	80%	70%	60%	50%	40%	30%	20%	10%

* ***Diamondback .22 cal. Blue w/2 1/2 In. Barrel***

N/A $4,000 $3,200 $2,000 $1,825 $1,550 $1,350 $1,100 $995 $850 $750 $650

A factory letter is now advisable on this configuration.

* ***Diamondback .22 cal. Nickel w/2 1/2 In. Barrel***

N/A $3,500 $3,150 $2,750 $2,250 $1,825 $1,550 $1,350 $1,100 $995 $850 $750

Extreme rarity factor precludes accurate pricing on this model. Currently, values can range from $4,000-$9,000 depending on condition, and if the gun will letter.

A factory letter is now advisable on this configuration.

* ***Diamondback .22 cal. Blue w/4 in. Barrel***

N/A $1,750 $1,450 $1,300 $1,100 $995 $850 $750 $650 $550 $475 $350

* ***Diamondback .22 cal. Nickel w/4 in. Barrel***

N/A $2,500 $2,300 $1,950 $1,700 $1,475 $1,300 $1,100 $995 $850 $750 $650

* ***Diamondback .22 cal. Blue w/6 in. Barrel***

N/A $1,750 $1,450 $1,300 $1,100 $995 $850 $750 $650 $550 $475 $350

* ***Diamondback .22 cal., Nickel w/6 in. Barrel*** – approx. 2,200 mfg. circa 1979.

N/A $2,500 $2,300 $1,950 $1,700 $1,475 $1,300 $1,100 $995 $850 $750 $650

DIAMONDBACK .38 SPL. – .38 Spl. cal., 2 1/2 (scarce), 4, or 6 in. VR barrel, blue or nickel finish, adj. sights, steel frame, checkered walnut grips. Mfg. 1966-1991.

For definitive information on Diamondbacks and variations, please refer to the new book *Seven Serpents - The History of Colt's Snake Guns* by Gurney Brown. Visit bluebookofgunvalues.com for more information, sample pages, and how to order.

* ***Diamondback .38 Spl. 4 or 6 in. Barrel***

N/A $1,450 $1,300 $1,100 $995 $850 $750 $650 $550 $475 $350 $275

Last MSR was $461.

Add 20% for nickel finish.

* ***Diamondback .38 Spl. 2 1/2 in. Barrel***

N/A $2,250 $1,750 $1,450 $1,300 $1,100 $995 $850 $750 $650 $550 $475

Add 20% for nickel finish.

COLT .357 MAG – 4 in. or 6 in. barrel, heavy frame, Accro rear sight, blue or nickel finish, checkered walnut grips. Mfg. 1953-61.

* ***Colt .357 Mag. Standard hammer***

N/A $1,000 $850 $775 $625 $475 $450 $350 $285 $270 $255 $240

Add 35% for nickel.

* ***Colt .357 Mag. Wide hammer w/target grips***

N/A $1,050 $900 $825 $675 $525 $475 $350 $300 $250 $225 $215

Add 35% for nickel.

In 1962, this model was absorbed into the Trooper line.

100%	98%	95%	90%	80%	70%	60%	50%	40%	30%	20%	10%

TROOPER – .22 LR (4 in. only, scarce), .357 Mag., or .38 Spl. cal., 4 or 6 in. barrel, blue or nickel finish, quick draw ramp front sight, adj. rear sight, checkered walnut grips. Mfg. 1953-69.

Add $100-$200 for .22 LR cal. (4 in. barrel only), depending on condition.

Add 25% for nickel finish.

* *Trooper Standard hammer*

$1,350	$1,100	$750	$675	$525	$350	$325	$295	$225	$195	$185	$175

* *Trooper Wide hammer and target grips*

$1,450	$1,250	$950	$800	$550	$400	$350	$300	$250	$200	$190	$180

Add 35% for nickel.

MSR	100%	98%	95%	90%	80%	70%	60%

TROOPER MK III – .22 LR, .22 WMR, .357 Mag., or .38 Spl. cal., 4, 6, or 8 in. solid rib barrel, adj. rear sight, walnut target grips, redesigned lock work to reduce amount of hand fitting needed on earlier Trooper versions. Mfg. 1969-1983.

Blue finish	$1,000	$950	$775	$575	$450	$325	$225
Nickel finish	$1,150	$850	$650	$525	$400	$300	$250

Add 50% for .22 WMR cal.

Add $300 for Custom Shop Model w/rosewood grips and factory tuned action.

TROOPER MK V – .357 Mag. cal. only, 4, 6, or 8 in. barrel, adj. rear sight, walnut target grips, improved version of Mark III action, vent. rib barrel, a few made with solid rib, redesigned 1982. Disc. 1986.

Blue finish	$1,000	$950	$775	$575	$450	$325	$225
Nickel finish	$1,150	$850	$650	$525	$400	$300	$250

Last MSR was $362 for Blue finish.

Last MSR was $396 for Nickel finish.

LAWMAN SKY MARSHAL – .38 Spl. cal., 2 in. barrel, experimental revolver with a replaceable plastic cylinder preloaded with plastic bullets, blue finish, checkered walnut grips, this model was designed to be carried on airliners by Federal Marshals during the 1970s.

N/A	$925	$850	$775	$700	$625	$550

Be wary of non-original alterations on this model as it can be modified very easily.

LAWMAN MK III – .357 Mag. cal., 2 in. and 4 in. barrel, unshrouded or shrouded ejector rod for 2 in. barrel, fixed sights, checkered walnut grips. Mfg. 1969-83.

Blue finish	$850	$750	$550	$450	$375	$300	$180
Nickel finish	$900	$850	$650	$550	$450	$350	$250

LAWMAN MK V – .357 Mag. cal., 2 or 4 in. barrel, shrouded ejector rod for 2 in. barrel, fixed sights, checkered walnut grips, improved version of MK III action. Mfg. 1984 and 1991 only.

Blue finish	$850	$750	$550	$450	$375	$325	$180

MSR	100%	98%	95%	90%	80%	70%	60%
Nickel finish	$900	$850	$650	$550	$450	$350	$250

Last MSR was $309 for Blue finish.

Last MSR was $328 for Nickel finish.

BORDER PATROL (SECOND ISSUE) - .357 Mag. cal., 4 in. heavy barrel, similar to Trooper Mark III frame, less polishing of frame. Limited mfg. 1970-75.

* ***Border Patrol Blue Finish*** - 5,356 mfg.

$975 $700 $600 $450 $375 $325 $275

* ***Border Patrol Nickel Finish*** - 1,152 mfg.

$1,150 $850 $650 $525 $400 $300 $250

PEACEKEEPER - .357 Mag. cal. only, similar to Trooper MK V, 4 or 6 in. barrel w/Python type rib, matte blue finish, rubber combat grips, adj. rear sight, about 42 oz. Mfg. 1985-1989.

$1,000 $950 $775 $575 $450 $325 $225

Last MSR was $330.

BOA - .357 Mag. cal., deep blue polish, Python type barrel w/full length ejector shroud and rib fitted to a Mark V action, 600 each mfg. in 4 and 6 in. barrel lengths. Entire production run was purchased by Lew Horton Distributing Co., Inc. located in Southboro, MA. 1985 retail was $525.

N/A $9,500 $8,500 $6,500 $5,500 $4,500 $3,500

100% values on the following Boa models have been intentionally omitted, as ascertaining accurate values is very difficult and not predictable.

For definitive information on Boas and variations, please refer to the new book *Seven Serpents - The History of Colt's Snake Guns* by Gurney Brown. Visit bluebookofgunvalues.com for more information, sample pages, and how to order.

* ***Boa Set*** - 100 sets mfg. including 4 and 6 in. barrels with Python type fully shrouded ejector rod housing and rib, consecutive serial numbers, cases were supplied by Lew Horton. 1985 retail was $1,200.

N/A $22,500 $18,500 $15,000 $12,500 $10,000 $8,500

DETECTIVE SPECIAL (FOURTH ISSUE) - .38 Spl. cal., 6 shot, 2 in. shrouded barrel, steel frame, blue finish, black composition grips with gold medallions, 21 oz. Mfg. 1993-1995.

$700 $600 $500 $400 $375 $300 $200

Last MSR was $400.

* ***Bobbed Detective Special*** - .38 Spl. cal., double action only with bobbed hammer, front night sight, honed action, choice of hard chrome or standard blue finish. Mfg. 1994-1995.

$850 $725 $600 $500 $375 $300 $250

Last MSR was $599.

Add $30 for hard chrome finish.

MSR	100%	98%	95%	90%	80%	70%	60%

COLT .38 SF-VI - .38 Spl. cal., 6 shot, 2 or 4 in. barrel, transfer bar safety, choice of matte (2 in.), bright polished (4 in.), or black (4 in.) finish, stainless steel, regular or bobbed (4 in. barrel only) hammer, fixed sights, black composition combat grips, 21 oz. Mfg. 1995-96.

	$850	$725	$600	$500	$375	$300	$250

Last MSR was $408.

* *Colt .38 Special Lady* - while advertised during 1996, this model had very limited mfg.

Extreme rarity factor precludes accurate values on this model.

COLT .38 DSII - .357 Mag. (new 1998) or .38 Spl. cal., 6 shot, 2 or 3 in. barrel, stainless steel, service hammer, rubber combat style checkered grips, 21 oz. Mfg. 1997-1998.

Nickel finish	$900	$850	$650	$550	$450	$350	$250

Last MSR was $435.

This model featured a redesigned trigger fire control group and is capable of shooting .38+P ammo.

COLT MAGNUM CARRY - .357 Mag. cal., 6 shot, 2 in. barrel, transfer bar safety, satin stainless steel, wraparound rubber grips with finger grooves, ramp front sight, 21 oz. Mfg. 1999 only.

	N/A	$2,100	$1,750	$1,450	$1,150	$925	$725

Last MSR was $460.

PYTHON & VARIATIONS - .357 Mag. cal., 2 1/2 (disc. 1994), 3 (a.k.a Combat Python, disc., very scarce), 4, 6, or 8 in. barrel with vent. rib, Royal blue, polished nickel, or Electroless Nickel (known as Royal Coltguard) satin nickel finish, fully shrouded ejector rod, adj. rear sight, checkered walnut grips (standard prior to 1991, and fitted on some SKUs much later), rubber Hogue monogrips (2 1/2 or 4 in. barrel), or rubber target (6 or 8 in. barrel) grips, 38-48 oz. A few late production guns included both a wood and rubber grip set. Mfg. 1955-1996.

As one of the few hand fitted revolvers ever produced, Python values have risen dramatically in recent years, especially early revolvers and any that remain in NIB or near NIB condition. 100% values on the following Python models have been intentionally omitted, as ascertaining accurate values is very difficult and not predictable. Over time, the value distinctions group the Python into 4 overall groups by period. These four groups are as follows: Early (circa 1950s) production with full checkered grips and high polish Royal blue, other early pre-suffix serial numbers up to about 1969, other production up to about 1990, and finally, 1990s production. In general, the older the Python, the higher the value.

For definitive information on all Pythons and variations, please refer to the new book *COLT'S PYTHON - King of the Seven Serpents* by Gurney Brown and *Seven Serpents - The History of Colt's Snake*

MSR	100%	98%	95%	90%	80%	70%	60%

Guns by Gurney Brown. Visit bluebookofgunvalues.com for more information, sample pages, and how to order.

* ***Python Blue or Royal Blue Finish (Mfg. 1955-1969)*** – first letter prefix or suffix used in ser. no., began in mid-1969 with the letter "E".

	MSR	100%	98%	95%	90%	80%	70%
4 or 6 in. barrel	N/A	$3,500	$2,650	$2,000	$1,500	$1,100	$900
2 1/2 in.	N/A	$4,250	$3,750	$2,675	$2,250	$1,750	$1,200

Add 50% for 3 in. barrel - purchase only with factory letter. 3 in. barreled Pythons were first (but not exclusively) mfg. for Lew Horton with "K" prefix.

Early production Pythons (serial numbered without letter prefix or suffix) with 4 or 6 in. barrels, fully checkered walnut grips with gold Colt medallions, and Accro flat-top sights will command a substantial premium.

* ***Python Blue or Royal Blue Finish (Mfg. circa 1970-1996)***

	MSR	100%	98%	95%	90%	80%	70%
4 or 6 in. barrel	N/A	$2,950	$2,450	$2,000	$1,550	$1,100	$900
2 1/2 in.	N/A	$3,750	$3,250	$2,675	$2,250	$1,750	$1,200
8 in.	N/A	$3,350	$2,750	$2,150	$1,750	$1,250	$975

Last MSR was $815.

Add 50% for 3 in. barrel with factory letter.

Beware of loose 3 in. barrel models sold by GPC and others during the 1990s.

The standard Python was manufactured 1955-1996, and 1997-recent production was through the Colt Custom Shop by special order only (see Python Elite listing).

During 2001-2002, Colt shipped some Pythons to dealers with prices in $1,100 - $1,200 retail range. These guns had a slightly different (rougher) line checkering pattern on the cylinder release and hammer parts.

There also exist a few Pythons mfg. in calibers other than .357 Mag., including .22 LR, .22 WMR, and .256 Win. Mag. (circa 1961), .41 Mag., and .44 Spl. cals. While the .22 LR and the .22 WMR (.22 Mag.) were advertised in earlier factory catalogs, they were never mass-produced - only a few prototypes exist. At least one known example of a .22 cal. Python was found at an auction, but it had only a special factory barrel sleeve for photographic purposes, and was not a shootable gun. The amount of premium on these cals. depends if the gun factory letters and how serious (and deep-pocketed) the Python collector is.

A California distributor special ordered a quantity of the first 3 in. barreled Pythons, which at the time were not available directly from the factory. This variation is called the California Combat Python, with the words "CALIFORNIA COMBAT" underneath the "PYTHON 357" marking on the left side of the barrel. Later, Colt made a special limited edition of 500 Combat Pythons, so marked for Lew

MSR	100%	98%	95%	90%	80%	70%	60%

Horton. These Lew Horton 3 inch Pythons are referred to as "Combat Pythons". A small number of the Combat Pythons were mfg. in nickel finish, and are very rare.

* ***Combat Python*** – .357 Mag cal., 3 in. barrel marked "COMBAT PYTHON." Rare.

	MSR	100%	98%	95%	90%	80%	70%
	N/A	$9,500	$8,500	$6,500	$5,500	$4,500	$3,500

* ***California Combat Python*** – .357 Mag cal., 3 in. barrel marked "PYTHON 357 MAG" over "CALIFORNIA COMBAT", made up from Python Targets with 8 in. barrels.

	MSR	100%	98%	95%	90%	80%	70%
	N/A	$6,500	$5,500	$4,500	$3,250	$2,500	$1,750

* ***Python Nickel Finish*** – available in traditional polished nickel or a satin nickel, called both Electroless Nickel and Royal Coltguard by Colt. Disc. 1985.

	MSR	100%	98%	95%	90%	80%	70%
4 or 6 in. barrel	N/A	$3,850	$3,250	$2,750	$2,250	$1,550	$1,250
4 or 6 in. Electroless Nickel	N/A	$5,250	$4,500	$4,150	$3,350	$2,750	$2,100
2 1/2 in. barrel	N/A	$4,400	$3,850	$2,950	$2,500	$1,950	$1,500
2 1/2 in. Electroless Nickel	N/A	$6,500	$5,650	$5,150	$4,750	$3,375	$2,600
3 in. barrel	N/A	$9,500	$8,500	$6,500	$5,500	$4,500	$3,500
8 in. barrel	N/A	$4,000	$3,500	$2,650	$2,150	$1,500	$1,250
8 in. Electroless Nickel	N/A	$5,500	$4,750	$4,350	$3,450	$2,850	$2,200

Last MSR was $693.

Satin nickel finish is so designated on original boxes as "Royal Coltguard" or "E NICK" (electroless nickel).

A Colt factory letter for the 3 in. barrel is mandatory if purchasing.

* ***Python Stainless Steel*** – stainless steel construction, matte or high polish finish, neoprene target or combat stocks, 2 1/2 (disc. 1994), 4, 6, or 8 (new 1989) in. barrel. Mfg. 1983-96.

	MSR	100%	98%	95%	90%	80%	70%
4 or 6 in. barrel	N/A	$3,500	$3,150	$2,500	$1,950	$1,350	$950
2 1/2 in. barrel	N/A	$7,500	$4,650	$3,150	$2,350	$1,600	$1,350
8 in. barrel	N/A	$3,950	$3,500	$3,000	$2,500	$2,000	$1,500

Last MSR was $904.

Add 100% for 2.5 inch ported barrel, Lew Horton edition of 1995.

Add 100% for Python Silver Snake (Factory Model #13060ESS), from Colt Custom Shop, 1982, laser etched.

Later production of the 6 in. barrel includes neoprene target stocks.

* ***Python "Ultimate" Bright Stainless Steel*** – deluxe, highly polished stainless model, 2 1/2 (disc.), 4, 6, or 8 in. VR barrel. Mfg. 1985-disc.

	MSR	100%	98%	95%	90%	80%	70%
4 or 6 in. barrel	N/A	$3,950	$3,500	$3,000	$2,500	$2,000	$1,500
2 1/2 in. barrel	N/A	$4,950	$4,500	$3,950	$3,250	$2,500	$1,750
8 in. barrel	N/A	$4,500	$4,000	$3,500	$2,750	$2,000	$1,500

Last MSR was $935.

MSR	100%	98%	95%	90%	80%	70%	60%

PYTHON ELITE - .357 Mag. cal., 4 or 6 in. VR barrel, choice of Royal Blue or stainless steel, adj. rear sight, rubber service style (disc.) or smooth walnut finger groove grips, roll-marked "PYTHON ELITE" on barrel, 38 or 43 1/2 oz. Mfg. 1997-1998, reintroduced 1999, again during 2002-2006.

This model was available by custom order only through the Colt Custom Shop.

Some early production models have Colt-Elliason rear sights, and recent production used Colt Accro sights. Some guns were shipped with both wood and hard rubber grips until 1999.

* ***Python Elite Blue***

	MSR	100%	98%	95%	90%	80%	70%	60%
	N/A	$3,750	$3,250	$2,750	$2,250	$1,750	$1,250	

Last MSR was $1,150.

* ***Python Elite Stainless*** - similar to Python Elite, except is stainless steel. Mfg. 1997-99, reintroduced 2002-2006.

	MSR	100%	98%	95%	90%	80%	70%	60%
	N/A	$3,950	$3,500	$3,000	$2,500	$2,000	$1,500	

Last MSR was $1,150.

A few examples from the first production run of Python Elite revolvers with "PN" serial number prefix are in Bright Stainless. Box end labels on these revolvers are marked "Stainless Steel Finish".

ULTIMATE PYTHON - .357 Mag. cal., 6 in. barrel only, specially tuned by the custom shop, supplied with both Colt-Elliason target and Accro white outline sighting systems, walnut and rubber grips also included, choice of Colt Royal Blue or Ultimate Stainless finish. Mfg. 1991-1993.

	MSR	100%	98%	95%	90%	80%	70%	60%
Royal Blue	N/A	$3,950	$3,500	$3,000	$2,500	$2,000	$1,500	
Ultimate Stainlesss	N/A	$4,500	$3,950	$2,750	$2,250	$1,950	$1,625	

Last MSR was $1,140.

Guns were delivered with 2 sets of Colt Python factory grips. Prices assume guns include both sets and accessories at time of resale.

PYTHON HUNTER - .357 Mag. cal., 8 in. barrel, includes Leupold 2x scope, Halliburton aluminum case, and accessories. Mfg. 1980-1981.

	MSR	100%	98%	95%	90%	80%	70%	60%
	N/A	$4,500	$3,950	$2,750	$2,250	$1,950	$1,625	

Last MSR was $995.

Subtract 10% if missing luggage case and accessories.

Values assume undamaged Halliburton case, scope and accessories including plastic cartridge box. Carefully observe the finish on this model as the foam rubber insert inside the Halliburton case can react with the metal finish if the revolver is left unprotected inside over a long period of time.

MSR	100%	98%	95%	90%	80%	70%	60%

PYTHON SILHOUETTE - .357 Mag. cal., 8 in. barrel, includes Leupold 2x scope, similar to Python Hunter, except barrel is roll marked with Silhouette name and scope position has been moved rearward, black luggage type case. Mfg. circa 1983.

N/A	$4,150	$3,750	$2,450	$1,950	$1,800	$1,500

Subtract 10% if missing luggage case and accessories.

Values assume undamaged black luggage case, scope and accessories.

PYTHON STALKER - .357 Mag. cal., 8 in. barrel, stainless steel, black combat style rubber grips with finger grooves and Colt medallions, left side of barrel marked "Silhouette", includes Leupold 2x scope, unfluted cylinder. Cased.

N/A	$3,950	$3,500	$2,200	$1,800	$1,650	$1,500

PYTHON TARGET - .38 Spl. cal., 8 in. barrel, blue (3,489 mfg.) or nickel (251 mfg.) finish, marked "PYTHON TARGET" on the barrel, sometimes referred to as "California Target Model." Disc.

Blue	N/A	$3,150	$2,600	$1,950	$1,700	$1,475	$1,300
Nickel	N/A	$3,950	$3,500	$2,200	$1,800	$1,650	$1,500

PYTHON TEN POINTER - .357 Mag. cal., 8 in. barrel, includes 3x Burris scope, wooden grips, extra set of neoprene composite grips, carrying case. Disc.

N/A	$3,750	$3,250	$2,750	$2,250	$1,750	$1,250

Deduct 15% if missing original case.

GRIZZLY - .357 Mag. cal., 6 in. Magna-Ported barrel, non-fluted cylinder, Pachmayr Decelerator rubber grips with Colt medallions, matte stainless, 999 mfg. 1994-1995.

N/A	$4,500	$3,950	$2,750	$2,250	$1,950	$1,625

This model was mfg. by the Colt Custom Shop using a King Cobra frame with a Python barrel and shipped in a blue box.

WHITETAILER - .357 Mag. cal., 8 in. barrel, blue or matte stainless finish, black plastic case, Burris 1.5-4x scope. 500 issued by Outdoor Sports Headquarters 1987.

N/A	$3,500	$2,650	$2,000	$1,500	$1,100	$900

Deduct 15% if original factory case is missing.

The Whitetailer Model was mfg. by the Colt Custom Shop using a Trooper MK V Model revolver.

* ***Whitetailer II*** - .357 Mag. cal., 8 in. barrel, matte stainless finish, Burris 1.5-4x scope and Colt soft case.

N/A	$3,250	$2,500	$1,750	$1,350	$1,000	$800

The Whitetailer II Model was mfg. by the Colt Custom Shop using a King Cobra Model revolver.

MSR	100%	98%	95%	90%	80%	70%	60%

KODIAK - .357 Mag. (rare), or .44 Mag. cal., 4 or 6 in. Mag-na-ported barrel with non-fluted cylinder, stainless steel, Pachmayr grips, built on Anaconda frame, "Colt Kodiak .44 Magnum" with outline of bear's footprint on left side of barrel, ser. nos. start with CKA. Approx. 2,000 mfg. in 1993 by Custom Shop.

.44 Mag. cal.	N/A	$3,950	$3,500	$2,200	$1,800	$1,650	$1,500
.357 Mag. cal. (rare)	N/A	$4,500	$3,950	$2,750	$2,250	$1,950	$1,625

ANACONDA - .44 Mag. or .45 LC (mfg. 1992-99) cal., 4 (new 1991), 5 (not factory cataloged, special edition only, mfg. 1998), 6, or 8 in. VR barrel, transfer bar safety system, 6 shot, choice of matte (disc. 2003), Realtree Grey camo (.44 Mag. with 8 in. barrel only, mfg. 1996 only) finish, or stainless steel, black neoprene combat grips with Colt medallion, red ramp front sight, full length ejector rod housing, white outline rear adj. sight, approx. 47-59 oz. Mfg. 1990-99, reintroduced 2002-2006.

100% values on the following Anaconda models have been intentionally omitted, as ascertaining accurate values is very difficult and not predictable.

For definitive information on Anacondas and variations, please refer to the new book *Seven Serpents - The History of Colt's Snake Guns* by Gurney Brown. Visit bluebookofgunvalues.com for more information, sample pages, and how to order.

* ***Anaconda 1st Edition*** - .44 Mag. cal., Ultimate Stainless finish, special rollmark on left side of barrel reads "Colt Anaconda First Edition", with aluminum carrying case, ser. no. range MM00001-MM01000, 1,000 mfg. 1990 only.

	N/A	$3,500	$3,000	$2,500	$2,000	$1,500	$1,000

* ***Anaconda 1990-1999 Mfg.*** - standard production, not mfg. by the Colt Custom Shop.

6 or 8 in. barrel	N/A	$1,900	$1,750	$1,500	$1,250	$1,000	$750
4 in. barrel	N/A	$2,500	$2,000	$1,750	$1,500	$1,250	$1,000

Add 20% for .45 LC cal.

* ***Anaconda 2002-2006 Mfg.*** - from 2002-2006, the Anaconda was only available through the Colt Custom Shop.

6 or 8 in. barrel	N/A	$1,900	$1,750	$1,500	$1,250	$1,000	$750
4 in. barrel	N/A	$2,000	$1,900	$1,750	$1,500	$1,250	$1,000

Last MSR was $1,000.

* ***Anaconda Camo*** - .44 Mag. cal. only, 8 in. barrel, Realtree Grey camo finish on gun and Redfield 2.5-7x scope, Hogue rubber grips w/Serpentine Colt logo, barrel marked "COLT-REALTREE" over "44 magnum". Mfg. 1996 only.

	N/A	$2,500	$2,250	$1,900	$1,600	$1,225	$800

Last MSR was $999.

MSR	100%	98%	95%	90%	80%	70%	60%

Revolver shipped with Realtree Gray camo soft case marked in yellow embroidery "TEAM COLT REALTREE".

* *Anaconda Hunter* - .44 Mag. cal., supplied with Leupold 2x scope, carrying case, cleaning accessories, and both walnut and rubber grips, 8 in. barrel only. Mfg. 1991-93.

MSR	100%	98%	95%	90%	80%	70%	60%
	N/A	$2,250	$2,100	$1,750	$1,350	$1,100	$750

Last MSR was $1,200.

* *Anaconda Custom Ported* - .44 Mag. cal., features 6 (disc.) or 8 in. Mag-na-ported barrel and Colt-Elliason rear sight, contoured trigger, and Pachmayr rubber grips, brushed stainless steel. Mfg. 1992-93, re-released 1995-96, again in 2002-2003.

MSR	100%	98%	95%	90%	80%	70%	60%
	N/A	$2,500	$2,250	$1,900	$1,600	$1,225	$800

Last MSR was $1,050.

100%	98%	95%	90%	80%	70%	60%	50%	40%	30%	20%	10%

RIFLES/CARBINES: PRE-1904

A Colt letter of provenance for the Colteer, Courier, and Stagecoach models listed below is $75.00 per gun. The charge for Lightning models listed below is $100 per gun (limited records). Colt-Burgess model factory letters are also available at $100 per gun.

The author wishes to express his thanks to Mr. Wilmer Kellogg and Mr. Michael Kelly for providing much of the information on Colt-Burgess and Lightning rifles in this section.

FIRST MODEL RING LEVER - .34, .36, .38, .40, or .44 cal., 8 or 10 shot revolving cylinder, 30 in. octagon barrel, walnut stock, no forend, 200 mfg., percussion. Mfg. 1837-1838.

* *First Model Ring Lever Standard Model*

100%	98%	95%	90%	80%	70%	60%	50%	40%	30%	20%	10%
N/A	N/A	N/A	$38,000	$28,500	$22,000	$17,000	$14,000	$11,500	$9,500	$8,000	$7,000

* *First Model Ring Lever Improved Model* - attached loading lever.

100%	98%	95%	90%	80%	70%	60%	50%	40%	30%	20%	10%
N/A	N/A	N/A	$41,500	$30,150	$23,250	$18,000	$15,000	$12,500	$10,500	$9,000	$8,000

SECOND MODEL RING LEVER - similar to First Model, w/o top strap over cylinder, .44 caliber only, percussion, 500 mfg., 1838-1841.

* *Second Model Ring Lever Standard Model*

100%	98%	95%	90%	80%	70%	60%	50%	40%	30%	20%	10%
N/A	N/A	N/A	$34,000	$30,000	$20,000	$15,000	$13,000	$11,000	$10,000	$7,800	$6,150

* *Second Model Ring Lever Improved Model*

100%	98%	95%	90%	80%	70%	60%	50%	40%	30%	20%	10%
N/A	N/A	N/A	$34,000	$30,000	$20,000	$15,000	$13,000	$11,000	$10,000	$7,800	$6,150

MODEL 1839 CARBINE - .52 smoothbore cal., 6 shot cylinder, 24 in. barrel, exposed hammer for cocking, blue finish, walnut stock, percussion, approx. 950 mfg. 1838-1841.

* *Model 1839 Carbine Early Model* - no loading lever.

100%	98%	95%	90%	80%	70%	60%	50%	40%	30%	20%	10%
N/A	N/A	N/A	$41,000	$39,000	$29,500	$22,500	$18,000	$15,250	$12,000	$9,850	$8,250

* *Model 1839 Carbine Standard Model*

100%	98%	95%	90%	80%	70%	60%	50%	40%	30%	20%	10%
N/A	N/A	N/A	$35,000	$31,500	$21,000	$16,000	$14,000	$11,000	$10,000	$7,800	$6,150

100% 98% 95% 90% 80% 70% 60% 50% 40% 30% 20% 10%

MODEL 1855 REVOLVING – .36, .44, or .56 cal., various barrel lengths and stock styles, 5 or 6 shot cylinder, blue with walnut buttstock, no forend, percussion. Mfg. 1856-1864.

* ***Model 1855 Revolving First Model w/o Forearm Wood*** – 15, 18, 21, 24 27, or 30 in. barrel, no forearm wood, non-fluted roll engraved cylinder ser. no. range 1-1,000, approx. 1,000 mfg.

N/A N/A N/A $12,000 $9,500 $8,350 $7,500 $7,000 $6,500 $6,000 $5,600 $5,250

* ***Model 1855 Revolving 1/2 Stock Sporter*** – 24, 27, or 30 in. barrel approx. 1,500 mfg.

N/A N/A N/A $12,000 $9,500 $8,350 $7,500 $7,000 $6,500 $6,000 $5,600 $5,250

* ***Model 1855 Revolving Full Stock Sporter*** – 21, 24, 27, 30, or 31 in barrel, approx. 2,000 mfg.

N/A N/A N/A $14,000 $12,000 $9,650 $9,000 $8,000 $7,450 $7,000 $6,600 $6,250

* ***Model 1855 Revolving Military Model, U.S.*** – martially marked, 21-37 in. barrel, 9,310 mfg.

N/A N/A N/A $18,000 $15,000 $12,400 $11,000 $10,300 $9,550 $9,000 $8,400 $8,000

* ***Model 1855 Revolving .36 Caliber Carbine Model*** – 15, 18, or 21 in. barrel, 4,400 mfg.

N/A N/A N/A $18,000 $15,000 $12,400 $11,000 $10,300 $9,550 $9,000 $8,400 $8,000

* ***Model 1855 Revolving .56 Caliber Artillery Carbine*** – 5 shot, 21 in. barrel with bayonet lug and forestock, approx. 64 mfg.

N/A N/A N/A $19,500 $17,000 $14,000 $11,375 $10,350 $9,600 $8,900 $8,450 $8,000

BERDAN – .42 bottle-necked CF cal., breechloading, approx. 30,000 mfg. 1866-circa 1870. Scarce since most were sent to Russia and have Russian barrel markings, approx. 50-100 are Hartford marked.

* ***Berdan Rifle*** – 32 1/2 in. barrel, approx. 10 lbs.

N/A N/A N/A $6,300 $5,300 $4,300 $3,800 $3,550 $3,300 $2,300 $1,650 $1,300

* ***Berdan Carbine*** – half stock, 18 1/4 in. barrel, approx. 50 mfg., both Russian and Hartford marked.

N/A N/A N/A $8,600 $7,900 $7,025 $6,400 $5,800 $5,050 $4,250 $3,575 $3,050

MODEL 1861 MUSKET – .58 cal., percussion, muzzle loader, 40 in. barrel, with 3 bands, white metal parts, white walnut stock. 75,000 mfg., 1861-65.

N/A N/A N/A $7,300 $5,300 $4,300 $3,800 $3,550 $3,300 $2,300 $1,650 $1,300

COLT-BURGESS LEVER ACTION – .44-40 WCF cal., 25 1/2 in. barrel, 15 shot tube mag., blue with case hardened lever and hammer, walnut stock. 6,403 mfg., 1883-1885.

N/A N/A N/A $12,900 $9,775 $6,600 $5,600 $4,500 $4,000 $3,450 $2,950 $1,890

COLT-BURGESS CARBINE – similar to Rifle, with 20 in. barrel.

N/A N/A N/A $19,200 $16,500 $12,900 $10,800 $8,700 $7,150 $5,600 $4,000 $2,950

100%	98%	95%	90%	80%	70%	60%	50%	40%	30%	20%	10%

COLT-BURGESS LIGHT CARBINE - lightened version of Carbine.

N/A N/A N/A $22,575 $19,425 $16,275 $14,175 $12,075 $9,975 $7,875 $4,725 $3,675

LIGHTNING SLIDE ACTION RIFLE (CLMR) - SMALL FRAME - .22 S or L cal., 24 in. barrel, open sights, walnut straight stock, round or octagon barrel. Approx. 90,000 mfg. 1887-1904.

N/A N/A N/A $5,700 $4,275 $3,800 $3,325 $2,850 $2,550 $2,150 $1,600 $950

Add 25% for deluxe model.

LIGHTNING SLIDE ACTION RIFLE (CLMR) - MEDIUM FRAME - .32 CLMR (.32-20 WCF), .38 CLMR (.38-40 WCF), or .44 CLMR (.44-40 WCF) cal., similar to Small Frame, except with 26 in. barrel and larger frame. Serial range 1-23,000, id not have a dust cover. Approx. 90,000 mfg. 1884-1902.

N/A N/A N/A $6,175 $5,500 $4,850 $4,500 $3,325 $2,850 $2,500 $1,900 $1,700

Add 25% for deluxe model.

23 Medium Frame rifles were shipped to A.G. Spalding and Brothers during 1897, a major sporting goods supplier located in Chicago. Most of these guns are factory engraved, and were probably used for display during the Chicago Exposition. These deluxe rifles represent some of the finest Colt rifles ever manufactured.

LIGHTNING CARBINE MEDIUM FRAME - similar to Medium Frame Rifle, with 20 in. barrel.

N/A N/A N/A $8,075 $7,125 $6,175 $5,225 $4,275 $3,800 $3,325 $2,850 $1,900

LIGHTNING BABY CARBINE MEDIUM FRAME - lightened version of Medium Frame Carbine, one pound lighter.

N/A N/A N/A $9,250 $7,125 $6,175 $5,225 $4,275 $3,800 $3,325 $2,850 $2,375

Add 50% for .50-95 Express cal.

LIGHTNING SLIDE ACTION RIFLE (CLMR) - LARGE FRAME - .38-56 WCF, .40-60 Marlin (most common), .45-60 WCF (rarest), .45-85 Marlin, or .50-95 Express (rare) cal., large version of previously described Lightnings, approx. 4,600 mfg. 1887-1894.

N/A N/A N/A $11,000 $9,000 $7,600 $6,650 $5,225 $4,275 $3,325 $2,375 $1,900

Add 25% for .50-95 Express cal.

Add 25% for deluxe model.

Add 25% for .45-60 cal. (approx. 8% mfg. in this cal.).

There may be a gap in the serial range of this model from ser. no. 2435 to 4444.

LIGHTNING CARBINE LARGE FRAME - similar to Large Frame Rifle, 22 in. barrel.

N/A N/A N/A $13,000 $10,150 $8,250 $6,350 $5,425 $4,450 $3,750 $3,500 $3,050

LIGHTNING BABY CARBINE LARGE FRAME - lightened version of Large Frame Carbine, one pound lighter.

N/A N/A N/A $13,000 $10,165 $8,250 $6,350 $5,400 $4,450 $3,750 $3,500 $3,050

Add 50% for .50-95 Express cal.

100%	98%	95%	90%	80%	70%	60%	50%	40%	30%	20%	10%

LIGHTNING MILITARY STYLE MUSKET - similar to Medium Frame Rifle, with bayonet lug.

N/A	N/A	N/A	N/A	N/A	N/A	$5,225	$4,275	$3,325	$2,375	$1,900	$1,425

Approximately 250 of these rifles with 27 in. round barrels, swivels, and carbine buttstocks, in serial ranges 50,000 and 51,000 were shipped to Costa Rica.

LIGHTNING SAN FRANCISCO POLICE - .44 CLMR (.44-40 WCF) cal., 26 in. round barrel Medium Frame rifle, with S.F.P. Police and rack numbers on lower tang. Ser. no. range S.F.P. 1-S.F.P. 401.

N/A	$9,975	$8,800	$7,350	$6,500	$5,000	$4,000	$3,550	$3,000	$2,500	$1,875	$1,500

DOUBLE RIFLE SxS - various cals. in the .45 range, hammers, very limited production between 1878-1880. Most guns were owned by friends of Caldwell Colt - Sam Colt's son, the original designer. Colt Double Rifles are extremely rare and desirable, and should be examined carefully.

Prices typically range between $80,000-$110,000, if all original.

MSR	100%	98%	95%	90%	80%	70%	60%

RIFLES: BOLT ACTION, CENTERFIRE

COLT "57" - .243 Win. or .30-06 cal., FN Mauser action, mfg. by Jefferson Mfg. Co. in N. Haven, CT during 1957, approx. 5,000 mfg. starting at ser. no. 1, checkered American Monte Carlo walnut stock, rear aperture and wraparound front sight, drilled and tapped for scope.

	$695	$650	$600	$550	$500	$450	$400

This model was also available in a deluxe version with deluxe hand checkered walnut stock - add 15%.

COLTSMAN STANDARD RIFLE - .223 Rem., .243 Win., .264 Win. Mag., .30-06, .300 Win. Mag., or .308 Win. cal., mfg. by Kodiak, Mauser or Sako action, 22 or 24 (.300 Win. Mag.) in. barrel, 5 or 6 shot mag. Approx. 10,000 (both models) mfg. 1958-66.

	$495	$450	$425	$400	$350	$325	$300

COLTSMAN CUSTOM RIFLE - deluxe variation including deluxe walnut stock with skipline checkering and rosewood forearm cap.

	$695	$650	$600	$550	$500	$450	$400

COLT SAUER RIFLE (STANDARD ACTION) - .25-06 Rem., .270 Win., or .30-06 cal., non-rotating bolt action, manufactured in Germany by J. P. Sauer & Sohn, 24 in. barrel, 4 shot detachable mag., no sights, checkered walnut stock with rosewood forend tip and pistol grip cap, recoil pad. Mfg. 1974-1985.

	$2,175	$1,875	$1,650	$1,475	$1,325	$1,075	$850

Last MSR was $1,257.

Add 20% for .25-06 Rem. cal.

MSR	100%	98%	95%	90%	80%	70%	60%

COLT SAUER SHORT ACTION - similar to the standard except in .22-250 Rem., .243 Win., or .308 Win. cal. Mfg. 1976-85.

	$2,750	$2,375	$1,975	$1,750	$1,425	$1,150	$875

Last MSR was $1,257.

Add 25% for .22-250 Rem. or .308 Win. cal.

COLT SAUER MAGNUM - similar to the standard except in 7mm Rem. Mag., .300 Win. Mag., or .300 Weatherby Mag. cal. Mfg. 1974-1985.

	$2,695	$2,350	$2,025	$1,835	$1,475	$1,225	$950

Last MSR was $1,300.

Subtract 20% for 7mm Rem. Mag. cal.

COLT SAUER GRADE III - similar to Grade IV, except scroll engraved nitride/nickel receiver w/o game scenes, "Colt" stamped on flat knob or standard round knob.

	$4,995	$4,375	$3,750	$3,395	$2,750	$2,250	$1,750

Add 10% for Magnum cals.

COLT SAUER GRADE IV - similar to the Magnum except has silver receiver, each caliber featured a different engraved animal.

	$5,995	$5,250	$4,495	$4,075	$3,295	$2,700	$2,100

Add 10% for Magnum cals.

COLT SAUER GRAND ALASKAN - heavier version in .375 H&H cal., adj. sights. Mfg. 1978-1985.

	$2,895	$2,535	$2,175	$1,975	$1,595	$1,300	$1,050

COLT SAUER GRAND AFRICAN - .458 Win. Mag. cal., 4 round capacity, 9 lb. 12 oz. Mfg. 1974-1985.

	$2,895	$2,535	$2,175	$1,975	$1,595	$1,300	$1,050

Last MSR was $1,400.

COLT LIGHT RIFLE - .243 Win., .260 Rem., .270 Win., .280 Rem., .25-06 Rem., .30-06, .308 Win., 7x57mm, .300 Win. Mag., 7mm-08 Rem., or 7mm Rem. Mag. cal., short or long action, matte black synthetic stock, matte metal finish, adj. trigger, 3 position side-swing safety, approx. 5.4 lbs. in short action. Mfg. by Saco Defense in the U.S. 2000-disc.

	$675	$550	$500	$450	$400	$350	$295

Last MSR was $779.

COLT PRECISION RIFLE (M2012SA308) - .308 Win. cal., tactical configuration featuring 22 in. heavy match grade spiral fluted stainless steel barrel with muzzle brake, skeletonized adj. forged aluminum stock, pistol grip, vent. aluminum handguard with 2/3 length Picatinny rail, 5 or 10 shot mag., black finish, Timney single stage adj. trigger, 13.2 lbs. Mfg. by Cooper Firearms of Montana 2013-2015.

	$3,300	$2,950	$2,600	$2,300	$2,000	$1,850	$1,625

Last MSR was $3,799.

MSR	100%	98%	95%	90%	80%	70%	60%

COLT M2012LT260G/308G – .260 Rem. or .308 Win. cal., 22 in. 6-groove button rifled medium heavy match grade chrome moly fluted barrel with Cooper Firearms muzzle brake, 5 or 10 shot mag., Timney adj. single stage trigger, custom grey laminated wood stock, 8 1/2 lbs. Mfg. 2013-2015.

	$2,375	$2,075	$1,775	$1,625	$1,300	$1,075	$825

Last MSR was $2,799.

COLT M2012MT308T – .308 Win. cal., 22 in. 6-groove button rifled heavy match grade stainless fluted barrel with Cooper Firearms muzzle brake, 5 or 10 shot mag., Timney adj. single stage trigger, custom Manners composite stock, Coyote Tan finish, 10 1/4 lbs. Mfg. mid-2013-2015.

	$2,775	$2,400	$2,050	$1,850	$1,500	$1,225	$950

Last MSR was $3,199.

RIFLES: BOLT/SEMI-AUTO ACTION, RIMFIRE

COLTEER 1-22 – .22 LR or .22 WMR cal., single shot bolt action, 20, 22, or 24 (.22 WMR only, w/o sights) in. round barrel, adj. rear sight (20 or 22 in. barrel), plain walnut stock. Approx. 50,000 mfg. 1957-66.

	$400	$325	$265	$225	$200	$175	$150

Add 10% for .22 WMR cal.

STAGECOACH – .22 LR cal., semi-auto, 16 1/2 in. barrel, 13 shot mag., deluxe walnut stock, saddle ring w/leather thong, roll-engraved hold-up scene. Over 25,000 mfg. 1965-mid 1970s.

	$400	$325	$265	$225	$200	$175	$150

Subtract 5% if wood and finish are scratched in front of the barrel/forearm band.

Subtract 5-10% if w/o the front sight hood.

Subtract 10% if gold color is missing in stagecoach scene.

This model has a soft aluminum alloy painted receiver which was very easily scratched. It is quite common to find these guns in 80 to 85% condition with very little market interest. It is becoming common place to find these guns with the receiver repainted. There is a limited market interest in guns that are 98% condition and better. On the models that have the band around the barrel and forearm, it is common to see the wood and finish scratched where the band has been slid forward.

COLTEER – .22 LR cal., similar to Stagecoach, except 19 3/8 in. barrel, 15 shot mag., no engraving and plain walnut stock. Over 25,000 mfg. 1965-mid 1970s.

	$350	$325	$265	$225	$200	$175	$150

Subtract 5% if wood and finish are scratched in front of the barrel/forearm band.

Subtract 5-10% if w/o the front sight hood.

This model has a soft aluminum alloy painted receiver which was very easily scratched. It is quite common to find these guns in 80 to 85% condition with very little market interest. It is becoming common place to find these guns with the receiver repainted. There

MSR	100%	98%	95%	90%	80%	70%	60%

is a limited market interest in guns that are 98% condition and better. On the models that have the band around the barrel and forearm, it is common to see the wood and finish scratched where the band has been slid forward.

COURIER - similar to Colteer semi-auto, except pistol-grip stock and enlarged forearm. Mfg. 1970-mid-1970s.

	$400	$325	$265	$225	$200	$175	$150

Subtract 5% if wood and finish are scratched in front of the barrel/forearm band.

Subtract 5-10% if w/o the front sight hood.

This model has a soft aluminum alloy painted receiver which was very easily scratched. It is quite common to find these guns in 80 to 85% condition with very little market interest. It is becoming common place to find these guns with the receiver repainted. There is a limited market interest in guns that are 98% condition and better. On the models that have the band around the barrel and forearm, it is common to see the wood and finish scratched where the band has been slid forward.

RIFLES: SINGLE SHOT, CENTERFIRE

COLT-SHARPS STANDARD OR DELUXE RIFLE - .17 Rem., .222 Rem. (Mfg.), .22-250 Rem. (Mfg. 106), .243 Win. (Mfg.103), .25-06 Rem. (Mfg. 79), .270 Win. (Mfg. 1), 7mm Rem. Mag. (Mfg. 86), .30-06 (Mfg. 120), .375 H&H (Mfg. 2), .50-70 Govt. (two known) cal., 26 or 28 in. heavy (rare) barrel, Sharps falling block action with Timken roller bearings, high-gloss bluing, Canjar set trigger, deluxe Fleur-De-Lis checkered Monte Carlo walnut stock and forearm with cheekpiece and choice of beavertail or standard forearm, engraved cartridge trap door (Deluxe Models) in stock and trigger guard, wood case with accessories, all guns were shipped with a Leupold VARI-X II 3-9x40mm scope with a special scope mount, supplied with either a full length wood and leather case (most desirable) or a green fiberglass case. Approx. 502 were mfg. 1970-1977 serial numbered CS000-CS502.

	$6,250	$5,500	$5,000	$4,500	$3,750	$3,250	$2,750

Add 10% for 28 in. heavy barrel.

Subtract 10% for missing case and accessories or Leupold scope and mount.

Subtract 10% for Standard model (approx. 50 mfg. without Monte Carlo stock, cartridge trap, engraving, or case) - serial range starts at CS2000.

Above values are for the standard calibers .22-250 Rem., .243 Win., .25-06 Rem., .30-06, or 7mm Rem. Mag. with case, accessories, and Leupold scope and mount.

DRILLINGS

COLT SAUER DRILLING - 12 ga./.30-06, 16 ga./.30-06 (rare), or .243 Win. cal., 25 in. barrels, engraved receiver, 8 lbs. Disc. 1985.

	$4,850	$4,300	$3,600	$3,100	$2,675	$2,200	$1,800

Last MSR was $4,228.

MSR	100%	98%	95%	90%	80%	70%	60%

RIFLES: SEMI-AUTO, CENTERFIRE, AR-15 & VARIATIONS

The AR-15 rifle and variations are the civilian versions of the U.S. armed forces M-16 model, which was initially ordered by the U.S. Army in 1963. Colt's obtained the exclusive manufacturing and marketing rights to the AR-15 from the ArmaLite division of the Fairchild Engine and Airplane Corporation in 1961.

Factory Colt AR-15 receivers are stamped with the model names only (Sporter II, Government Model, Colt Carbine, Sporter Match H-Bar, Match Target), but are not stamped with the model numbers (R6500, R6550, R6521, MT6430, CR6724). Because of this, if an AR-15 rifle/carbine does not have its original box, the only way to determine whether the gun is pre-ban or not is to look at the serial number and see if the configuration matches the features listed below within the two pre-ban subcategories.

AR-15 production included transition models, which were made up of obsolete and old stock parts. These transition models include: blue label box models having large front takedown pins, no internal sear block, 20 in. barrel models having bayonet lugs, misstamped nomenclature on receivers, or green label bolt assemblies.

Rifling twists on the Colt AR-15 have changed throughout the years, and barrel twists are stamped at the end of the barrel on top. They started with a 1:12 in. twist, changed to a 1:7 in. twist (to match with the new, longer .223 Rem./5.56mm SS109-type bullet), and finally changed to a 1:9 in. twist in combination with 1:7 in. twist models as a compromise for bullets in the 50-68 grain range. Current mfg. AR-15s/Match Targets have rifling twists/turns incorporated into the model descriptions.

Colt's never sold pre-ban lower receivers individually. It only sold completely assembled rifles.

A Colt letter of provenance for the following AR-15 models is $100 per gun.

AR-15, Pre-Ban, 1963-1989 Mfg. w/Green Label Box

Common features of 1963-1989 mfg. AR-15s are bayonet lug, flash hider, large front takedown pin, no internal sear block, and no reinforcement around the magazine release button.

AR-15 boxes during this period of mfg. had a green label with serial number affixed on a white sticker. Box is taped in two places with brown masking tape. NIB consists of the rifle with barrel stick down the barrel, plastic muzzle cap on flash hider, factory tag hanging from front sight post, rifle in plastic bag with ser. no. on white sticker attached to bag, cardboard insert, accessory bag with two 20 round mags., manual, sling, and cleaning brushes. Cleaning rods are in separate bag.

Pre-ban parts rifles are rifles which are not assembled in their proper factory configuration. Counterfeit pre-ban rifles are rifles using post-ban receivers and assembled into a pre-ban configuration (it is a felony to assemble or alter a post-ban rifle into a pre-ban configuration).

Add $100 for NIB condition.

Add $300 for early green label box models with reinforced lower receiver.

SP-1 (R6000) - .223 Rem. cal., GIO, original Colt tactical configuration without forward bolt assist, 20 in. barrel with 1:12 in. twist, identifiable by the triangular shaped handguards/forearm, no case deflector, A1 sights, finishes included parkerizing and electroless nickel, approx. 6 3/4 lbs. Ser. no. range SP0001-SP16000 through 1976. Mfg. 1963-1984.

	100%	98%	95%	90%	80%	70%	60%
	$2,450	$2,150	$1,850	$1,650	$1,500	$1,350	$1,200

MSR	100%	98%	95%	90%	80%	70%	60%

Add 40%-60% for mint original models with early two and three digit serial numbers.

Pre-ban serialization is ser. no. SP360,200 and lower.

Early SP-1s were packaged differently than later standard green box label guns.

* ***SP-1 Carbine (R6001)*** - .223 Rem. cal., similar to SP-1, except has 16 in. barrel, ribbed handguards, collapsible buttstock, high gloss finish.

	100%	98%	95%	90%	80%	70%	60%
	$3,000	$2,600	$2,250	$1,950	$1,800	$1,500	$1,350

Mint original condition models with early two and three digit serial numbers are selling in the $3,250 - $3,500 range.

Pre-ban serialization is ser. no. SP360200 and lower.

Early SP-1s were packaged differently than later standard green box label guns.

SPORTER II (R6500) - .223 Rem. cal., GIO, various configurations, receiver stamped "Sporter II", 20 in. barrel, 1:7 twist, A1 sights and forward assist, disc.

	100%	98%	95%	90%	80%	70%	60%
	$1,850	$1,650	$1,450	$1,250	$1,100	$950	$850

Serial numbers SP360200 and below are pre-ban.

* ***Sporter II Carbine (R6420)*** - .223 Rem. cal., similar to Sporter II, except has 16 in. barrel, A1 sights and collapsible buttstock.

	100%	98%	95%	90%	80%	70%	60%
	$2,500	$2,200	$1,900	$1,750	$1,600	$1,400	$1,250

Serial numbers SP360200 and below are pre-ban.

GOVERNMENT MODEL (R6550) - .223 Rem. cal., GIO, receiver is stamped Government Model, 20 in. barrel with 1:7 in. twist and bayonet lug, A2 sights, forward assist and brass deflector, very desirable because this model has the closest configurations to what the U.S. military is currently using.

	100%	98%	95%	90%	80%	70%	60%
	$2,250	$1,950	$1,800	$1,650	$1,400	$1,200	$950

In 1987, Colt replaced the AR-15A2 Sporter II Rifle with the AR-15A2 Govt. Model. This new model has the 800 meter rear sighting system housed in the receiver's carrying handle (similar to the M-16 A2).

Serial numbers GS008000 and below with GS prefix are pre-ban.

* ***Government Model (6550K)*** - .223 Rem. cal., similar to R6550, except does not have bayonet lug, originally supplied with .22 L.R. cal. conversion kit.

	100%	98%	95%	90%	80%	70%	60%
	$2,100	$1,900	$1,750	$1,600	$1,450	$1,250	$1,000

Subtract $300 w/o conversion kit.

Serial numbers GS008000 and below with GS prefix are pre-ban.

* ***Government Model (R6550CC)*** - .223 Rem. cal., similar to R6550, except has Z-Cote tiger striped camo finish, very scarce (watch for cheap imitation paint jobs).

	100%	98%	95%	90%	80%	70%	60%
	$3,500	$3,350	$3,100	$2,800	$2,600	$2,400	$2,000

Serial numbers GS008000 and below with GS prefix are pre-ban.

MSR	100%	98%	95%	90%	80%	70%	60%

H-BAR MODEL (R6600) - GIO, HBAR model with 20 in. heavy barrel, 1:7 *twist, forward assist, A2 sights, brass deflector, 8 lbs. New 1986.*

	$2,100	$1,900	$1,750	$1,600	$1,450	$1,250	$1,000

Serial numbers SP360200 and below are pre-ban.

* ***H-Bar (R6600K)*** - similar to R6600, except has no bayonet lug, supplied with .22 LR cal. conversion kit.

	$1,850	$1,650	$1,450	$1,250	$1,100	$950	$850

Subtract $300 if w/o conversion kit.

Serial numbers SP360200 and below are pre-ban.

* ***Delta H-Bar (R6600DH)*** - similar to R6600, except has 3-9x rubber armored scope, removable cheekpiece, adj. scope mount, and black leather sling, test range selected for its accuracy, aluminum transport case. Mfg. 1987-1991.

	$2,500	$2,200	$1,900	$1,750	$1,600	$1,400	$1,250

Last MSR was $1,460.

Serial numbers SP360200 and below are pre-ban.

AR-15, Pre-Ban,1989-Sept. 11,1994 Mfg. w/Blue Label Box

Common features of 1989-1994 AR-15 production include a small front takedown pin, internal sear block, reinforcement around the mag. release button, flash hider, no bayonet lug on 20 in. models, A2 sights, brass deflector, and forward bolt assist. Models R6430 and 6450 do not have A2 sights, brass deflector, or forward bolt assist.

Blue label boxed AR-15s were mfg. between 1989-Sept. 11, 1994. Please refer to box description under Pre-1989 AR-15 mfg.

Pre-ban parts rifles are rifles which are not assembled in their proper factory configuration. Counterfeit pre-ban rifles are rifles using post-ban receivers and assembled into a pre-ban configuration.

Add $100 for NIB condition.

AR-15A3 TACTICAL CARBINE (R-6721) - .223 Rem. cal., GIO, M4 flat-top with 16 in. heavy barrel, 1:9 twist, A2 sights, pre-ban configuration with flash hider, bayonet lug, and 4-position, collapsible stock, removable carry handle, 134 were sold commercially in the U.S., most collectible AR-15. Mfg. 1994 only.

S/N 134 and lower	$3,000	$2,500	$2,275	$2,050	$1,900	$1,775	$1,600
S/N 135 and higher	$2,000	$1,850	$1,700	$1,450	$1,225	$1,050	$900

On the R-6721, serial numbers BD000134 and below are pre-ban.

Please note the serial number cutoff on this model, as Colt shipped out a lot of unstamped post-ban law enforcement only "LEO" rifles before finally stamping them as a restricted rifle.

GOVERNMENT CARBINE (R6520) - .223 Rem cal., GIO, receiver is stamped Government Carbine, two-position collapsible buttstock, 800 meter adj. rear sight, 16 in. barrel with bayonet lug, 1:7 twist, shortened forearm, 5 lbs. 13 oz. Mfg. 1988-94.

$2,275 $2,125 $2,000 $1,850 $1,650 $1,500 $1,250

Last MSR was $880.

Add $200 for green label box.

On the R6520, serial numbers GC018500 and below are pre-ban.

Please note the serial number cutoff on this model, as Colt shipped out a lot of unstamped post-ban law enforcement only "LEO" rifles before finally stamping them as a restricted rifle.

This model was manufactured in both green and blue label configurations.

COLT CARBINE (R6521) - receiver is stamped Colt Carbine, similar to R6520, except has no bayonet lug, 16 in. barrel, 1:7 twist. Disc. 1988.

$2,275 $2,125 $2,000 $1,850 $1,650 $1,500 $1,250

Last MSR was $770.

Serial numbers CC001616 and below are pre-ban.

SPORTER LIGHTWEIGHT (R6530) - .223 Rem. cal., GIO, receiver is stamped Sporter Lightweight, 16 in. barrel, 1:7 twist, similar to R6520, except does not have bayonet lug or collapsible stock.

$2,000 $1,850 $1,700 $1,450 $1,225 $1,050 $900

Last MSR was $740.

Serial numbers SI027246 and below are pre-ban.

9mm CARBINE (R6430) - 9mm Para. cal., similar to R6450 Carbine, except does not have bayonet lug or collapsible stock. Mfg. 1992-1994.

$2,150 $2,050 $1,950 $1,800 $1,600 $1,450 $1,150

Serial numbers NL004800 are pre-ban.

9mm CARBINE (R6450) - 9mm Para. cal., GIO, carbine model with 16 in. barrel, 1:10 twist, bayonet lug, w/o forward bolt assist or brass deflector, two-position collapsible stock, 20 shot mag., 6 lbs. 5 oz.

$2,250 $2,100 $2,000 $1,800 $1,600 $1,500 $1,250

Last MSR was $696.

On the R6450, serial numbers TA010100 are pre-ban.

Please note the serial number cutoff on this model, as Colt shipped out a lot of unstamped post-ban law enforcement only "LEO" rifles before finally stamping them as a restricted rifle.

This model was manufactured with either a green or blue label.

7.62x39mm CARBINE (R6830) - 7.62x39mm cal., GIO, 16 in. barrel w/o bayonet lug, 1:12 twist, fixed buttstock. Mfg. 1992-1994.

$1,850 $1,700 $1,550 $1,400 $1,200 $1,025 $875

Serial numbers LH011326 are pre-ban.

MSR	100%	98%	95%	90%	80%	70%	60%

TARGET COMPETITION H-BAR RIFLE (R6700) - .223 Rem. cal., GIO, flat-top upper receiver for scope mounting, 20 in. H-Bar barrel (1:9 in. twist), quick detachable carry handle with a 600-meter rear sighting system, dovetailed upper receiver grooved to accept Weaver style scope rings, 8 1/2 lbs.

$1,850 $1,700 $1,550 $1,400 $1,200 $1,025 $875

Serial numbers CH019500 and below are pre-ban.

COMPETITION H-BAR CUSTOM SHOP (R6701) - .223 Rem. cal., similar to the R6700, but with detachable scope mount, custom shop enhancements added to trigger and barrel, 2,000 mfg. from Colt Custom Shop.

$1,950 $1,800 $1,650 $1,500 $1,350 $1,200 $1,000

MATCH H-BAR (R6601) - GIO, heavy 20 in. HBAR barrel with 1:7 twist, fixed buttstock. 8 lbs.

$1,850 $1,700 $1,550 $1,400 $1,200 $1,025 $875

* ***Delta H-Bar (R6601DH)*** - similar to R6601, except has 3-9x rubber armored variable scope, removable cheekpiece, adj. scope mount, black leather sling, test range selected for its accuracy, aluminum transport case. Mfg. 1987-91.

$2,500 $2,300 $2,150 $2,000 $1,800 $1,600 $1,450

Last MSR was $1,460.

Serial numbers MH086020 and below are pre-ban.

SPORTER TARGET (R6551) - similar to R6601, except had 20 in. barrel with reduced diameter underneath handguard, 7 1/2 lbs.

$1,850 $1,700 $1,550 $1,400 $1,200 $1,025 $875

On the R6551, serial numbers ST038100 and below are pre-ban.

AR-15, Post-Ban, Mfg. Sept. 12, 1994-Present

During 2007, Colt released the M-5 Military Carbine and the LE 10-20, with 11 1/2, 14 1/2, or 16 in. barrel. These guns were only available for military and law enforcement.

During 2013, Colt released a line of competition rifles, manufactured under license by Bold Ideas, located in Breckenridge, TX. Every rifle/carbine comes with a 100 yard target.

State compliant variations are not listed in this text. Values are typically similar to the models from which they were derived.

Add $368 for Colt Scout C-More Sight (disc.).

Add $444 for Colt Tactical C-More Sight (disc.).

COMPETITION CRP-18 WITH GUNGODDESS TOUCH - .223 Rem. cal., GIO, 18 in. match grade stainless steel fluted barrel with triple port muzzle brake, 30 shot Magpul mag., enlarged trigger guard, Geissele two-stage match trigger, Magpul CTR 6-pos. adj. stock with locking adjustments, Magpul MOE grip, matched bolt and carrier with H-buffer, GunGoddess 15 in. free float handguard, one 2 in. accessory rail, Colt

MSR	100%	98%	95%	90%	80%	70%	60%

Competition charging handle with extended tactical latch, black finish, 7.22 lbs. New 2015.

MSR $1,995	$1,800	$1,550	$1,350	$1,200	$1,000	$800	$650

Add $130 for Robin Egg Blue, Pink, Bright Purple, Snow White, Crimson, Zombie Green, Brushed Nickel, or Crushed Silver furniture.

COMPETITION PRO – .223/5.56 Wylde chamber, GIO, 18 in. match grade stainless steel fluted barrel, fully adj. gas block, triple chamber or SureFire muzzle brake, forged upper and lower receiver, flat-top with Picatinny rail, 30 shot mag., matte black finish, Geissele two-stage match trigger, Magpul adj. stock, grip, and forend, approx. 7 lbs. Mfg. 2013.

	$1,850	$1,600	$1,400	$1,250	$1,000	$850	$650

Last MSR was $2,029.

EXPERT CRE-16 – 5.56 NATO cal., similar to Expert CRE-18, except has 16 in. barrel. Mfg. 2014-2015.

	$1,400	$1,200	$1,050	$950	$750	$650	$500

Last MSR was $1,599.

EXPERT CRE-16T GEN2 – .223 Rem. cal., mid-length gas system, 16 in. stainless steel HBAR contour match grade barrel, steel muzzle brake, Magpul 30 shot PMAG, Magpul enlarged trigger guard, no sights, Hogue overmolded collapsible stock, Hogue rubber beavertail grip, low profile fixed gas block, extended charging handle, M-LOK 12 in. aluminum-alloy float tube handguard, matte black finish, 6.66 lbs.

MSR $1,599	$1,400	$1,200	$1,050	$950	$750	$650	$500

EXPERT CRE-16T GEN3 PRECISION CARBINE – .223/5.56 Wylde chamber, fixed gas block, 16 in. stainless steel HBAR mid-weight barrel, 3-chamber muzzle brake, 30 shot mag., Hogue stock with buttpad, Hogue grip, 15 in. M-LOK float-tube handguard with sling swivel mount. New 2017.

MSR $1,699	$1,500	$1,350	$1,150	$1,050	$850	$700	$550

EXPERT CRE-18/CRE-18 RR – 5.56 NATO cal., GIO, low profile gas block, forged and precision fitted upper and lower receivers, matte black finish, 18 in. midweight match grade air gauged polish stainless steel barrel, 10 or 30 shot Magpul mag., competition nickel Teflon coated match target trigger, enlarged Magpul trigger guard, Magpul MOE four position adj. stock or CTR adj. stock (Model CRE-18 RR, new 2014), Expert Brake (CRE-18) or ProBrake (CRE-18 RR, mfg. 2014-2015), 15 in. vented modular float tube handguard, 5 1/2 in. top mounted Picatinny handguard rail with 11 slots, two 3 in. accessory rails with five slots each or quad rails (CRE-18 RR, disc. 2015), Hogue rubber finger groove grip, competition charging handle with extended tactical latch, matched bolt and bolt carrier with H-buffer, 13 slot Picatinny rail on flat-top upper receiver. New 2013.

MSR $1,599	$1,400	$1,200	$1,050	$950	$750	$650	$500

Add $100 for CRE-18 RR model with quad rails and ProBrake (mfg. 2014-2015).

MSR	100%	98%	95%	90%	80%	70%	60%

EXPERT CRE-18T GEN2 - .223 Rem. cal., rifle length gas system, 18 in. stainless steel HBAR contour match grade barrel, steel muzzle brake, Magpul 30 shot PMAG, Magpul enlarged trigger guard, no sights, Hogue overmolded collapsible stock, Hogue rubber beavertail grip, low profile fixed gas block, extended charging handle, M-LOK 15 in. aluminum-alloy float tube handguard, matte black finish, 7 lbs.

MSR $1,599	$1,400	$1,200	$1,050	$950	$750	$650	$500

EXPERT CRE-18T GEN3 LONG RANGE RIFLE - .223/5.56 Wylde chamber, fixed gas block, 18 in. stainless steel HBAR mid-weight barrel, 3-chamber muzzle brake, 30 shot mag., Hogue stock with buttpad, Hogue grip, 15 in. M-LOK float-tube handguard with sling swivel mount. New 2017.

MSR $1,699	$1,500	$1,350	$1,150	$1,050	$850	$700	$550

MARKSMAN CRX-16/CRX-16E - .223 Rem. cal., GIO, low profile gas block, 16 in. midweight match grade manganese phosphate chrome moly steel barrel, Expert brake, 10 or 30 shot Magpul mag., competition match target nickel Teflon coated trigger, enlargd Magpul trigger guard, carbine style four position adj. buttstock or Magpul MOE fixed rifle stock (CRX-16E), checkered A2 style finger groove grip, forged and precision fitted upper and lower receivers, 12 in. vented modular float tube handguard, 5 1/2 in. top mounted Picatinny handguard rail with 11 slots, two 3 in. accessory rails with five slots each, matched bolt and bolt carrier with H-buffer, 13 slot Picatinny rail on flat-top upper receiver, matte black finish. Mfg. 2013-2015.

	$1,250	$1,100	$950	$850	$700	$550	$450

Last MSR was $1,399.

MARKSMAN CRX-16 GEN2 - 5.56 NATO cal., carbine length fixed gas system, blackened 16 in. HBAR contour barrel, triple chamber steel muzzle brake, Magpul 30 shot PMAG, Magpul enlarged trigger guard, no sights, Hogue overmolded collapsible stock, Hogue beavertail grip, extended charging handle, M-LOK 12 in. aluminum alloy float tube handguard, matte black finish, 6.65 lbs. New 2016.

MSR $1,199	$1,075	$950	$800	$750	$600	$475	$375

MARKSMAN CRX-16 GEN3 LIGHT CARBINE - 5.56 NATO cal., fixed gas block, 16 in. chrome moly, mid-weight barrel, 3-chamber muzzle brake, 30 shot mag., Hogue stock with buttpad, Hogue grip, 15 in. M-LOK float-tube handguard with sling swivel mount. New 2017.

MSR $1,249	$1,125	$1,000	$850	$750	$600	$500	$400

MARKSMAN CRZ-16 GEN2 - 5.56 NATO cal., low profile fixed gas block, blackened 16 in. HBAR contour barrel, twin chamber steel muzzle brake, Magpul 30 shot PMAG, Magpul enlarged trigger guard, no sights, M4 collapsible stock, A2 grip, extended charging handle, M-LOK 10 in. aluminum-alloy float tube handguard, matte black finish, 6 lbs. New 2016.

MSR $999	$900	$800	$700	$600	$500	$400	$325

MSR	100%	98%	95%	90%	80%	70%	60%

PRO CRB-16 – .300 AAC Blackout or .300 Whisper (new 2014) cal., GIO, patented low profile adj. gas block, forged and precision fitted upper and lower receivers, matte black finish, 16 in. match grade air gauged stainless steel barrel with Colt competition triple port muzzle brake, 10 or 30 shot aluminum mag., Geissele two-stage match trigger, Magpul enlarged trigger guard, Magpul STR six position adj. stock with locking adjustments, Magpul MOE grip with extended backstrap, Hogue 12 in. multi-piece slotted free floated tubular handguard, Competition charging handle with extended tactical latch, matched bolt and bolt carrier with H-buffer, 13 slot Picatinny rail on flat-top upper receiver, 6.7 lbs. Mfg. 2013-2015.

	$1,600	$1,400	$1,200	$1,100	$900	$700	$550

Last MSR was $1,799.

PRO CRC-22 – 6.5mm Creedmoor cal., 22 in. fluted stainless steel HBAR+ match barrel, ProBrake, 20 shot Magpul mag., PRS adj. stock, 3 rails, 15 in. float tube modular handguard. Mfg. 2014-2015.

	$2,675	$2,350	$2,000	$1,800	$1,450	$1,200	$950

Last MSR was $2,979.

PRO CRC-22 GEN2 – 6.5mm Creedmoor cal., rifle length adj. gas system, 22 in. polished HBAR contour heavy fluted stainless steel barrel, triple chamber steel muzzle brake, Magpul 20 shot PMAG, enlarged integral trigger guard, no sights, Luth-AR stock, Ergo tactical beavertail grip, extended charging handle, M-LOK 15 in. aluminum alloy float tube handguard, matte black finish, 11.2 lbs. New 2016.

MSR $2,899	$2,600	$2,300	$1,950	$1,750	$1,450	$1,150	$900

PRO CRG-20 – 6.5mm Grendel cal., GIO, patented low profile adj. gas block, forged and precision fitted upper and lower receivers, matte black finish, 20 in. match grade air gauged chrome moly steel custom barrel with black Nitride finish, 10 or 25 shot aluminum mag., Colt competition match target trigger, nickel Teflon coated, 15 in. vented modular free floated tubular handguard, 10 in. top mounted Picatinny handguard rail with 23 slots and 2-3 accessory rails, oversized trigger guard, Magpul CTR 6-position adj. buttstock with locking adjustments, Magpul MOE pistol grip with extended backstrap, competition charging handle with extended tactical latch, matched bolt and bolt carrier with H-buffer, 13 slot Picatinny rail on flat-top upper receiver. Limited mfg. 2013 only.

	$1,450	$1,300	$1,100	$1,000	$800	$650	$500

Last MSR was $1,649.

PRO CRL-16 – .308 Win. cal., GIO, low profile adj. gas block, CNC machined and precision fitted upper and lower receivers, matte black finish, 16 in. tapered midweight match grade air gauged polished stainless steel custom barrel with triple port muzzle brake, 10 or 20 shot Magpul mag., integral enlarged trigger guard, Geissele two-stage SSA-E match trigger, Magpul CTR six position adj. stock with locking adjustments, Magpul MOE pistol grip with extended backstrap, 12 1/2 in. free floated tubular handguard,

MSR	100%	98%	95%	90%	80%	70%	60%

top mounted Picatinny handguard rail, two 3 in. accessory rails, competition charging handle with extended tactical latch, matched bolt and bolt carrier, 18 slot Picatinny rail on flat-top upper receiver. Mfg. 2013-2015.

	$2,100	$1,850	$1,600	$1,450	$1,150	$950	$750

Last MSR was $2,339.

PRO CRL-16 GEN2 – .308 Win. cal., adj. mid-length gas system, 16 in. polished HBAR contour heavy tapered stainless steel barrel, triple chamber vented muzzle brake, Magpul 20 shot PMAG, SST, enlarged integral trigger guard, no sights, Hogue overmolded 6-pos. collapsible stock, Hogue rubber beavertail grip, M-LOK 12 in. aluminum-alloy float tube handguard, extended charging handle, matte black finish, 8.67 lbs. New 2016.

	$2,050	$1,800	$1,550	$1,400	$1,150	$900	$700

PRO CRL-20 – .308 Win. cal., adj. rifle length gas system, 20 in. match barrel with six flutes, 3-chamber muzzle brake, 20 shot Magpul mag., Geissele match trigger, Magpul PRS stock, 15 in. float tube handguard, 3 rails. Mfg. 2013-2015.

	$2,675	$2,350	$2,000	$1,800	$1,450	$1,200	$950

Last MSR was $2,979.

PRO CRL-20 GEN2 – .308 Win. cal., rifle length adj. gas system, 20 in. polished HBAR contour heavy fluted stainless steel barrel, triple chamber steel muzzle brake, Magpul 20 shot PMAG, enlarged trigger guard, no sights, Luth-AR stock, Ergo tactical beavertail grip, extended charging handle, M-LOK 15 in. aluminum alloy float tube handguard, matte black finish, 10.8 lbs. New 2016.

MSR $2,899	$2,600	$2,300	$1,950	$1,750	$1,450	$1,150	$900

PRO CRP-16 – 5.56 NATO cal., GIO, low profile adj. gas block, forged and precision fitted upper and lower receivers, matte black finish, 16 in. two-diameter heavy weight match grade air gauged polished stainless steel barrel, triple port muzzle brake, 10 or 30 shot Magpul mag., Geissele two-stage match trigger, Magpul enlarged trigger guard, Magpul CTR 6-position adj. stock with locking adjustments, Magpul MOE grip with extended backstrap, competition 12 in. vented modular float tube handguard, 5 1/2 in. top mounted Picatinny handguard rail with 11 slots, two 3 in. accessory rails, competition charging handle with extended tactical latch matched bolt and bolt carrier with H-buffer, 13 slot Picatinny rail on flat-top upper receiver. New 2013.

MSR $1,899	$1,700	$1,500	$1,300	$1,150	$950	$750	$600

PRO CRP-18 THREE-GUN MATCH RIFLE – 5.56 NATO cal., similar to CRP-16, except has 18 in. custom fluted mid-weight barrel, 15 in. vented modular float tube handguard, and full length Picatinny top handguard rail with one 2 in. accessory rail. Mfg. 2013-2015.

	$1,850	$1,600	$1,400	$1,250	$1,000	$850	$650

Last MSR was $2,019.

MSR	100%	98%	95%	90%	80%	70%	60%

PRO CRP-18LV (LIGHT VARMINT RIFLE) – .223 Rem. cal., adj. rifle length gas system, 18 in. stainless steel HBAR match barrel, 3-chamber muzzle brake, 30 shot Magpul mag., Geissele match trigger, Magpul CTR 6-pos. stock, 15 in. float tube modular handguard, 4 rails. Disc. 2015.

	$1,700	$1,500	$1,300	$1,150	$950	$750	$600

Last MSR was $1,899.

PRO CRP-18 GEN2 – .223 Rem. cal., rifle length adj. gas system, 18 in. polished HBAR stainless steel barrel, triple chamber muzzle brake, Magpul 30 shot PMAG, Magpul enlarged trigger guard, no sights, Luth-AR stock, Ergo tactical beavertail grip, extended charging handle, M-LOK 15 in. aluminum alloy float tube handguard, matte black finish, 7 lbs. New 2016.

MSR $1,999	$1,800	$1,550	$1,350	$1,200	$1,000	$800	$650

PRO CRP-18 GEN3 3-GUN COMPETITION – .223/5.56 Wylde chamber, fully adj. gas block, 18 in. stainless steel HBAR mid-weight barrel, 3-chamber fluted muzzle brake, 30 shot mag., Hogue stock with buttpad, Hogue grip, 15 in. M-LOK float-tube handguard with sling swivel mount. New 2017.

MSR $1,999	$1,800	$1,550	$1,350	$1,200	$1,000	$800	$650

PRO CRP-20/20L/22RR – .223 Rem. cal., adj. rifle length gas system, 20 in. stainless steel extra heavy match barrel, 3-chamber vented muzzle brake, 30 shot Magpul mag., Geissele match trigger, Magpul CTR 6-position (CRP-20) or Magpul PRS adj. sniper (CRP-20L or CRP-20RR) stock, forged receivers, 15 in. float tube modular handguard with 3 rails, polished barrel (CRP-20 or CRP-20L) or blackened barrel (CRP-20RR) finish. Mfg. 2013-2015.

	$1,700	$1,500	$1,300	$1,150	$950	$750	$600

Last MSR was $1,899.

Add $100 for CRP-20L or CRP-20SS model.

PRO CRP-20VR (VARMINT RIFLE) – .223 Rem. cal., adj. rifle length gas system, 20 in. stainless steel HBAR match barrel, 3-chamber muzzle brake, 30 shot Magpul mag., Geissele match trigger, Magpul MOE fixed stock, forged receivers, 15 in. float tube modular handguard, 4 rails. New 2013.

MSR $1,899	$1,700	$1,500	$1,300	$1,150	$950	$750	$600

SPORTING RIFLE CSR-1516/CSR-1518 – .223 Rem. or 5.56 NATO cal., GIO, 16 (CSR-1516) or 18 (CSR-18) in. midweight match grade chrome moly black manganese phosphate threaded steel barrel with standard flash suppressor, 10 or 30 shot mag., nickel Teflon coated match target trigger, adj. 6-position carbine (CSR-16) or rifle stock with wide cheekpiece (CSR-18), rubber over-molded finger groove grip with integral beavertail, solid steel machined low profile gas block, forged alloy upper and lower receivers, 12 in. float tube handguard, standard charging handle, bolt, and bolt carrier, top mounted seven slot accessory rail, matte black finish. Mfg. 2013-2015.

	$900	$800	$700	$600	$500	$400	$325

Last MSR was $990.

Add $59 for CSR-18.

MSR	100%	98%	95%	90%	80%	70%	60%

TACTICAL PATROL CARBINE CRX-16 RR - 5.56 NATO cal., low pro gas system, 16 in. chrome moly M4 contour barrel, ProBrake, quad rails CTR stock, 6 lb. trigger, 30 shot mag. Mfg. 2014-2015.

	$1,250	$1,100	$950	$850	$700	$550	$450

Last MSR was $1,379.

COLT ACCURIZED RIFLE (CR6720/CR6724) - .223 Rem. cal., GIO, 20 (CR6720) or 24 (CR6724, disc. 2012, reintroduced 2014) in. stainless match barrel, matte finish, accurized AR-15, 8 (disc. 1998) or 9 (new 1999) shot mag., 9.41 lbs. New 1997.

MSR $1,374	$1,250	$1,100	$950	$850	$700	$550	$450

MATCH TARGET COMPETITION H-BAR RIFLE (MT6700/MT6700C) - .223 Rem. cal., GIO, features flat-top upper receiver for scope mounting, 20 in. barrel (1:9 in. twist), quick detachable carry handle which incorporates a 600-meter rear sighting system, counterbored muzzle, dovetailed upper receiver is grooved to accept Weaver style scope rings, supplied with two 5 (disc.), 8 (disc.), or 9 (new 1999) shot mags., cleaning kit, and sling, matte black finish, 8 1/2 lbs. Mfg. 1992-2013.

	$1,125	$1,000	$850	$750	$600	$500	$400

Last MSR was $1,230.

Add $57 for compensator (MT6700C, mfg. 1999-disc).

MATCH TARGET COMPETITION H-BAR II (MT6731) - .223 Rem. cal., GIO, flat-top, 16.1 in. barrel (1:9 in.), 9 shot mag., matte finish, 7.1 lbs. Mfg. 1995-2012.

	$1,050	$900	$800	$700	$600	$475	$375

Last MSR was $1,173.

MATCH TARGET LIGHTWEIGHT (MT6430, MT6530, or MT6830) - .223 Rem. (MT6530, 1:7 in. twist), 7.62x39mm (MT6830, disc. 1996, 1:12 in. twist), or 9mm Para. (MT6430, disc. 1996, 1:10 in. twist) cal., GIO, features 16 in. barrel (non-threaded per C/B 1994), initially shorter stock and handguard, rear sight adjustable for windage and elevation, includes two detachable 5, 8, or 9 (new 1999) shot mags., approx. 7 lbs. Mfg. 1991-2002.

	$1,000	$850	$750	$700	$550	$450	$350

Last MSR was $1,111.

Add $200 for .22 LR conversion kit (disc. 1994).

MATCH TARGET M4 CARBINE (MT6400/MT6400R) - .223 Rem. cal., GIO, similar to current U.S. armed forces M4 model, except semi-auto, 9 or 10 shot mag., 16.1 in. barrel, 1:7 in. twist, matte black finish, fixed tube buttstock, A3 detachable carrying handle, 7.3 lbs. Mfg. 2002-2013.

	$1,100	$950	$800	$750	$600	$500	$375

Last MSR was $1,211.

Add $341 for quad accessory rail (MT6400R).

MSR	100%	98%	95%	90%	80%	70%	60%

MATCH TARGET 6400001 - 5.56 NATO cal., GIO, 16.1 in. M4 barrel with flash suppressor, 10 shot mag., flat-top receiver, fixed tube stock, Magpul Gen. II rear backup sight, two-piece ribbed handguard with post front sight, black finish, 7 lbs. Mfg. 2013 only.

$1,325 $1,150 $1,000 $900 $750 $600 $475

Last MSR was $1,461.

MATCH TARGET 6400R001 - 5.56 NATO cal., 16.1 in. M4 barrel with flash suppressor, 10 shot mag., flat-top receiver with Picatinny rail integrated with quad rail handguard, Magpul Gen. II rear sight and flip-up adj. post front sight, black finish, 7.2 lbs. Mfg. 2013 only.

$1,650 $1,450 $1,250 $1,100 $900 $750 $600

Last MSR was $1,825.

MATCH TARGET H-BAR RIFLE (MT6601/MT6601C) - .223 Rem. cal., GI, heavy 20 in. HBAR barrel, 1:7 in. twist, A2 sights, 8 lbs. Mfg. 1986-2010.

$1,100 $950 $800 $750 $600 $500 $375

Last MSR was $1,218.

Add $200 for .22 LR conversion kit (mfg. 1990-94).

Add $1 for compensator (MT6601C, new 1999).

TACTICAL ELITE MODEL (TE6700) - .223 Rem. cal., GIO, 20 in. heavy barrel, 1:8 in. twist, Hogue finger groove pistol grip, Choate buttstock, fine tuned for accuracy, scope and mount included, approx. 1,000 rifles made by the Custom Shop circa 1996-97.

$2,450 $2,150 $1,850 $1,650 $1,350 $1,100 $850

TARGET GOVT. MODEL RIFLE (MT6551) - .223 Rem. cal., GIO, semi-auto version of the M16 rifle with forward bolt assist, 20 in. barrel (1:7 in.), straight line black nylon stock, aperture rear and post front sight, 5, 8, or 9 (new 1999) shot mags., 7 1/2 lbs. Disc. 2002.

$1,050 $900 $800 $700 $600 $475 $375

Last MSR was $1,144.

Add $200 for .22 LR conversion kit (mfg. 1990-94).

SPORTER CARBINE (SP6920) - .223 Rem. cal., GIO, has M-4 features including flat-top receiver with A3 removable carry handle, 16.1 in. barrel with flash hider, 4-position collapsible buttstock, ribbed oval handguard, matte black finish, 5.95 lbs. Mfg. 2011 only.

$1,050 $900 $800 $700 $600 $475 $375

Last MSR was $1,155.

Add 15% for the legal LE6920 variation that were sold to civilians.

The last 100 carbines of the Model LE6920 marked "Law Enforcement Carbine" and "Restricted" were sold as commercial guns to FFL dealers. Each of these has a factory letter stating as such.

MSR	100%	98%	95%	90%	80%	70%	60%

COLT SPORTER (SP6940) – .223 Rem. cal., GIO, 16.1 in. fully floated barrel, 20 shot mag., *flip-up adj. sights, 4-position collapsible stock,* one-piece monolithic upper receiver, flat-top receiver with full-length quad Picatinny rails, matte black metal finish, 6.1 lbs. Mfg. 2011 only.

	$1,350	$1,200	$1,000	$900	$750	$600	$475

Last MSR was $1,500.

Add 15% for the legal LE6940 variation that were sold to civilians.

The last 100 carbines of the Model LE6940 marked "Law Enforcement Carbine" and "Restricted" were sold as commercial guns to FFL dealers. Each of these has a factory letter stating as such.

SP901 RIFLE – .308 Win. cal., GIO, 16 in. full floated heavy chrome-lined barrel, direct gas system, locking bolt, matte black finish, one-piece monolithic upper receiver with rail, upper receiver can be swapped out for .223, ambidextrous operating controls, flip-up post sights, bayonet lug and flash hider. Mfg. mid-2011.

While advertised in 2011, this model never went into production (see LE901-16S).

COLT CARBINE AR6450 – 9mm Para. cal., GIO, 16.1 in. barrel with flash suppressor, A3 detachable carrying handle, 32 shot mag., grooved aluminum handguard, A2 post front sight, adj. Rogers Super-Stoc, matte finish, 6.35 lbs. Mfg. 2012 only.

	$1,050	$900	$800	$700	$600	$475	$375

Last MSR was $1,176.

COLT CARBINE AR6520TRI – 5.56 NATO cal., GIO, 16.1 in. barrel, matte black finish, 30 shot mag., adj. sights. Mfg. 2013 only.

	$1,125	$1,000	$850	$750	$600	$500	$400

Last MSR was $1,223.

LIGHTWEIGHT CARBINE (AR6720) – 5.56 NATO cal., GIO, 16.1 in. light barrel with flash hider and A2 front sight, 30 shot PMAG, ribbed aluminum forearm, A3 detachable carrying handle, MBUS Gen 2 rear sight, matte black finish, adj. stock, 6.2 lbs. Mfg. 2012-2018.

	$900	$800	$700	$600	$500	$400	$325

Last MSR was $999.

COLT CARBINE AR6720LECAR – 5.56 NATO cal., GIO, 16.1 in. barrel, Magpul Gen. II rear sight with adj. post front sight, 30 shot mag., matte black finish, 6 lbs. Mfg. 2013 only.

	$1,325	$1,150	$1,000	$900	$750	$600	$475

Last MSR was $1,468.

TACTICAL CARBINE (AR6721) – 5.56 NATO cal., GIO, 16.1 in. heavy barrel with flash hider and A2 front sight, 30 shot PMAG, MBUS Gen 2 rear sight, ribbed aluminum forearm, A3 detachable carrying handle, matte black finish, adj. stock, 7.3 lbs. Mfg. 2012 - 2017.

	$825	$700	$600	$550	$450	$375	$300

Last MSR was $929.

MSR	100%	98%	95%	90%	80%	70%	60%

9MM CARBINE (AR6951) – 9mm Para. cal., GIO, 16.1 in. barrel with flash suppressor, 32 shot mag., folding rear sight, adj. Rogers Super-Stoc, flat-top receiver, A3 detachable carrying handle, grooved aluminum handguard, choice of matte black or Muddy Girl (AR6951MPMG, limited mfg. 2015 only) finish, 6.4 lbs. Mfg. 2012-2018.

	$975	$850	$750	$650	$550	$450	$350

Last MSR for Muddy Girl finish was $1,567 in 2015.

Last MSR in 2018 was $1,099.

Add $319 for Muddy Girl camo finish (limited mfg. 2015 only).

AR15 A4 RIFLE – 5.56 NATO cal., GIO, 20 in. barrel with flash suppressor, 30 shot mag., flat-top receiver with removable carry handle, A2 style buttstock and front sight, ribbed handguard, black finish, 7.7 lbs. New 2013.

MSR $1,099	$975	$850	$750	$650	$550	$450	$350

AR15 A4MP-FDE – 5.56 NATO cal., GIO, 20 in. barrel with flash suppressor, Flat Dark Earth (FDE) furniture, 30 shot mag., 2/3 quad rail with cover, A2 front sight with Magpul Gen. II rear sight, fixed stock, matte black barrel, matte black or FDE (new 2014) receiver finish, 7 1/2 lbs. Mfg. 2013-2014.

	$1,175	$1,050	$900	$800	$650	$550	$400

Last MSR was $1,304.

Add $35 for FDE receiver finish.

COLT CARBINE AR-6821/AR-6821MP-R – .300 AAC Blackout cal., AR-6821 is similar to AR-6720, AR-6821MP-R has Magpul furniture and accessory rail. Mfg. 2015 only.

	$1,050	$900	$800	$700	$600	$475	$375

Last MSR was $1,155.

Add $113 for Magpul furniture and accessory rail.

COLT CARBINE CR6724001 – 5.56 NATO cal., GIO, 24 in. stainless barrel without sights, one-piece flat-top upper receiver with integrated 2/3 length quad Picatinny rail, fixed non-adj. stock, 10 shot mag., black finish, 8.8 lbs. Mfg. 2013-2015.

	$1,500	$1,350	$1,150	$1,050	$850	$700	$550

Last MSR was $1,653.

AR-15 SCOPE (3X/4X) AND MOUNT – initially offered with 3x magnification scope, then switched to 4x. Disc.

	$395	$300	$240	$185	$160	$130	$115

Last MSR was $344.

LE901-16S (SP901) – .308 Win. cal., GIO, 16.1 in. heavy full floated barrel with bayonet lug and flash hider, flat-top with Picatinny rail, one-piece upper receiver with BUIS, ambidextrous controls, flip-up adj. front sight post, flip-up adj. rear sight, 20 shot mag., fixed stock, matte black finish, 9.4 lbs. Mfg. 2012-2015.

	$2,350	$2,050	$1,750	$1,600	$1,300	$1,050	$800

Last MSR was $2,544.

MSR	100%	98%	95%	90%	80%	70%	60%

M.A.R.C.901 MONOLITHIC – .308 Win. cal., GIO, 16.1 or 18 (LE901-18SE, mfg. 2015 only) in. heavy full floated barrel with bayonet lug and flash hider, 20 shot mag., one-piece monolithic flat-top upper receiver with Picatinny rail, BUIS, ambidextrous controls, adj. VLTOR buttstock, matte black or FDE (LE901FDE-16SE) finish, 9.4 lbs. Mfg. 2015-17.

	$1,800	$1,550	$1,350	$1,200	$1,000	$800	$650

Last MSR was $1,999.

Add $100 for FDE finish (model LE901FDE-16SE), disc. 2015.

M.A.R.C.901 CARBINE (AR901-16S) – .308 Win. cal., 16.1 in. heavy free floating barrel with muzzle brake, 20 shot mag., retractable B5 Bravo buttstock, flat-top receiver with full length Picatinny rail, vent tubular handguard with 3 Picatinny rails. Mfg. 2015 -2016.

	$1,250	$1,100	$950	$850	$700	$550	$450

Last MSR was $1,399.

LE6900 – 5.56 NATO cal., GIO, 16.1 in. barrel, no sights, 30 shot mag., matte black finish, 6 lbs. Mfg. 2012-mid-2013.

	$800	$700	$600	$550	$450	$350	$275

Last MSR was $899.

LE6920 M4 CARBINE – 5.56 NATO cal., GIO, 16.1 in. barrel with bayonet lug and flash hider, 30 shot mag., adj. front sight post, ribbed handguard, Magpul Gen2 backup rear sight, flat-top receiver with Picatinny rail, collapsible stock, matte black finish, 6.9 lbs. New 2012.

MSR $1,099	$975	$850	$750	$650	$550	$450	$350

LE6920AE – 5.56 NATO cal., 16.1 in. barrel, ambidextrous mag. release, bolt catch and fire selector, 30 shot PMAG, MBUS rear Gen. 2 sights, collapsible stock, matte black finish, 6.38 lbs. Mfg. 2014-2016.

	$1,250	$1,100	$950	$850	$700	$550	$450

Last MSR was $1,374.

LE6920-OEM1/OEM2 M4 – 5.56 NATO cal., 16.1 in. barrel with muzzle brake, includes pistol grip and rear buffer tube, flat-top receiver with Picatinny rail, no furniture, OEM1 (disc. 2016) includes A2 style front sight. Mfg. 2015-2018.

	$765	$650	$600	$500	$425	$350	$275

Last MSR was $849.

LE6920 SOCOM – 5.56 NATO cal., GIO, 16.1 in. barrel with bayonet lug and flash hider, 30 shot mag., flat-top receiver with BUIS, Knights Armament rail system, adj. front sight post, flip-up adj. rear sight, non-adj. tube stock, matte black finish, 7.2 lbs. Mfg. 2012-2014.

	$1,450	$1,300	$1,100	$1,000	$800	$650	$500

Last MSR was $1,602.

MSR	100%	98%	95%	90%	80%	70%	60%

LE6920MP-R - 5.56 NATO cal., 16.1 in. barrel, 30 shot PMAG, MBUS rear Gen. 2 sight, Troy rail, Magpul MOE furniture, black finish, 7.11 lbs. Mfg. 2014-2015.

	$1,150	$1,000	$850	$800	$650	$500	$400

Last MSR was $1,268.

LE6920MP & VARIATIONS - 5.56 NATO cal., GIO, 16.1 in. barrel with bayonet lug and flash hider, 30 shot PMAG, adj. front sight post, MBUS Gen2 backup rear sight, Magpul MOE carbine collapsible stock with MOE handguard and pistol grip, flat-top receiver with Picatinny rail, MOE trigger guard, Magpul MOE furniture in black (LE6920MP-B), A-TACS Foliage/Green (LE6920MPFG, new 2013), Olive Drab (LE6920MP-OD), USA One Nation Hydro-dipped (LE6920MP-USA, new 2014), ATAC camo hydro-dipped (LE6920MPATAC, new 2014), or Steel Gray (LE6920MP-STG, new 2015), 6.9 lbs. Mfg. 2012-mid-2015.

	$1,125	$1,000	$850	$750	$600	$500	$400

Last MSR was $1,229.

Add $87 for USA One Nation Hydro-Dipped Magpul furniture (LE6920-USA, new 2014).

Add $166 for ATACS Foliage/Green finish (LE6920MPFG).

Add $247 for ATAC camo Hydro-Dipped Magpul furniture (LE6920MPATAC, new 2014).

* ***LE6920MPG*** - 5.56 NATO cal., similar to LE6920MP, except features Olive Drab Green upper and lower receivers, OD Green Magpul furniture (LE6920MPG-OD) or Black Magpul furniture (LE6920MPG-B, new 2014), vertical grip. Mfg. 2012-mid-2015.

	$1,225	$1,050	$900	$850	$700	$550	$425

Last MSR was $1,361.

* ***LE6920MPFDE*** - 5.56 NATO cal., similar to LE6920MP, except features Flat Dark Earth Magpul MOE furniture with vertical grip, Flat Dark Earth finish. Mfg. 2012-mid-2015.

	$1,225	$1,050	$900	$850	$700	$550	$425

Last MSR was $1,361.

* ***LE6920MPFDE-R*** - 5.56 NATO cal., similar to LE6920MP, except features Flat Dark Earth coated upper and lower receivers, FDE Troy Rail, FDE Magpul furniture. Mfg. 2014-mid-2015.

	$1,400	$1,200	$1,050	$950	$750	$650	$500

Last MSR was $1,572.

LE6920MPS-B/FDE - 5.56 NATO cal., 16.1 in. barrel, 30 shot round PMAG, MBUS Gen 2 rear sight, Magpul MOE SL carbine vertical pistol grip stock, Magpul MOE SL handguard, Black or FDE (disc. 2018) furniture.

MSR $1,199	$1,075	$950	$800	$750	$600	$475	$375

MSR	100%	98%	95%	90%	80%	70%	60%

LE6920-R TROOPER – 5.56 NATO cal., GIO, 16.1 in. barrel, 30 shot mag., single stage trigger, milled aluminum receiver, full-length top Picatinny rail, anodized black finish, 6 1/2 lbs. Mfg. 2018 only.

	$925	$800	$700	$650	$500	$425	$325

Last MSR was $1,049.

LE6940 M4 MONOLITHIC – 5.56 NATO cal., GIO, 16.1 in. full floated barrel with bayonet lug and flash hider, 1-piece upper receiver, 30 shot mag., flip-up adj. front sight post, Magpul Gen2 backup rear sight, collapsible stock, matte black finish, 6.9 lbs. New 2012.

MSR $1,399	$1,250	$1,100	$950	$850	$700	$550	$450

LE6940P – 5.56 NATO cal., GPO, 16.1 in. full floated barrel with bayonet lug and flash hider, one-piece upper receiver, 30 shot mag., flip-up adj. front sight post, Magpul Gen2 backup rear sight, collapsible stock, matte black finish, 6.9 lbs. Mfg. 2012-mid-2015.

	$1,950	$1,700	$1,450	$1,300	$1,100	$900	$700

Last MSR was $2,105.

* ***LE6940MPFG*** – 5.56 NATO cal., similar to LE6940P, except features A-TACS Forest Green Camo. Mfg. 2012-2013.

	$1,250	$1,100	$950	$850	$700	$550	$450

Last MSR was $1,395.

LE6940AE-3G – 5.56 NATO cal., 16.1 in. barrel, 30 shot PMAG, Colt articulating piston system, lower receiver features ambidextrous operating controls and 3 operating controls on both sides, monolithic upper is fully modular with smooth handguard allowing for different rail locations, A2 grip, M4 buttstock, MBUS rear Gen. 2 sight, black furniture, 7.2 lbs. Mfg. 2014-2015.

	$1,750	$1,550	$1,300	$1,200	$950	$800	$600

Last MSR was $1,945.

LE6960-CCU (COMBAT UNIT CARBINE) – 5.56 NATO cal., GIO, 16 in. chrome-lined barrel, 30 shot mag., SST, optic ready, Magpul MOE SL buttstock, Magpul MOE SL pistol grip, ambidextrous safety, aluminum receiver, mid-length gas system, hardcoat anodized black finish, 6.47 lbs. Mfg. 2016-2017.

	$1,150	$1,000	$850	$800	$650	$500	$400

Last MSR was $1,299.

LT6720-R – 5.56 NATO cal., 16.1 in. barrel, 30 shot PMAG, MBUS front and rear Gen 2 sights, Troy rail, Magpul ACS telescoping stock, black Magpul furniture, matte black finish, 6.48 lbs. Mfg. 2014 - 2016.

	$1,175	$1,050	$900	$800	$650	$550	$400

Last MSR was $1,321.

MSR	100%	98%	95%	90%	80%	70%	60%

* ***LT6720MPMG*** – 5.56 NATO cal., 16.1 in. light contour barrel with birdcage flash hider, 30 shot mag., Magpul MBUS sights, Magpul ACS Muddy Girl camo telescoping stock, trigger guard, and pistol grip, Muddy Girl camo finish, 6.2 lbs. Mfg. 2014-mid-2015.

	$1,300	$1,150	$1,000	$900	$700	$600	$450

Last MSR was $1,448.

EXPANSE M4 – 5.56 NATO cal., GIO, 16.1 in. barrel, 30 shot round aluminum mag., adj. front sight post, flat-top Picatinny rail, matte black finish, 6.44 lbs. Mfg. 2016-2017.

	$700	$650	$550	$500	$400	$325	$275

Last MSR was $799.

CRM 16A1 CLASSIC SERIES – 5.56 NATO cal., 20 in. barrel, 20 shot mag., single stage trigger, A1 style fixed sights, gray furniture (including triangular forearm), A1 style buttstock, A1 style grips, semi-auto reproduction of the Vietnam era M16A1, left side of mag. well marked "COLT AR-15/PROPERTY OF U.S. GOVT./M16A1/CAL. 5.56 MM", 6.37 lbs. New mid-2016.

MSR $2,499	$2,250	$1,950	$1,700	$1,550	$1,250	$1,000	$800

M4A1 SOCOM – 5.56 NATO cal., gas operated, 14 1/2 in. heavy SOCOM barrel with extended A2 flash hider pinned and welded to make non-NFA 16.1 in. barrel length, 30 shot mag., A2 front and Matech folding rear sights, 4-pos. collapsible stock, ambi safety selector, lower receiver features PROPERTY OF THE US GOVT, M4A1 CARBINE, and CAL. 5.56 MM, includes KAC RAS rail, side sling swivel, matte black finish, 6.95 lbs. New mid-2018.

MSR $1,499	$1,325	$1,150	$975	$850	$700	$550	$450

MODULAR CARBINE – 7.62 NATO or 6.5CM cal., 16 or 18 in. chrome-lined barrel, 20 shot mag., flip-up front and adj. rear sights, telescoping VLTOR stock, 15 in. M-LOK rail system, matte black finish. New mid-2018.

MSR $2,299	$1,875	$1,100	$895	$650	$575	$495	$425

XM177E2 RETRO CARBINE – 5.56 NATO cal., 11 1/2 in. barrel with extended flash hider (to make legal 16 in. length), 20 shot USGI mag., A1 fixed front and rear sights, Vinyl-Acetate coated aluminum synthetic stock, safety selector switch, Retro Classic Carbine built to the original Colt Model 629 specifications from the 1960s, matte black finish, 6 1/2 lbs. New 2019.

MSR $2,599	$2,325	$2,000	$1,750	$1,575	$1,275	$1,050	$875

RIFLES: SEMI-AUTO, RIMFIRE, AR-15 & VARIATIONS

The following models are manufactured by Carl Walther, located in Ulm, Germany, under license from New Colt Holding Corp., and imported/distributed by Walther Arms.

MSR	100%	98%	95%	90%	80%	70%	60%

M4 CARBINE – .22 LR cal., GIO, 16.2 in. shrouded barrel, flat-top receiver 10 or 30 shot mag., detachable carry handle, single left-side safety lever, four position retractable stock, ribbed aluminum handguard, black finish, approx. 6 lbs. Mfg. by Umarex under license from Colt and imported by Walther Arms. Imported 2009-2016.

	$475	$400	$350	$315	$285	$250	$225

Last MSR was $569.

* ***M4 Ops*** – .22 LR cal., GIO, 16.2 in. barrel, 10 or 30 shot mag., aluminum upper and lower receiver, black finish, quad tactical rail interface system with elongated Picatinny rail on top of barrel and frame, inline barrel/stock design, cartridge case deflector, muzzle compensator, detachable rear sight, four position collapsible stock, ejection port cover, approx. 6 1/2 lbs. Mfg. by Umarex under license from Colt and imported by Walther Arms. Imported 2009-2016.

	$515	$435	$375	$340	$310	$285	$250

Last MSR was $599.

M16 – .22 LR cal., GIO, 21.2 in. barrel, 10 or 30 shot mag., flat-top receiver with detachable carry handle, fixed stock, elongated ribbed aluminum handguard, removable rear sight, ejection port cover, single left-side safety lever, black finish, approx. 6 1/4 lbs. Mfg. 2009-2010.

	$575	$525	$475	$425	$395	$375	$350

Last MSR was $599.

* ***M16 SPR (Special Purpose Rifle)*** – .22 LR cal., GIO, 21.2 in. barrel, 30 shot mag., black finish, fixed stock, aluminum upper and lower receiver, quad tactical rail interface system with Picatinny rail, flip-up front and rear sights, inline barrel/stock design, cartridge case deflector, muzzle compensator. Mfg. 2009-2010.

	$625	$575	$525	$475	$450	$415	$395

Last MSR was $670.

RIFLES: SEMI-AUTO, MISC. CENTERFIRE

COLT 1918 SELF LOADING RIFLE – .30-06 cal., gas operated w/three position regulator, 20 shot staggered mag., uncheckered walnut stock and forearm w/horizontal finger grooves, lock breech, closed bolt, hammer fired, sling swivels, includes leather display case, blue metal finish, 16 lbs. Mfg. by Ohio Ordnance Works under license from Colt Manufacturing Company.

MSR $8,799	$8,500	$7,750	$7,000	$6,250	$5,500	$4,750	$4,000

SHOTGUNS: O/U

ARMSMEAR – 12 ga. only, 2 3/4 in. chambers, a few prototypes were mfg. by Worshipful Co. Gunmakers of London, boxlock action with engraved sideplates, checkered high-grade European walnut stock and forearm, 28 (HE) or 30 (LE) in. VR barrels with screw-in chokes, choice of light (Armsmear 12 LE) or heavy (Armsmear 12 HE) engraving, 7 1/2 lbs. This model was originally advertised in 1995.

While advertised, only several prototypes of this model were manufactured.

SHOTGUNS: PERCUSSION

MODEL 1855 REVOLVING SHOTGUN MODEL - 16 gauge or .60 cal., 10 ga. or .75 cal., smoothbore, 27, 30, 33, or 36 in. barrels, 1,100 mfg.

100%	98%	95%	90%	80%	70%	60%	50%	40%	30%	20%	10%
N/A	N/A	N/A	$17,500	$15,000	$12,000	$9,000	$8,000	$7,500	$6,800	$6,500	$6,100

PATERSON MODEL 1839 SHOTGUN - 16 gauge, percussion, center hammer, revolving, 6 shot cylinder with scene, browned finished in a Damascus pattern 24 or 32 in. barrel marked on right side of lug "-Patent Arms M'g. Co. Paterson, NJ.-Colt's Pt. -" in one line, front pin and either dovetailed block or brazed half moon shape on breech end with U-shaped notch, blue finish, walnut butt stock with minor crescent shaped butt plate, 9 1/4 lbs. Approx. 225 mfg. circa 1839-1841.

100%	98%	95%	90%	80%	70%	60%	50%	40%	30%	20%	10%
N/A	N/A	N/A	N/A	$35,000	$30,000	$25,000	$20,000	$15,000	$11,500	$10,000	$8,500

SHOTGUNS: SxS, DISC.

Strong, original case colors and vivid damascus barrel patterning will make the difference when determining values on the Models 1878 and 1883. Remember, the models listed below were designed to shoot black powder loads only, not smokeless powder.

A Colt letter of provenance for the models listed below is $100 per gun.

MODEL 1878 HAMMER SHOTGUN - 10 or 12 ga., 28-32 in. blue or browned damascus barrels, double triggers, sideplates, case hardened breech, extractors, semi-pistol grip stock, 22,683 mfg. between 1878-89. Many of these guns were ordered with special features - these original guns command premiums above the prices listed below.

100%	98%	95%	90%	80%	70%	60%	50%	40%	30%	20%	10%
$12,500	$10,000	$8,000	$4,500	$3,000	$2,600	$2,300	$1,975	$1,600	$1,275	$750	$600

MODEL 1883 HAMMERLESS - 8, 10, or 12 ga., 28-32 in. damascus barrels, many deluxe custom orders mfg. in this model from 1883-1895. Approx. serial range is 1-3,050 and 4,055-8,365. Seldom encountered in mint condition. Most guns were custom ordered.

100%	98%	95%	90%	80%	70%	60%	50%	40%	30%	20%	10%
$17,500	$15,000	$11,500	$7,500	$3,500	$3,000	$2,500	$1,650	$1,475	$1,200	$750	$450

Subract 15% for 10 ga.

This model was generally a custom order gun with no standard grades being designated. Quality was extremely high, and the high cost of manufacture is a large reason why the gun never sold in large numbers commercially. The Model 1883 was discontinued after only 12 years of manufacture (it was one of the most expensive shotguns during its day). Values above assume moderate engraving and above average walnut.

* ***Model 1883 Hammerless 8 Ga.*** - 8 ga.

Rarity precludes accurate pricing for this model. Extremely rare.

MSR	100%	98%	95%	90%	80%	70%	60%

SxS SHOTGUN MFG. 1961-62 – 12 or 16 ga., various barrel lengths, DTs, checkered stock and forearm, mfg. in France 1961-62 by Fabrication Mechanique, estimated total between 25-50 guns in serial range 467,000-469,000.

	$675	$595	$525	$450	$400	$360	$320

SHOTGUNS: SEMI-AUTO

STANDARD AUTO SHOTGUN – 12 or 20 ga. (also available in Magnum), aluminum frame, 26, 28, 30, or 32 in. plain or VR barrel. Almost 5,300 mfg. (both models) mfg. by Franchi of Italy 1962-66.

	$375	$350	$325	$295	$260	$230	$200

Add $50 for VR barrel.

CUSTOM AUTO SHOTGUN – similar to Standard Model, except deluxe walnut, hand engraved receiver. Mfg. 1962-1966.

	$475	$425	$375	$350	$325	$295	$260

SHOTGUNS: SLIDE ACTION

COLTSMAN PUMP SHOTGUN – 12, 16, or 20 ga., Manufrance frame assembled by both Kodiak and Montgomery Wards, 26 or 28 in. plain barrel, aluminum frame. Approx. 2,000 mfg. 1961-1965.

	$325	$295	$260	$230	$200	$180	$165

Add 30% for Riot model with extended magazine and 20 in. barrel (not cataloged).

FACTORY COMMEMORATIVES & SPECIAL/LIMITED EDITIONS

During the course of a year, we receive many phone calls and letters on Colt non-factory special editions and limited editions that do not appear in this section. It should be noted that Colt factory commemoratives and special/limited editions are guns that has been manufactured, marketed, and sold through the auspices of the specific trademark (in this case Colt). There have literally been hundreds of non-factory special and limited editions which, although mostly made by Colt (some were subcontracted), were not marketed or retailed by Colt. These guns are NOT factory Colt commemoratives or special/limited editions and for the most part, do not have the desirability factor that the factory commemoratives and special/limited editions have. Your best alternative to find out more information about the multitude of these special/limited editions is to write: COLT ARCHIVE PROPERTIES, LLC, 1295 Blue Hills Avenue, Bloomfield, CT 06002. If anyone could have any information, it will be the factory. Their research fee is $100 per gun, with a premium charge for factory engraving. If they cannot obtain additional information on the variation you request, they will refund $50. Unfortunately, in some cases, a special/limited edition may not be researchable. In situations like this, do not confuse rarity with desirability.

Typically, non-factory special and limited editions are made for distributors. These sub-contracts seem to be mostly made to signify/commemorate an organization, state, special event or occasion, personality, etc. These are typically marketed and sold through a distributor to dealers, or a company/individual to those people who want to purchase them. These non-factory special/limited editions may or may not have a retail price and often times, since demand is regional, values may decrease rapidly in other areas of the country. In some cases, if the distributor/wholesaler who ordered the initial non-factory special/

limited edition is known (and still in business), you may be able to find more information by contacting them directly (i.e. Lew Horton, Davidson's, etc.). Overall desirability is the key to determining values on these non-factory special/limited editions.

The word commemorative as it applies to firearms is almost an obsolete term - kind of like calling a flight attendant a stewardess these days. The last factory gun Colt designated a "Colt Commemorative" was manufactured back in the mid-1980s. One of the biggest reasons Colt dropped its commemorative program was because during this time period, it became more advantageous for Colt to sell large domestic distributors special order guns with the features these distributors wanted. This way Colt did not have to inventory, market, and sell these guns through the company. In today's marketplace, Colt is now producing factory special/limited editions which are marketed and sold through the auspices of Colt, so a line in the sand has now been drawn between factory Colt commemoratives and special/limited editions versus non-factory special/limited editions. The word commemorative has never applied to non-factory guns. In this text, recent Colt factory special/limited editions will appear as listings in those sections where their standard models are listed. Older factory special/limited editions will appear in this section.

Because the commemorative consumer is now more in charge (consumers now own most of the guns since distributor/dealer inventories are depleted) than during the 1980s, commemorative firearms are possibly as strong as they have ever been. When the supply side of commemorative economics has to be purchased from knowledgable collectors or savvy dealers and demand stays the same or increases slightly, prices have no choice but to go up. If and when the manufacturers crank up the commemorative production runs again (and it won't be like the good old days), the old marketplace characteristics may reappear. Until then, however, the commemorative marketplace remains steady, with values having become more predictable.

As a reminder on commemoratives, I would like to repeat a few facts, especially for the beginning collector, but applicable to all manufacturers of commemoratives. Commemoratives are current production guns designed as a reproduction of an historically famous gun model, or as a tie-in with historically famous persons or events. They are generally of very excellent quality and often embellished with select woods and finishes such as silver, nickel, or gold plating. Obviously, they are manufactured to be instant collectibles and to be pleasing to the eye. As with firearms in general, not all commemorative models have achieved collector status, although most enjoy an active market. Consecutive-numbered pairs as well as collections based on the same serial number may bring a premium. Remember that handguns usually are in some type of wood presentation case, and that rifles may be cased or in packaging with graphics styled to the particular theme of the collectible. The original factory packaging and papers should always accompany the firearm, as they are necessary to realize full value at the time of sale, and get more important every year.

NIB commemorative firearms should be absolutely new, unfired, and as issued, since any obvious use or wear removes it from collector status and lowers its value significantly. Many owners have allowed their commemoratives to sit in their boxes while encased in plastic wrappers for years without inspecting them for corrosion or oxidation damage. This is risky, especially if stored inside a plastic wrapper for long periods of time, since any accumulated moisture cannot escape. Periodic inspection should be implemented to ensure no damage occurs - this is important, since even light "freckling" created from touching the metal surfaces can reduce values significantly. A mint or unfired gun

100%	Issue Price	Qty. Made

without its original packaging can lose as much as 50% of its normal value - many used commemoratives get sold as "fancy shooters" with little, if any, premiums being asked.

A final note on commemoratives: One of the characteristics of commemoratives/special editions is that over the years of ownership, most of them stay in the same NIB condition. Thus, if supply always is constant and in one condition, demand has to increase before price appreciation can occur. After 47 years of commemorative/special edition production, many model's performance records can be accurately analyzed and the appreciation (or depreciation) can be compared against other purchases of equal vintage. You be the judge.

1961 GENESEO, ILLINOIS 125TH ANNIVERSARY DERRINGER - ser. no. range, 87150D-87253D.

$650	$28	104

1961 125TH ANNIVERSARY MODEL SAA - ser. no. range, 1AM-7390AM.

$1,595	$150	7,390

1961 CIVIL WAR CENTENNIAL PISTOL .22 SHORT - ser. no. range, 50W-24189W (numbers 1W-49W and 124W-149W were not mfg.).

$250	$33	24,114

1961 KANSAS STATEHOOD CENTENNIAL FRONTIER SCOUT - ser. no. range, 001G-6201G.

$595	$75	6,201

1961 PONY EXPRESS CENTENNIAL FRONTIER SCOUT - ser. no. range, 1W-550W, 1E-500E.

$695	$80	1,007

1961 SHERIFF'S MODEL - blue and case hardened, 3 in. barrel, "SM" suffix, w/two-piece box.

$4,000	$130	478

1961 SHERIFF'S MODEL NICKEL - nickel, 3 in. barrel, "SM" suffix, w/ two-piece box.

$9,500	$140	25

1962 COLUMBUS, OHIO SESQUICENTENNIAL SCOUT - ser. no. range, 001CS-200CS.

$750	$100	200

1962 FORT FINDLAY CASE PAIR - .22 LR and .22 WMR cals., ser. no. range, FF0001-FF0150, one hundred revolvers shipped as singles, forty shipped as cased pairs.

$2,750	$185	20

1962 FORT FINDLAY, OHIO SESQUICENTENNIAL SCOUT - ser. no. range, FF0001-FF0150, 110 revolvers shipped as singles, 40 shipped as cased pairs.

$750	$90	110

100%	Issue Price	Qty. Made

1962 FORT MCPHERSON, NEBRASKA CENTENNIAL DERRINGER - ser. no. range, 001McP-300McP.

$595	$29	300

1962 NEW MEXICO GOLDEN ANNIVERSARY SCOUT - ser. no. range, 001NMA-1000NMA.

$695	$80	1,000

1962 ROCK ISLAND ARSENAL CENTENNIAL MODEL - ser. no. range, 1RIA-550RIA.

$250	$39	550

1962 WEST VIRGINIA STATEHOOD CENTENNIAL SCOUT - ser. no. range, WV5, WV8, WV9, WV50, and WV100-WV3546, not all shipped.

$595	$75	3,452

1963 WEST VIRGINIA STATEHOOD CENTENNIAL SAA .45 - ser. no. range, 25WVC-624WVC, not all shipped.

$1,595	$150	600

1963 ARIZONA TERRITORIAL CENTENNIAL SCOUT - ser. no. range, AT001-AT5355.

$695	$75	5,355

1963 ARIZONA TERRITORIAL CENTENNIAL SAA .45 - ser. no. range, 100AT-129AT, and 24AC-1273AC.

$1,595	$150	1,280

1963 BATTLE OF GETTYSBURG CENTENNIAL SCOUT - ser. no. range, 0001GC-1019GC.

$695	$90	1,019

1963 CAROLINA CHARTER TERCENTENARY SCOUT - ser. no. range, 001CT-300CT.

$595	$75	300

1963 CAROLINA CHARTER TERCENTENARY 22/45 COMBO - ser. no. range, Scout: 301CT-550CT and SAA: 301CCT-550CCT.

$2,195	$240	251

1963 FORT STEPHENSON, OHIO SESQUICENTENNIAL SCOUT - ser. no. range, 001FS-200FS, records indicate 150 cased singles and 25 cased doubles.

$695	$75	200

1963 GEN. JOHN HUNT MORGAN INDIANA RAID SCOUT - ser. no. range, 1JHM-100JHM.

$795	$75	100

100%	Issue Price	Qty. Made

1963 H. COOK "1 OF 100" 22/45 COMBO - ser. no. range, Scout: 001HCK-100HCK and SAA: 001HC-100HC.

$2,750	$275	100

1963 IDAHO TERRITORIAL CENTENNIAL SCOUT - ser. no. range, 0001TC-0902TC.

$695	$75	902

1964 CALIFORNIA GOLD RUSH SCOUT - ser. no. range, 0001GR-0500GR.

$695	$80	500

1964 CHAMIZAL TREATY SCOUT - ser. no. range, 0001CS-0500CS, 350 singles and 50 cased pairs.

$695	$85	450

1964 CHAMIZAL TREATY SAA .45 - ser. no. range, 0001CP-0100CP, 50 singles and 1 cased pair.

$1,795	$170	50

1964 CHAMIZAL TREATY 22/45 COMBO - ser. no. range, Scout: 0001CS-0500CS and SAA: 0001CP-0100CP.

$2,500	$280	50

1964 CHERRY'S SPORTING GOODS 35TH ANNIVERSARY 22/45 COMBO - ser. no. range, Scout: REC1-REC100 and SAA: EPC1-EPC100.

$2,500	$275	100

1964 COL. SAM COLT SESQUI. PRESENTATION SAA .45 - ser. no. range, 0001SC-5000SC.

$1,595	$225	4,750

1964 COL. SAM COLT SESQUI. DELUXE PRES. SAA .45 - ser. no. range, 2000SC-2200SC.

$3,500	$500	200

1964 COL. SAM COLT SESQUI. SPEC. DELUXE PRES. SAA .45 - ser. no. range, 0001SC-5000SC, only numbers ending with 00 or 000.

$5,500	$1,000	50

1964 GENERAL HOOD CENTENNIAL SCOUT - ser. no. range, 0001GH-1503GH.

$695	$75	1,503

1964 MONTANA TERRITORIAL CENTENNIAL SCOUT - ser. no. range, 0001MF-2300MF.

$695	$75	2,300

1964 MONTANA TERRITORIAL CENTENNIAL SAA .45 - ser. no. range, 0001MA-0850MA.

$1,650	$150	851

100%	Issue Price	Qty. Made

Approx. 100-200 sets (including the Scout) were sold with matching ser. numbers.

1964 NEVADA STATEHOOD CENTENNIAL SCOUT - ser. no. range, 0001NS-1752NS, 1846NS, 1964NS, and 2001NS-4996NS.

$595	$75	3,984

1964 NEVADA STATEHOOD CENTENNIAL SAA .45 - ser. no. range, 0001NC-1752NC, 1864NC, 1964NC, and 2001NC-2700NC.

$1,595	$150	1,688

1964 NEVADA STATEHOOD CENTENNIAL 22/45 COMBO - ser. no. range, Scout: 0001NS-1752NS, 1846NS, 1964NS, and 2001NS-4996NS, SAA: 0001NC-1752NC, 1864NC, 1964NC, and 2001NC-2700NC.

$2,195	$240	189

1964 NEVADA ST. CENT. 22/45 COMBO W/EXTRA ENGR. CYLS. - ser. no. range, Scout 0001NS-1752NS, 1846NS, 1964NS, and 2001NS-4996NS, SAA 0001NC-1752NC, 1864NC, 1964NC, and 2001NC-2700NC, records do not indicate how revolvers were cased.

$2,395	$350	577

1964 NEVADA "BATTLE BORN" SCOUT - ser. no. range, 001BB-1001BB.

$695	$85	981

1964 NEVADA "BATTLE BORN" SAA .45 - ser. no. range, 001NB-100NB, .45 cal., cased singles and cased pairs shipped.

$1,895	$175	80

1964 NEVADA "BATTLE BORN" 22/45 COMBO - ser. no. range, Scout: 001BB-100BB and S.A.A.: 001NB-100NB.

$2,595	$265	20

1964 NEW JERSEY TERCENTENARY SCOUT - ser. no. range, 0001NJ-1001NJ.

$595	$75	1,001

1964 NEW JERSEY TERCENTENARY SAA .45 - ser. no. range, 0001JT-0250JT.

$1,595	$150	250

1964 PONY EXPRESS PRESENTATION SAA .45 - ser. no. range, 1W-500W and 1E-500E also 0E, 00E, 0W, 00W, X1-W, X1-E, and CAL-1.

$1,750	$250	1,004

100% value assumes all accessory items included.

1964 ST. LOUIS BICENTENNIAL SCOUT - ser. no. range, 0251SL-1051SL.

$595	$75	802

100%	Issue Price	Qty. Made

1964 ST. LOUIS BICENTENNIAL SAA .45 – ser. no. range, 0251SB-0450SB.

$1,595	$150	200

1964 ST. LOUIS BICENTENNIAL 22/45 COMBO – ser. no. range, Scout: 0001SL-0250SL and SAA: 0001SB-0250SB.

$2,195	$240	250

1964 WYATT EARP BUNTLINE SAA .45 – ser. no. range, 0001WE-0150WE.

$2,995	$250	150

1964 WYOMING DIAMOND JUBILEE SCOUT – ser. no. range, 001DJ-2357DJ.

$695	$75	2,357

1965 APPOMATTOX CENTENNIAL SCOUT – ser. no. range, 1000AK-2000AK.

$595	$75	1,001

1965 APPOMATTOX CENTENNIAL SAA .45 – ser. no. range, 1000AP-1249AP.

$1,595	$150	250

1965 APPOMATTOX CENTENNIAL 22/45 COMBO – ser. no. range, Scout: 0001AK-0250AK and SAA: 0001AP-0250AP.

$2,195	$240	250

1965 FORTY-NINER MINER SCOUT – ser. no. range, 0001FN-0500FN.

$695	$85	500

1965 GENERAL MEADE CAMPAIGN SCOUT – ser. no. range, 1GM-1197GM.

$595	$75	1,197

1965 JOAQUIN MURIETTA 22/45 COMBO – ser. no. range, Scout: 001JMK-100JMK and SAA: 001JMP-100JMP.

$2,500	$350	100

1965 OREGON TRAIL SCOUT – ser. no. range, 0001OT-1995OT.

$695	$75	1,995

1965 OLD FT. DES MOINES RECONSTRUCTION SCOUT – ser. no. range, 0101DM-0800DM.

$695	$90	700

1965 OLD FT. DES MOINES RECONSTRUCTION SAA .45 – ser. no. range, 0101FD-0200FD.

$1,695	$170	100

100%	Issue Price	Qty. Made

1965 OLD FT. DES MOINES RECONSTRUCTION 22/45 COMBO - ser. no. range, Scout: 0001DM-0100DM and SAA: 0001FD-0100FD.

$2,195	$290	100

1965 ST. AUGUSTINE QUADRACENTENNIAL SCOUT - ser. no. range, 1AQ-500AQ.

$695	$85	500

1965 KANSAS COWTOWN SERIES - Wichita Scout, ser. no. range, 1KW-500KW.

$595	$85	500

1966 ABERCROMBIE & FITCH "TRAILBLAZER" CHICAGO - Chicago, ser. no. range, 201AF-300AF.

$1,595	$275	100

1966 ABERCROMBIE & FITCH "TRAILBLAZER" NEW YORK - New York, ser. no. range, 001AF-200AF.

$1,595	$275	200

1966 ABERCROMBIE & FITCH "TRAILBLAZER" SAN FRANCISCO - San Francisco, ser. no. range, 301AF-400AF.

$1,595	$275	100

1966 CALIFORNIA GOLD RUSH SAA .45 - ser. no. range, 0001GP-0500GP, not all shipped.

$1,695	$175	130

1966 COLORADO GOLD RUSH SCOUT - ser. no. range, 0CG-1350CG.

$695	$85	1,350

1966 DAKOTA TERRITORY SCOUT - ser. no. range, 1DT-1000DT.

$695	$85	1,000

1966 GENERAL MEADE SAA .45 - ser. no. range, 0001MC-0200MC.

$1,595	$165	200

1966 INDIANA SESQUICENTENNIAL SCOUT - ser. no. range, 1IS-1745IS.

$695	$85	1,500

1966 KANSAS COWTOWN SERIES ABILENE - Abilene Scout, ser. no. range, 1KA-500KA.

$595	$95	500

1966 KANSAS COWTOWN SERIES - Dodge City Scout, ser. no. range, 1KD-500KD.

$595	$85	500

1966 OKLAHOMA DIAMOND JUBILEE - ser. no. range, 1OK-1343OK.

$695	$85	1,343

100%	Issue Price	Qty. Made

1966 PONY EXPRESS .45 SAA 4-SQUARE SET (4 GUNS) – ser. no. range with backstrap marking, PE001E-PE250E "SACRAMENTO TO FRIDAY'S STATION", PE251E-PE500E "SALT LAKE CITY TO FORT LARAMIE", PE001W-PE250W "ST. JOSEPH TO MARYSVILLE"' PE251W-PE500W "FORT KEARNEY TO JULESBURG".

$7,500	$1,400	unknown

1967 ALAMO SCOUT – ser. no. range, cased single 1051A22-4500A22 and cased pairs 251A22-1050A22.

$595	$85	4,250

1967 ALAMO SAA .45 – ser. no. range, 251A45-1000A45, 450 singles and 300 cased pairs.

$1,595	$165	750

1967 ALAMO 22/45 COMBO – ser. no. range, 1A22-250A22 and 1A45-250A45.

$2,095	$265	250

1967 KANSAS COWTOWN SERIES – Coffeyville Scout, ser. no. range, 1KC-500KC.

$595	$95	500

1967 KANSAS TRAIL SERIES – Chisolm Trail Scout, ser. no. range, 1CH-500CH.

$595	$100	500

1967 LAWMAN SERIES SAA – Bat Masterson SAA .45, ser. no. range, 1LMP-500LMP.

$1,995	$180	500

1967 LAWMAN SERIES SCOUT – Bat Masterson Scout, ser. no. range, 1LM-3000LM.

$750	$90	3,000

1967 WWI SERIES – .45 ACP cal., Chateau Thierry, ser. no. range, 101CT-7500CT.

$995	$200	7,400

1967 WWI SERIES DELUXE – Chateau Thierry Deluxe, ser. no. range, 26CT-100CT.

$1,995	$500	75

1967 WWI SERIES SPECIAL DELUXE – Chateau Thierry Spec. Deluxe, ser. no. range, 1CT-25CT.

$3,000	$1,000	25

1968 GEN. NATHAN BEDFORD FORREST SCOUT – ser. no. range, 1NBF-3000NBF.

$595	$110	3,000

100%	Issue Price	Qty. Made

1968 KANSAS TRAIL SERIES PAWNEE TRAIL - Pawnee Trail Scout, ser. no. range, 1PT-500PT.

$595	$110	501

1968 KANSAS TRAIL SERIES SANTA FE TRAIL - Santa Fe Trail Scout, ser. no. range, 1SF-500SF.

$595	$120	501

1968 LAWMAN SERIES SAA - Pat Garrett .45 SAA, ser. no. range, 1PGP-500PGP.

$1,795	$220	500

1968 LAWMAN SERIES SCOUT - Pat Garrett Scout, ser. no. range, 1PG-3000PG.

$750	$110	3,000

1968 NEBRASKA CENTENNIAL SCOUT - ser. no. range, 1NEB-7000NEB.

$595	$100	7,001

1968 WWI SERIES - .45 ACP cal., Belleau Wood, ser. no. range, 1BW-100BW and 201BW-7500BW.

$995	$200	7,400

1968 WWI SERIES DELUXE - Belleau Wood Deluxe, ser. no. range, 126BW-200BW.

$1,995	$500	75

1968 WWI SERIES SPECIAL DELUXE - Belleau Wood Special Deluxe, ser. no. range, 101BW-125BW.

$3,000	$1,000	25

1968 WWI SERIES BATTLE OF THE MARNE - .45 ACP cal., 2nd Battle of the Marne, 1M2-200M2 and 301M2-7500M2.

$995	$220	7,400

1968 WWI SERIES BATTLE OF THE MARNE DELUXE - 2nd Battle of the Marne Deluxe, ser. no. range, 226M2-300M2.

$1,995	$500	75

1969 ALABAMA SESQUICENTENNIAL SCOUT - ser. no. range, 1AS-3098AS, not all shipped.

$595	$110	3,001

1969 ALABAMA SESQUICENTENNIAL .45 SAA - ser. no. ALA1P.

$17,500	unknown	1

1969 ARKANSAS TERRITORIAL SESQUICENTENNIAL SCOUT - ser. no. range, 1ARK-3500ARK.

$595	$110	3,500

100%	Issue Price	Qty. Made

1969 CALIFORNIA BICENTENNIAL SCOUT – ser. no. range, 1CBI-5000CBI.

$595	$135	5,000

1969 GOLDEN SPIKE SCOUT – ser. no. range, 1GS-11000GS.

$695	$135	11,000

1969 KANSAS TRAIL SERIES – Shawnee Trail Scout, ser. no. range, 1ST-500ST.

$595	$120	501

1969 LAWMAN SERIES SAA – .45 SAA Wild Bill Hickok, ser. no. range, 1WBH-500WBH.

$1,795	$220	500

1969 LAWMAN SERIES SCOUT – Wild Bill Hickok Scout, ser. no. range, 1WB-3000WB.

$750	$117	3,000

1969 WWI SERIES BATTLE OF THE MARNE DELUXE – 2nd Battle of the Marne Spec. Deluxe, ser. no. range, 201M2-225M2.

$3,000	$1,000	25

1969 WWI SERIES MEUSE-ARGONNE – .45 ACP cal., Meuse-Argonne, ser. no. range, 1MA-300MA and 401MA-7500MA.

$995	$220	7,400

1969 WWI SERIES MEUSE-ARGONNE DELUXE – Meuse-Argonne Deluxe, ser. no. range, 326MA-400MA.

$1,995	$500	75

1969 WWI SERIES MEUSE-ARGONNE SPECIAL DELUXE – Meuse-Argonne Spec. Deluxe, ser. no. range, 301MA-325MA.

$3,000	$1,000	25

1970 KANSAS FORT HAYS – Ft. Hays Scout, ser. no. range, 1FH-500FH.

$595	$130	500

1970 KANSAS FORT LARNED – Ft. Larned Scout, ser. no. range, 1FL-500FL.

$595	$120	500

1970 KANSAS FORT RILEY – Ft. Riley Scout, ser. no. range, 1FR-500FR.

$595	$130	500

1970 LAWMAN SERIES SAA – Wyatt Earp .45 SAA, ser. no. range, 1WYE-500WYE.

$2,995	$395	500

1970 LAWMAN SERIES SCOUT – Wyatt Earp Scout, ser. no. range, 1LWE-3000LWE.

$750	$125	3,000

100%	Issue Price	Qty. Made

1970 MAINE SESQUICENTENNIAL SCOUT - ser. no. range, 1MES-3000MES.

$595	$120	3,000

1970 MISSOURI SESQUICENTENNIAL SCOUT - ser. no. range, 1MOS-3000MOS.

$595	$125	3,000

1970 MISSOURI SESQUICENTENNIAL .45 SAA - ser. no. range, P1MOS-P900MOS.

$1,595	$220	900

1970 TEXAS RANGER SAA .45 - ser. no. range, N/A.

$2,500	$650	1,000

1970 TEXAS RANGER GRADE I (95% ENGRAVING COVERAGE) - ser. no. range, N/A.

$6,000	N/A	90

1970 TEXAS RANGER GRADE II (75% ENGRAVING COVERAGE) - ser. no. range, N/A.

$5,500	$2,250	80

1970 TEXAS RANGER GRADE III (50% ENGRAVING COVERAGE) - ser. no. range, N/A.

$5,000	$2,950	90

1970 WWII SERIES EUROPEAN THEATRE - European Theatre, ser. no. range, 0001ETO-9959ETO, not all shipped.

$995	$250	11,500

1970 WWII SERIES PACIFIC THEATRE - Pacific Theatre, ser. no. range, 0001PTO-9960PTO, not all shipped.

$995	$250	11,500

Note: A complete set of the WWI and WWII Series standard grade models (6 guns) with matching serial numbers in NIB condition is currently selling in the $4,750-$5,500 range.

1971 KANSAS SERIES - Ft. Scott Scout, ser. no. range, 1FSC-500FSC.

$595	$130	500

1971 NRA CENTENNIAL GOLD CUP .45 ACP - ser. no. range, 1NRA-2500NRA, not all shipped.

$1,495	$250	2,500

1971 NRA CENTENNIAL .45 SAA - ser. no. range, NRA1-NRA7000, not all shipped.

$1,595	$250	5,000

100%	Issue Price	Qty. Made

1971 NRA CENTENNIAL .357 SAA – ser. no. range, NRA1-NRA7000, not all shipped.

$1,495	$250	5,000

1971 1851 NAVY LEE-GRANT – Lee-Grant Set, ser. no. range, 1LGP-250LGP.

$1,595	$500	250

1971 1851 NAVY U.S. GRANT – U.S. Grant, ser. no. range, 251USG-4398USG, not all shipped.

$795	$250	4,750

1971 1851 NAVY ROBERT E. LEE – Robert E. Lee, ser. no. range, 251REL-4900REL.

$795	$250	4,750

1972 ARIZONA RANGER SCOUT – ser. no. range, 1AR-3000AR.

$695	$135	3,001

1972 FLORIDA TERRITORY SESQUICENTENNIAL SCOUT – ser. no. range, 1FLA-2000FLA.

$695	$125	2,001

1975 PEACEMAKER CENTENNIAL .45 – ser. no. range, PC501-PC2000.

$1,795	$300	1,500

1975 PEACEMAKER CENTENNIAL 44.40 – ser. no. range, 501PC-2000PC.

$1,795	$300	1,500

1975 PEACEMAKER CENT. CASED PAIR – ser. no. range, .44-40 cal.: 1MPC-500MPC and .45 cal.: MPC1-MPC500.

$3,250	$625	500

USS TEXAS BATTLESHIP SPECIAL EDITION (1975) – .45 ACP cal., Model 1911A1 with special embellishments, nickel finish, this model is not a factory commemorative, ser. no. range N/A.

$1,250	unknown	500

USS ARIZONA BATTLESHIP SPECIAL EDITION (1975) – .45 ACP cal., Model 1911A1 with special embellishments, nickel finish, this model is not a factory commemorative, ser. no. range N/A.

$1,250	unknown	500

1976 U.S. BICENTENNIAL SET – ser. no. range, SAA .45: 0001PM-1776PM, Python .357 Mag.: 0001PY-1776PY, and black powder Dragoon: 0001DG-1776DG, in walnut display case with drawers.

$5,250	$1,695	1,776

1976 BICENTENNIAL SAA FREEDOM COLTS – consisted of A, B, and C sets, set As were engraved, Bs had gold work and accessories, Cs were

100%	Issue Price	Qty. Made

similar to Bs, but had shoulder stock. Set A prices averaged $1,500-$3,000 in 1976, set B prices varied between $3,500-$20,000, and set C prices started at $5,000. Total mfg. was 4 set As, 6 set Bs, and 1 set C. These sets in today's marketplace are too rare to accurately evaluate and pricing is literally "what the market will bear."

These guns were all engraved by Dwain Wright located in Applegate, OR.

1977 2ND AMENDMENT .22 - ser. no. range, G0001RB-G3020RB.

$595	$195	3,020

1977 U.S. CAVALRY 200TH ANNIVERSARY SET - ser. no. range, US0001-US3020 and 0001US-3020US, not all shipped.

$1,450	$995	3,000

1978 STATEHOOD 3RD MODEL DRAGOON - ser. no. range, N/A.

$7,500	$12,500	52

1979 NED BUNTLINE .45 SAA - ser. no. range, NB0001-NB3000.

$1,395	$895	3,000

OHIO PRESIDENT'S SPECIAL EDITION (1979) - .45 ACP cal., Model 1911A1 with special Ohio embellishments, this is not a factory commemorative, ser. no. range N/A.

$1,250	unknown	250

1979 TOMBSTONE CENTENNIAL .45 SAA - .45 LC cal., 7 1/2 in. barrel, nickel finish, two-piece walnut stocks, P-1876 Model, etched with scroll engraving and Western scenes. 300 mfg. (200 singles and 50 pairs), ser. no. range N/A.

$2,500	$995	300

This model was not sold retail through the auspices of Colt.

1980 DRUG ENFORCEMENT AGENCY (DEA) .45 AUTO - ser. no. range N/A.

$1,250	$550	910

This model was not sold at retail through the auspices of Colt.

1980 OLYMPICS ACE MODEL SPECIAL EDITION - ser. no. range N/A.

$1,600	$1,000	200

This model was not sold at retail through the auspices of Colt.

1980 HERITAGE-WALKER .44 PERCUSSION - ser. no. range, 0001 C CO-1850 C CO.

$950	$1,475	1,847

1981 "JOHN M. BROWNING" .45 ACP SEMI-AUTO - ser. no. range, CJMBC0001-CJMBC3000.

$995	$1,100	3,000

100%	Issue Price	Qty. Made

1980-81 .45 ACP GOVT. SIGNATURE SERIES - .45 ACP cal., blue finished Govt. with gold auroplated or nickel finish. 250 mfg. in both finishes, ser. no. range N/A.

$1,250	$833	250

Add $50 for blue finish.

1980-81 ACE SIGNATURE SERIES - .22 LR cal., cocobolo grips with medallions, blue finish with photo engraving, cased. 1,000 mfg., ser. no. range N/A.

$1,500	$955	1,000

1981 BUFFALO BILL SPECIAL EDITION - .44-40 WCF cal., 7 1/2 in. barrel, gold and silver plating, Class C engraved, scrimshaw ivory grips featuring Buffalo Bill and his TE Wyoming Ranch brand, leather cased, 250 mfg. serialized 1BB-250BB.

$4,975	$3,750	250

This model was a special edition (not commemorative), which was made specifically for the Buffalo Bill Historical Center.

1982 JOHN WAYNE SAA STANDARD - ser. no. range, CJWC0001-CJWC3100.

$2,250	$2,995	3,100

While advertising literature indicated 3,100 were mfg., 3,041 were sold.

1982 JOHN WAYNE SAA DELUXE - ser. no. range, JWD001-JWD500.

$8,000	$10,000	500

While advertising literature indicated 500 were mfg., only 90 were sold.

1982 JOHN WAYNE SAA PRESENTATION - ser. no. range, JWP001-JWP100.

$13,500	$20,000	100

While advertising literature indicated 100 were mfg., only 47 were sold.

1983 BUFFALO BILL WILD WEST SHOW CENTENNIAL SAA .45 - ser. no. range, CBC0001-CBBC1236, not all shipped.

$1,695	$1,350	500

1983 CCA LIMITED EDITION SAA - .44-40 WCF cal., 4 3/4 in. barrel, nickel finish, fleur-de-lis checkered walnut grips, two line barrel address and Colt Frontier Six Shooter roll marking. 250 mfg. in 1983 to commemorate Colt Collector's Assn., ser. no. range N/A.

$1,895	$825	250

This model was not sold at retail through the auspices of Colt.

100%	Issue Price	Qty. Made

1983 "ARMORY MODEL" SAA .45 ACP – this model had limited production, and should not be considered a commemorative. So-called because it was shipped with extra .45 LC cylinder and the "Colt Armory Edition" book by E. Grant. 250 mfg. with nickel finish, 250 mfg. with blue finish, presentation cased, smooth ivory grips, ser. no. range N/A.

$2,500	$1,125	500

20 Armory Models were available with class A engraving - $2,995, B engraving - $3,500, C engraving - $3,995, D engraving - $4,500.

1983 PYTHON SILVER SNAKE SPECIAL EDITION – .357 Mag. cal., 6 in. barrel, stainless steel with black chrome finish, Pachmayr grips with custom shop pewter medallions, etched engraving, includes custom gun pouch, ser. no. range N/A.

$13,000	$1,150	250

1984 1ST EDITION GOVT. MODEL .380 ACP – ser. no. range, RC00000-RC01000.

$850	$425	1,000

1984 JOHN WAYNE "DUKE" FRONTIER .22 – ser. no. range N/A.

$895	$475	5,000

1984 COLT/WINCHESTER SET – 1 ea. of the Model 1894 Winchester carbine and Colt Peacemaker, serial numbered 1WC-4440WC, .44-40 WCF cal., elaborate gold etching, cased. Pistol became available for sale individually in 1986 - see individual listing below for values.

$3,500	$3,995	2,300

Approx. 2,300 sets were actually put together in this combination. Some sets were split up with individual prices being discounted.

1984 COLT SAA ONLY FROM SET – .44-40 WCF cal., 7 1/2 in. barrel, gold etching, this commemorative was originally made as part of the 1984 Winchester/Colt rifle-pistol set, but was later able to be purchased individually. Originally mfg. 1984, ser. no. range N/A.

$1,595	N/A	4,000

1984 USA EDITION SAA – .44-40 WCF cal., 7 1/2 in. barrel, old style black powder frame, bullseye ejector rod head, 3 line patent date, high polished blue with gold line engraving. 100 guns total mfg. - 1 for each state and its capitol, ser. no. range N/A.

$3,250	$4,995	100

1984 KIT CARSON .22 NEW FRONTIER – 6 in. barrel, color case hardened frame, gold artwork, serial numbered KCC0001-KCC1000, cased.

$695	$550	1,000

1984 SECOND EDITION GOVT. MODEL .380 ACP – serial numbered 00000RC- 01000RC.

$850	$525	1,000

100%	Issue Price	Qty. Made

1984 OFFICER'S COMMENCEMENT ISSUE - Officer's ACP with Marine Corps emblem, rosewood grips, silver plated oak leaf scroll, cased, ser. no. range N/A.

$995	$700	1,000

This model was not sold retail through the auspices of Colt.

1984 THEODORE ROOSEVELT COMMEMORATIVE SAA - .44-40 WCF cal., 7 1/2 in. barrel, black powder frame, case colored receiver, factory "B" hand engraving, ivory stocks, cased, ser. no. range, TRC001-TRC500.

$2,250	$1,695	500

1984 NORTH AMERICAN OILMEN SAA BUNTLINE - .45 LC cal., 12 in. barrel, non-fluted cylinder, elaborate gold etching, ebony grips with ivory inlays, stand-up glass case, ser. nos. 1-100 mfg. for Canada, 101-200 for the U.S.

$3,250	$3,900	200

This model was not sold retail through the auspices of Colt.

1985 TEXAS 150th SESQUICENTENNIAL SAA - .45 cal., Sheriff's model, 4 3/4 in. barrel, mirror bright blue, gold etching, 24Kt. gold plated backstrap and trigger guard, smooth ivory grips, French fit oak presentation case. Mfg. 1985 only.

* ***1985 Texas 150th Sesquicentennial SAA Standard Model*** - 1,000 mfg., ser. no. range TX0001-TX1000.

$1,595	$1,836	1,000

* ***1985 Texas 150th Sesquicentennial SAA Premier Model*** - elaborate engraving, 75 mfg., ser. no. range TEXAS0001-TEXAS0096, not all shipped.

$5,000	$7,995	75

1986 150th ANNIVERSARY SAA - .45 LC cal., 10 in. barrel, 50% coverage engraving, royal blue finish, Goncalo Alves smooth grips, 150th anniversary logo in stocks, cherrywood case. 490 mfg. 1986 only, ser. no. range AM0001-AM1000, not all shipped.

$1,995	$1,595	490

1986 150th ANNIVERSARY ENGRAVING SAMPLER SAA - various cals. and barrel lengths, 4 different engraving styles featuring Nimschke, Helfricht, Henshaw, and Contemporary (these names are scrimshawed on the ivory grips), approx. 75% coverage signed by the engraver, available in either blue or nickel finish, no special serialization. Mfg. 1986.

$3,500	$1,613	unknown

1986 150th ANNIVERSARY ENGRAVING SAMPLER .45 M1911A1 - .45 ACP cal., 4 different engraving styles on metal surfaces, 75% coverage, ivory grips, signed by the engraver, available with either blue or nickel finish. New 1986, ser. no. range N/A.

$2,350	$1,155	unknown

Add $60 for nickel.

100%	Issue Price	Qty. Made

1986 MUSTANG FIRST EDITION - .380 ACP cal., 1,000 manufactured serialized MU00001-MU01000 (the first thousand of production), rosewood stocks, walnut presentation case. Mfg. 1986 only.

$850 $475 1,000

OFFICER'S ACP HEIRLOOM EDITION - .45 ACP cal., personalized with individual's choice for serial number (ie. John Smith 1), mirror brite bluing, jeweled barrel, hammer, and trigger, ivory grips, with historical letter and mahogany case. New 1986, ser. no. range N/A.

$1,550 $1,643 open

1986 DOUBLE DIAMOND SET - Python Ultimate .357 Mag. revolver and Officer's Model .45 ACP, both guns in stainless steel, smooth rosewood grips, presentation cased. 1,000 sets mfg. 1986 only, serial numbered 1-1,000 (matched).

$8,500 $1,575 1,000

DELTA MATCH H-BAR RIFLE - AR-15 A2 H-Bar rifle selectively chosen and equipped with 3-9x variable power rubber armored scope, leather sling, shoulder stock cheekpiece, cased. Mfg. 1987, ser. no. range N/A.

$1,500 $1,425 open

12TH MAN-'SPIRIT OF AGGIELAND' - .45 ACP cal., mfg. to commemorate Texas A&M University, serial numbered TAM001-TAM999, 24Kt gold plating including wreaths on left frame and inscription on right, cherrywood glass top presentation case, includes personalized class graduation inscription. Available 1987 only.

$1,150 $950 999

This model was not sold retail through the auspices of Colt.

COMBAT ELITE CUSTOM EDITION - .45 ACP cal., with ambidextrous thumb safety, wide grip safety, hand tuned action, and carrying case, ser. numbered CG00001-CG00500. Mfg. 1987.

$1,150 $900 500

1987 SHERIFF'S EDITION - set of 5 SAA Sheriff's configuration revolvers in .45 LC cal., barrel lengths include 2, 2 1/2, 3, 4, and 5 1/2 in., royal blue finish, smooth rosewood grips with medallions, supplied with glass top case which displays the revolvers in a circle around a brass sheriff's badge. Serialization has 3 numeral prefix (which is the same in each set), followed by the letters "SE", followed by 1 or 2 numerals (indicating barrel length) - i.e. serial number 002SE25 indicates the second set built, Sheriff's Edition (SE), and a barrel length of 2 1/2 inches.

$6,995 $7,500 200 sets

1989 SNAKE EYES LIMITED EDITION - includes two Python revolvers (2 1/2 in. barrels), one finished in brite stainless steel and the other in Royal Blue finish, grips are ivory-like with scrimshaw "snake eyes" dice on left side and royal flush poker hand on right, includes chips and

100%	Issue Price	Qty. Made

playing cards, 500 sets only of consecutive serial numbers. New 1989, ser. no. range N/A.

$12,000	$3,500	500

1990 SAA HEIRLOOM II EDITION - .45 LC cal., 7 1/2 in. barrel, color case hardened frame and hammer, balance of metal finished in Colt Royal Blue, one-piece American Walnut grips with cartouche on lower left side, personalized inscription on backstrap, walnut cased. Available 1990 only, ser. no. range N/A.

$1,795	$1,600	open

1990 JOE FOSS LIMITED EDITION .45 ACP GOVT. MODEL - .45 ACP cal., first limited edition in Colt's All American Hero Series, commemorates Joe Foss, famous American WWII Marine Fighter Pilot, gold etched scenes on slide sides, smooth walnut grips. While 2,500 were advertised, only 300+ were mfg. Serial numbered beginning with JF 0001. French fitted walnut presentation case, 38 oz. Mfg. 1990 only.

$1,850	$1,375	300+

1911A1 50th ANNIVERSARY BATTLE OF THE BULGE - .45 ACP cal., special edition commemorating the Battle of the Bulge, silver plated with gold inlays, 100 mfg. serialized BB001-BB100.

$1,595	$1,250	100

Add $150 for deluxe presentation case.

This special edition was sold exclusively by Cherry's located in Greensboro, NC.

1993 CCA LIMITED EDITION SAA - .38-40 WCF cal., 4 3/4 in. barrel, nickel finish, walnut grips, CCA markings on grip strap. 150 mfg. in 1993, ser. no. range N/A.

$1,750	$1,165	150

This model was not sold at retail through the auspices of Colt.

2014 SAA SAM COLT 200TH BIRTHDAY COMMEMORATIVE - .45 LC cal., 7 1/2 in. barrel with front and rear gold barrel bands and engraving, 100% Royal Blue finish, unfluted cylinder with gold-etched Sam Colt on left side and Colt dome on the right, scroll engraved frame and top strap, gold-plated hammer, trigger, and screws, hand-carved ivory grips, while advertised during 2014, Colt never manufactured this commemorative outside of prototypes.

*	Banned due to 1994-2004 Crime Bill (may be current again)
5R	Five (groove) Rifling
A	Standard Grade Walnut
A.R.M.S.	Atlantic Research Marketing Systems
A2	AR-15 Style/Configuration w/fixed carry handle
A3	AR-15 Style/Configuration w/detachable carry handle
AA	Extra Grade Walnut
AAA	Best Quality Walnut
ACB	Advanced Combat Bolt (LWRC)
ACP	Automatic Colt Pistol
ACR	Adaptive Combat Rifle
ACS	MAGPUL Adaptable Carbine/Storage (stock)
adj.	Adjustable
AE	Automatic Ejectors or Action Express
AECA	Arms Export Control Act
AFG	MAGPUL Angled Fore Grip
AK	Avtomat Kalashnikova rifle
AMU	Army Marksman Unit
AOW	Any Other Weapon (NFA)
appts.	Appointments
AR	Armalite Rifle
ASAP	MAGPUL Ambi Sling Attachment Point
ATACS	Advanced Tactical Concealment System (camo pattern)
ATR	All Terrain Rifle (Mossberg)
ATS	All Terrain Shotgun (Mossberg)
AWB	Assault Weapons Ban
AWR	Alaskan/African Wilderness Rifle
B	Blue
BAC	Browning Arms Company
BAD	MAGPUL Battery Assist Device (bolt catch lever)
BAN/CRIME BILL ERA	Mfg. between Nov. 1989 - Sept. 12, 2004
BAR	Browning Automatic Rifle
BASR	Bolt Action Sniper Rifle (H&K)
BB	Brass Backstrap
BBL	Barrel
BLR	Browning Lever Rifle
BMG	Browning Machine Gun
BOSS	Ballistic Optimizing Shooting System
BOSS-CR	BOSS w/o Muzzle Brake
BP	Buttplate or Black Powder
BPE	Black Power Express
BPS	Browning Pump Shotgun
BR	Bench Rest
BT	Beavertail
BT	Browning Trap shotgun
BUIS	Back-Up Iron Sight(s)
c.	Circa
C/B 1994	Introduced Because of 1994 Crime Bill
CAD	Computer Assisted Design
cal.	Caliber
CAR	Colt Automatic Rifle or Carbine
CAWS	Close Assault Weapons System
CB	Crescent Buttplate
CC	Case Colors
CCA	Colt Collectors Association
CDP	Custom Defense Package (Kimber)
CF	Centerfire
CFR	Code of Federal Regulations
CH	Cross Hair
CLMR	Colt Lightning Magazine Rifle
CMS	Cowboy Mounted Shooter
CMV	Chrome Moly Vanadium Steel
CNC	Computer Numeric Controlled (machining/machinery)
COMM.	Commemorative
COMP	Compensated/Competition
CQB	Close Quarter Battle
CQC	Close Quarter Combat
C-R	Curio-Relic
CRF	Controlled Round Feed
CRPF	Controlled Round Push Feed
CSAT	Combat Shooting & Tactics (accessories)
CTF	Copper/Tin Frangible (bullet)
CTG/CTGE	Cartridge
CTR	MAGPUL Compact/Type Restricted (stock)
CYL/C	Cylinder
DA	Double Action
DA/SA	Double Action/Single Action
DAGR	Dual aperture Gunsite rifle scope
DAK	Double Action Kellerman Trigger (SIG)
DAO	Double Action Only
DB	Double Barrel
DBM	Detachable Box Magazine
DCM	Director of Civilian Marksmanship
DI	Direct Impingement Gas System, see Glossary
DIGS	Delayed Impingement Gas System, see Glossary
DISC or disc.	Discontinued
DLC	Diamond Like Carbon (STI International)
DMR	Designated Marksman Rifle (U.S Army, LWRC)

DPMS	Defense Procurement Manufacturing Services
DSL	Detachable Side Locks
DST	Double Set Triggers
DT	Double Triggers
DWM	DeutscheWaffen and Munitions Fabriken
EGLM	Enhanced Grenade Launcher Module (FNH)
EJT	Ejector or Ejectors
EMAG	MAGPUL Export MAGazine
EMP	Enhanced Micro Pistol (Springfield Inc.)
EXC	Excellent
EXT	Extractor or Extractors
F	Full Choke
F&M	Full & Modified
FA	Forearm
FAL	Fusil Automatique Leger
FBT	Full Beavertail Forearm
FC	Full Choke
FDE	Flat Dark Earth (finish color)
FDL	Fleur-de-lis
FE	Forend/Fore End
FFL	Federal Firearms License
FIRSH	Free Floating Integrated Rail System Handguard
FK	Flat Knob
FKLT	Flat Knob Long Tang
FM	Full Mag
FMJ	Full Metal Jacket
FMOS	Full Mass Operating System
FN CAL	FN Carabine Automatique Leger
FN GP	FN Grande Puissance (pistol)
FN LAR	Fabrique Nationale Light Automatic Rifle
FN	Fabrique Nationale
FNAR	FN Automatic Rifle
FNC	Fabrique Nationale Carabine
FNH USA	Fabrique Nationale Herstal (U.S. sales and marketing)
FNH	Fabrique Nationale Herstal
FOL	Foliage (finish)
FPS	Feet Per Second
g.	Gram
ga.	Gauge
GCA	Gun Control Act
GIO	Gas Impingement Operation
G-LAD	Green Laser Aiming Device
GOVT	Government
GPO	Gas Piston Operation
gr.	Grain
H&H	Holland & Holland
HAMR	High accuracy multi-range rifle scope
HB	Heavy Barrel
H-BAR	H(eavy)-BARrel, AR-15/M16
HC	Hard Case
HK	Heckler und Koch
HMR	Hornady Magnum Rimfire
HP	High Power (FN/Browning pistol)
HP	Hollow Point
HPJ	High Performance Jacket
I	Improved
IAR	Infantry Automatic Rifle (LWRC)
IC	Improved Cylinder
ICORE	International Confederation of Revolver Enthusiasts
ILS	Integral Locking System (North American Arms)
IM	Improved Modified
IMI	Israel Military Industries
in.	Inch
intro.	Introduced
IOM	Individual Officer Model (FNH model suffix)
IPSC	International Practical Shooting Confederation
ISSF	International Shooting Sports Federation
ITAR	International Traffic (in) Arms Regulation
IVT	Italian Value-Added Tax
JCP	Joint Combat Pistol
KAC	Knight's Armament Co.
KMC	Knight's Manufacturing Co.
KSG	Kel Tec Shotgun
L	Long
LBA	Lightning Bolt Action (Mossberg)
LBC	Les Baer Custom (Inc.)
lbs.	Pounds
LC	Long Colt
LCW	Lauer Custom Weaponry
LDA	Light Double Action (PARA USA INC.)
LEM	Law Enforcement Model or Modification
LEO	Law Enforcement Only
LMT	Lewis Machine and Tool (Company)
LOP	Length of Pull
LPA	Lightning Pump Action (Mossberg)
LPI	Lines Per Inch
LR	Long Rifle
LT	Long Tang or Light
LTR	Light Tactical Rifle (Rem.)
LTRK	Long Tang Round Knob
LWRC	Land Warfare Resources Corporation
LWRC	Leitner-Wise Rifle Company, Inc.

LXX	Trigger by Weatherby (new 2016)
M (MOD.)	Modified Choke
M&P	Military & Police
M-4	Newer AR-15/M16 Carbine Style/Configuration
Mag.	Magnum Caliber
mag.	Magazine
MARS	Modular Accessory Rail System
MBUS	MAGPUL Back-Up Sight
MC	Monte Carlo
MCS	Modular Combat System (Rem.)
MFG or Mfg.	Manufactured/manufacture
MIAD	MAGPUL Mission Adaptable (grip, other)
mil	see Glossary
mil-dot	See Glossary
Mil-Spec	Mfg. to Military Specifications
Mil-Std	Mfg. to Military Standards
MK	Mark
mm	Millimeter
MOA	Minute of Angle
MOE	MAGPUL Original Equipment
MOS	Modular Optic System (Glock)
MOUT	Military Operations (on) Urbanized Terrain
MR	Matted Rib
MS2	MAGPUL Multi Mission Sling System
MSR	Manufacturer's Suggested Retail or Modern Sporting Rifle
MVG	MAGPUL MOE Vertical Grip
MWS	Modular Weapons System
N	Nickel
N/A	Not Applicable or Not Available
NATO	North Atlantic Treaty Org.
NE	Nitro Express
NFA	National Firearms Act (U.S. 1934)
NIB	New in Box
NM	National Match
no.	Number
NP	New Police
NP3/NP3 Plus	Nickel-Phosphorus (firearm coating)
NSST	Non Selective Single Trigger
NVD	Night Vision Device
O/U	Over and Under
OA	Overall
OAL	Overall Length
OB	Octagon Barrel
OBFM	Octagon Barrel w/full mag.
OBO	Or Best Offer
OCT	Octagon
ODG	Olive Drab Green (finish color)
ORB	Oil-Rubbed Bronze finish (Sig Sauer)
ORC	Optics Ready Carbine
oz.	Ounce
P	Police (Rem. rifle/shotgun)
P99AS	Pistol 99 Anti Stress (trigger, Walther)
PAD	Personal Anti-recoil Device (Savage)
Para.	Parabellum
PBR	Patrol Bolt Rifle (FNH)
PDA	Personal Defense Assistant (PARA USA INC.)
PFFR	Percantage of factory finish remaining
PG	Pistol Grip
PGF	Precision Guided Firearm
PK	Pistol Kompact (Walther)
PMAG	MAGPUL Polymer MAGazine
POR/P.O.R.	Price on Request
POST-'89	Paramilitary mfg. after Federal legislation in Nov. 1989
POST-BAN	Refers to production after Sept. 12, 2004
PPC	Pindell Palmisano Cartridge
PPD	Post Paid
PPK	Police Pistol Kriminal (Walther 1931 design)
PPKs	Police Pistol Kriminal (Walther 1968 design)
PPQ	Police Pistol Quick (defense trigger, Walther)
PRE-'89	Paramilitary mfg. before Federal legislation in Nov. 1989
PRE-BAN	Mfg. before September 13, 1994 per C/B or before Nov. 1989.
PRS/PRS2	MAGPUL Precision Rifle/Sniper (stock)
PSD	Personal Security Detail rifle (LWRC)
PSG	PrazisionSchutzenGewehr (H&K rifle)
PSR	Precision Shooting Rifle (FNH)
PXT	Power Extractor Technology (PARA USA INC.)
QD	Quick Detachable
RACS	Remington Arms Chassis System
RAS	Rail Adapter System
RB	Round Barrel/Round Butt
RCM	Ruger Compact Magnum
RCMP	Royal Canadian Mounted Police
RCP	Refined Carry Pistol (Kimber)
RDS	Rapid Deployment Stock
REC	Receiver
REM	Remington
REM. MAG.	Remington Magnum
REPR	Rapid Engagement Precision Rifle (LWRC)
RF	Rimfire
RFB	Rifle Forward (ejection) Bullpup

RFM	Rim Fire Magnum
RIS	Rail Interface system
RK	Round Knob
RKLT	Round Knob Long Tang
RKST	Round Knob Short Tang
RMEF	Rocky Mt. Elk. Foundation
RMR	Rimfire Magnum Rifle (Kel Tec)
RPD	Ruchnoy Pulemyot Degtyaryova (machine gun)
RR	Red Ramp
RSA	MAGPUL Rail Sling Attachment
RSUM	Remington Short-Action Ultra Magnum
RUM	Remington Ultra Magnum
RVG	MAGPUL Rail Vertical Grip
S	Short
S&W	Smith & Wesson
S/N	Serial Number
SA	Single Action
SAA	Single Action Army
SAAMI	Sporting Arms and Ammunition Manufacturers' Institute
SABR	Sniper/Assaulter Battle Rifle (LWRC)
SAE	Selective Automatic Ejectors
SAO	Single Action Only
SAS	SIG Anti Snag (pistol models)
SASS	Single Action Shooting Society or (U.S. Army) Semi Automatic Sniper System
SAUM	Short Action Ultra Magnum
SAW	Semiautomatic Assault Weapon
SAW	Squad Automatic Weapon
SB	Shotgun butt or Steel backstrap
SBR	Short Barrel Rifle
SCAR	Special (Operations Forces) Combat Assault Rifle (FNH)
SCW	Sub Compact Weapon (Colt)
SDT	Super Dynamic Technology (PARA USA INC.)
ser.	serial
SFO	Striker Fire Operation
SG	Straight Grip
SIG	Schweizerische Industriegesellschaft
SIM	Special Impact Munition
SK	Skeet
SLP	Self Loading Police (FNH shotgun)
SMG	Submachine Gun
SMLE	Short Magazine Lee Enfield Rifle
SNT	Single Non-Selective Trigger
SOCOM	Special Operations Command
SOPMOD	Special Operations Peculiar Modification
SP	Special Purpose
SPC	Special Purpose Cartridge
SPEC	Special
SPEC-OPS	Special Operations
SPG	Semi-Pistol Grip
Spl.	Special
SPLLAT	Special Purpose Low Lethality Anti Terrorist (Munition)
SPR	Special Police Rifle (FNH), Special Purpose Rifle
SPS	Special Purpose Synthetic (Remington)
SPS	Superalloy Piston System (LWRC)
sq.	Square
SR	Solid Rib
SRC	Saddle Ring Carbine
SRT	Short Reset Trigger
SS	Single Shot or Stainless Steel
SSA	Super Short Action
SSR	Sniper Support Rifle (FNH)
SST	Single Selective Trigger or Single Stage Trigger
ST	Single Trigger
SUR	Sport Utility Rifle - see Glossary
SWAT	Special Weapons Assault Team
SWAT	Special Weapons and Tactics
SxS	Side by Side
TAS	Tactical Adjustable Sight (STI International)
TB	Threaded Barrel
TBA	To be Announced
TBM	Tactical Box Magazine
TD	Takedown
TDR	Target Deployment Rifle (Rem.)
TFO	Tritium Fiber Optic (Sig Sauer)
TGT	Target
TH	Target Hammer
TiAIN	Titanium Aluminum Nitride finish (STI International)
TIR	Target Interdiction Rifle (Rem.)
TLE	Tactical Law Enforcement (Kimber)
TPS	Tactical Police Shotgun (FNH)
TRP	Tactical Response Pistol (Springfield Inc.)
TRPAFD	Take Red Pen Away From Dave!
TS	Target Stocks
TSOB	Scope Mount Rail Weaver Type
TSR XP USA	Tactical Sport Rifle - Extreme Performance Ultra Short Action (FNH)
TSR XP	Tactical Sport Rifle - Extreme Performance (FNH)

TT	Target Trigger
TTR	Tactical Target Rifle (PARA USA INC.)
TWS	Tactical Weapons System (Rem.)
UBR	MAGPUL Utility/Battle Rifle (stock)
UCIW	Ultra Compact Individual Weapon (LWRC)
UCP	Universal Combat Pistol (H&K)
UIT	Union Internationale de Tir
UMC	Union Metallic Cartridge Co.
UMP	Universal Machine Pistol (H&K)
URX	Upper Receiver Extending (free floating barrel system, Knight's Armament)
USA	Ultra Safety Assurance (Springfield Inc.)
USAMU	U.S. Army Marksmanship Unit
USC	Universal Self-Loading Carbine (H&K)
USG	United States Government (FNH model suffix)
USP	Universal Self-Loading Pistol (H&K)
USPSA	United States Practical Shooting Association
USR	Urban Sniper Rifle (Rem.)
USSOCOM	U.S. Special Operations Command
VAT	Value Added Tax
Vent.	Ventilated
VG	Very Good
VR	Ventilated Rib
VTAC	Viking Tactics, Inc. (accessories)
VTR	Varmint Triangular Profile Barrel (Remington)
w/	With
w/o	Without
WBY	Weatherby
WC	Wad Cutter
WCF	Winchester Center Fire
WD	Wood
WFF	Watch For Fakes
WIN	Winchester
WMR	Winchester Magnum Rimfire
WO	White Outline
WRA	Winchester Repeating Arms Co.
WRF	Winchester Rim Fire
WRM	Winchester Rimfire Magnum
WSL	Winchester Self-Loading
WSM	Winchester Short Magnum
WSSM	Winchester Super Short Magnum
WW	World War
X (1X)	1X Wood Upgrade or Extra Full Choke Tube
XD	Extreme Duty (Springfield Inc.)
XDM	Extreme Duty M Factor (Springfield Inc.)
XX (2X)	2X Wood Upgrade or Extra Extra Full Choke Tube
XXX (3x)	3X Wood Upgrade
YHM	Yankee Hill Machine

CONTACT INFORMATION

COLT

Colt's Manufacturing Company LLC

P.O. Box 1868
Hartford, CT 06144-1868
Toll Free: 800-962-COLT
Fax: 860-244-1449
Website: www.coltsmfg.com

Colt Defense LLC (Law Enforcement & Rifles)

P.O. Box 118
Hartford, CT 06141
Phone: 860-232-4489
Fax: 860-244-1442
Website: www.colt.com

Historical Research - Colt Archive Properties LLC

P.O. Box 1868
Hartford, CT 01644-1868
If mailing in a request, make sure the proper research fee is enclosed (please refer to appropriate Colt section for current fees and related information).

1st and 2nd Generation SAA phone service only

Phone: 800-962-COLT
(Ask for Historical Dept. Research fees start at $150.)

Colt Cavalry & Artillery Revolver Authentication Service

Mr. John Kopec, Historian
Phone/Fax: 530-222-4440
Website: www.johnakopec.com
Email: books@johnakopec.com (book sales only)